Quest for Clues

ISBN 0-929373-00-6

DEDICATION

For Lurline and Roland, my favorite parents.

The Quest Buster's CODE

b = a	i = h	p = o	w = v
c = b	j = i	q = p	x = w
d = c	k = j	r = q	y = x
e = d	l = k	s = r	z = y
f = e	m = l	t = s	a = z
g = f	n = m	u = t	
h = g	o = n	v = u	

Use this table to decode clues. To make this process more convenient, photocopy it and place it beside the coded sections.

(Origin Systems hereby authorizes you to photocopy this page, and no other portion of this book, exclusively for this purpose.)

Quest for Clues

the
table of
contents

1

The QuestBusters Guild

The QuestBusters Guild is a league of dedicated adventurers who don't quit after they've saved the land from the Evil Wizard, or rescued civilization as we know it from a star fleet of bug-eyed Betelgeusians. Instead, they prepare detailed walkthroughs to their most recent adventures, enabling others to get past the puzzles or monsters that have them stymied. This book would not have been possible without the contributions of the following members of the QuestBusters Guild, who went above and beyond the call of duty to provide solutions and maps for the indicated games. (Members also get the adventure game of their choice for each solution. If you'd like to join the Guild, write to QuestBusters for more information.)

William E. Carte: *Stationfall, Leather Goddesses of Phobos, Bureaucracy, Gunslinger, Roadwar 2000, Moonmist, Indiana Jones in Revenge of the Ancients, Hollywood Hijinx, Trinity, Might and Magic (maps), Star Trek II*

Brian Smith: *A View to a Kill, Goldfinger, Rambo, High Stakes, Neverending Story, The Mist, Oo-topos, Essex*

Aaron Chou: *Shard of Spring, Borrowed Time, Amnesia, Tass Times in Tonetown*

Eric Mitchell: *Wizard's Crown, Phantasie I, Phantasie II*

Michael R. Bagnall: *Bard's Tale I and II*

Tim Snider: *Mercenary, AutoDuel*

Brian Anderson: *Might and Magic*

Raymond Fong: *Rings of Zilfin*

Sandra K. Walton: *Ballyhoo*

Timothy Walsh: *Fraktured Faebles*

Lawrence T. Paprocki: *Wrath of Denethenor*

Thomas M. Kirby: *The Pawn*

Richard Rasmussen: *Moebius*

Scott Huang: *Nine Princes in Amber*

Stephen King: *Ultima IV*

Harold Bohn: *Breakers*

Juha Kahilainen: *King's Quest III*

Jerry Dattilo: *Labyrinth*

Brad Kinman: *Phantasie III*

Mark E. Revesman: *Spellbreaker*

Allen Reinwasser and Curt Weber: *Space Quest*

Douglas M. Campbell: *Shadowgate*

Shay Addams: *Universe II*

With hundreds of adventure games from which to choose, and four to five new ones each month, today's adventurer enjoys as wide a variety of exotic destinations as he or she would if considering vacation packages at a travel agency. In the "old days," however, the most difficult quest was not finding the Mystic Orb or Evil Wizard, but finding a

revelations as we step through the Time Door and visit the Golden Age of Adventure for a first-hand look at how it all began.

The First Adventure, The First Cave. If adventure has a name, it must be William Crowther. The Indiana Jones of interactive entertainment, Crowther wrote the first computer adventure game in the late Sixties, hacking a path through the silicon

name hints at the real-life model upon which Colossal Cave was based— Kentucky's Mammoth Cave, a sprawling limestone cavern.

"From 1963 until 1967, I was with the Cave Research Foundation," Crowther recalls. "We produced maps and conducted low-grade scientific research for the National Park Service. Much of that time was spent mapping Mammoth Cave in Kentucky, and the geography of the original half of the adventure matches a small part of that cave." His fascination with spelunking and cartography explains why contemporary adventurers must spend so much time exploring caves and drawing maps. But Crowther didn't set out to invent a new kind of game and wasn't planning to cash in on the commercial prospects of adventure games, which have since generated more gold than all the bullion in all the caves in all the adventures combined.

"I wrote it for my kids, Sandy and Laura, when I was on the research staff at a Cambridge consulting firm in 1967 or 1968," says Crowther, who graduated from nearby Massachusetts Institute of Technology with a B.S. in physics in 1953. He and his kids had often played "Mirkwood," a non-computer role-playing game that was a precursor to Gary Gygax's 1973 Dungeons & Dragons (itself a modified set of rules Dave

The Golden Age of Adventure

new adventure game. And when you finally did, the packaging usually consisted of a zip-loc bag and a photo-copied manual— and the graphics, sound effects, and other aspects were primitive by contemporary standards. Even so, the ability to enter a fantasy world inside your computer was wondrous enough to enthrall those who crossed that magical threshold.

Countless stories have sprung up about those days, some authentic and others as fanciful as the tales passed around a medieval tavern. Whether you're one of the pioneers who first mapped Colossal Cave, or a relative stranger in these enchanting lands, you'll discover a wealth of

jungle for countless programmers and designers to follow. Twenty years later, hundreds of alternative worlds have been crafted according to the formula conceived by Crowther when he created a place called Colossal Cave.

Called *Adventure* (often dubbed *Original Adventure* to distinguish it from the multitude of subsequent scenarios), it is still fondly referred to as "the cave" by Crowther. Myths and legends have sprung up around this fountainhead of the fantastic. The most common story said the rambling collection of caverns was an imaginary place dreamed up by Crowther and expanded by Don Woods. But its

Arnesson devised for playing games with miniature figures). Created by an associate of Crowther's, Mirkwood drew its name from a locale that was tangentially referred to in J. R. R. Tolkien's trilogy, *Lord of the Rings*. Tolkien's epic tale chronicled the quest of a hobbit named Frodo as he fought off legions of orcs and sought to rid Middle Earth of the evil Sauron, a theme echoed in countless computer games since.

Crowther elaborates: "I'd played Mirkwood with my kids, and since I'd done some caving, it seemed like an interesting combination. So I did it. It took about a month, working on weekends, to write the program in Fortran on the DEC PDP-10 at the office. [Fortran is a language usually reserved for scientific research and formula-related programming.] That became the first half of the original adventure. The dwarves, bird, the snake, black rod, some treasures and the magic words 'xyzzy' were in the original version. My kids, who were six and eight or nine at the time, played it from a teletype and modem at home. Sometimes they'd come in and play it at the office." There was no scoring system. Sandy and Laura—and a growing number of his colleagues at the office—played for the sheer pleasure of exploring the cave and solving its puzzles.

Adventure represented a new kind of computer program, a new form of entertainment. (A maze-exploration game called *Hunt the Wumpus* is sometimes cited as predating Crowther's game, but even its author, Gregory Yob, doesn't consider his 1972 *Wumpus* an adventure game.) Crowther's game consisted of pure text and used no joystick or other control device. All the descriptions of the caves, creatures and everything that can happen in response to the player's actions were stored in a data base. When Sandy or Laura typed, "go east," the parser, a sub-routine in the program, would analyze the words by looking to see if they were part of the game's vocabulary, also part of the data base. If so, a number assigned to each word in the vocabulary table would be sent to the logic/action tables. Everything Crowther had decided could happen in the cave was listed here, along with the conditions that must be in effect for each to be executed.

If other parts of the program, the variables that kept track of things like the player's location, inventory and other aspects of the game, established that Sandy was in Cobble Crawl when she'd typed "go east," the conditions for displaying the description of the Debris Room (which lies due east) were fulfilled. The program then retrieved its description from the database, displayed it on-screen or printed it out, and updated the appropriate variable to register the player's new position. Then it waited for another command. This simple yet classic design and implementation proved engaging to play because of the unusual degree of interaction between the player and the game's environment.

The consulting firm where Crowther worked was part of AR-PAnet, a pioneer telecommunications network, and he made the game available on it. *Adventure* soon attracted the all-night attention of America's earliest on-line hackers, who were hooked into the same network. (The term hacker has been assigned numerous definitions since then, but here it refers to anyone who devoted an inordinate amount of time to exploring data bases and other on-line resources

available in this manner.) "A lot of people saw it and liked it," Crowther's voice grows melancholy. "The system hackers thought it was a lot of fun. Then Don Woods found it. He doubled the size, adding exotic things like the giant's room and the volcano."

Twenty-three at the time, Woods was studying computer science and electrical engineering at SAIL (Stanford Artificial Intelligence Laboratory at Stanford University). "I was wandering around on the ARPAnet in February of 1976 or 1977," he says. Someone ran across *Adventure* on the Stanford Medical Center computer, which was also on ARPAnet. I brought it across to the Artificial Intelligence lab and looked at it there. I thought it was an interesting idea for a game. The program had a lot of bugs in it, but it was fun to play. In fact, I was playing it for awhile, struggling around with some of the problems, when I decided the easiest way to fix all these problems was to get hold of the author. Willie Crowther's name was mentioned in the introduction, so I sent a message to Crowther at every site on the ARPAnet until I found him."

Crowther furnished the source code, and Woods rewrote most

of the program to make it easier to add new things. "Coming up with new rooms was the hard part, but adding them to the program wasn't that hard. Friends and classmates helped. I had not played any D & D-type games, though I have since then. I had read Tolkien's trilogy, which influenced the description of one room, Breathtaking View. It was written by a friend, John Gilberth, and I, after we'd watched the sun rise on Mount Diablo. We came back and by then were in a fine state of mind for writing that sort of prose.

"One person, Bob Pariseau, helped a fair amount in coming up with new things to add. I finished rewriting it around April of 1976 or 1977 and, before going on vacation, created an account on the Stanford machine under my name so people could log-in and run this program. When I returned, much to my dismay, I found that people had been connecting to the machine from all over the place to play this game. The people who ran the computer at Stanford were kind of annoyed because of the workload that had been put on the machine in my absence. Meanwhile I'd gotten comments from people and incorporated a lot of them into the game. One was a situation in which someone had tried to do some really ridiculous thing and was disappointed that the program didn't provide a suitably snide message. So I began

sneaking in more snide messages in various places. I touched it up a bit and added a few small items here and there. Then I announced its general availability for people to copy onto their own machines, and was deluged by requests for it.

"This probably all happened in 1977 rather than 1976, but I always have trouble remembering the exact year. One reason is that I did get around to making a new version, *Adventure II*, with five additional treasures and a total of 430 points instead of 350. It hasn't spread quite as far because I was stricter about handing out copies of it. And that was roughly a year after the first release, so the two years seem to muddle in my mind. It's still on various machines today."

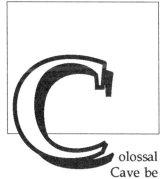

Colossal Cave became a midnight mecca for hackers who entered it from their terminals and teletypes. After crunching numbers for the accounting department or debugging a new program all day, engineers and programmers looked forward to escaping into this enchanting alternative universe. Solving the puzzles and grabbing the gold became an obsession for hundreds of America's most highly paid computer scientists, programmers and distinguished academicians. Many players, like Crowther himself, didn't see the game's text displayed on a screen but read its responses and descriptions on paper as they emerged from the teletype.

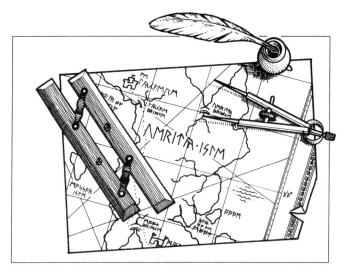

The Cave on Campus

When *Adventure* reached further into America's college campuses, students started squeezing through the grate into Colossal Cave. "Everyone was hooked," says Marc Blank, an Infocom founder, "because there was nothing like it— it was just a totally new type of game that happened to be very appealing. At the time no one thought of it as anything other than just a fun sort of thing. I don't think anyone planned for it to turn into real interactive stories or anything else." In fact, there weren't even any home computers at this stage, so the only people who could venture into the cave were those with access to an incredibly expensive mainframe computer or terminal.

Dave Lebling, now a consultant and author for Infocom, remembers exploring and mapping the cave when he was supposed to be studying political science at MIT. "Literally everyone played it. No work was done for weeks. You would look on the ma-

chines to see who was logged-in. If there were fifteen people at the terminals, twelve would be playing *Adventure*. I can remember playing it for hours at a time on many occasions, and I knew people who played it almost continuously until they solved it. They just beat their heads against a wall until they got past a problem. At lunchtime, groups of players would huddle and whisper things like, 'How do you get past the snake?' and exchange clues and hints. There were days when I sat down and played non-stop, with only occasional breaks to keep from falling asleep.

The Making of *Zork*

Lebling met Marc Blank, Stu Galley and Joel Berez in MIT's Computer Research Lab where they were doing computer science projects. They felt convinced an even more advanced adventure could be written. "Early on we decided that we wanted to have a full-sentence parser," Blank elaborates, "that would help the games by making them

more realistic and the problems more interesting and easier for people to play." With Al Vezza, who ran the lab, they and other students developed MDL, a computer language especially for writing adventures games. (MDL was the group's acronym for "muddle," which was how they jokingly say they managed to get through the project. Blank gives most of the credit for the language's development to Christopher Reeve.) They had *Zork* running on the campus mainframe by Christmas, 1977. Blank and Lebling, along with Tim Anderson and Bruce Daniels wrote the actual program and story of the mythical land of the Great Underground Empire.

"Lots of the text— especially what we called the 'purple stuff'—was written by whoever was doing a particular piece of code at the time," Lebling points out. Daniels modeled the Thief after *Original Adventure*'s Pirate. Blank devised the bizarrely humourous responses to unacceptable commands, inspired by the snide re-

6

sponses in *Original Adventure*. "Zork" itself was a nonsense expletive buzzing around campus then, circulating mainly in the computer science classes. Lebling dreamed up the grues, those fearsome creatures of the dark that haunt most of Infocom's worlds. "The grues were indirectly based on an old English word meaning blood," he explains. "But it's a direct homage to Jack Vance and his science fiction novel, *The Dying Earth* , which contained creatures called grues. There was some Dungeons & Dragons influence," Lebling muses, "like the fighting scene with the troll. I was the only D & D player in the group, though, and *Zork* was as much influenced by Tolkien and Jack Vance as by anything else."

Meanwhile, Floridian Scott Adams was writing the first commercial adventure game, an all-text scenario called *Adventureland*, on his TRS-80 Model I computer. Based on Crowther's model, *Adventureland* and the series that followed lacked the polished, vivid prose of the mainframe games, and the parser was crude. Still, his contribution helped establish the adventure game in the pioneer days of the entertainment software industry. During the same time frame, Gordon Letwin of Softwin Associates wrote *Microsoft Adventure* , which became the "industry standard" of the Crowther and Woods' game. Microsoft released it on cassette and disk for

TRS Model I and Apple II computers.

In 1979 Infocom's founders chipped in and rented time on a mainframe computer, and *Zork* surfaced as a commercial game in December, 1980. "The original *Zork* was over a megabyte—one million bytes—in size," Blank emphasizes, far too big for the memory of home computers even today. "So we turned it into all of *Zork I* , about two-thirds of *Zork II* and a piece of *Zork III* ." *Zork I* was initially distributed by Personal Software (which later became Visicorp, renowned for the VisiCalc spreadsheet.) The *Zork* Users Group sprang up in Milwaukee, Wisconsin, run by Michael Dornbrook, who was Infocom's first playtester and is now their Product Manager.

Anyone who has played *Sorcerer* will recall being chased through the glass maze by a "ferocious Dorn beast," which was named after Michael. The "vezza" spell in the same game is drawn from the name of Infocom's Chairman of the Board, Al Vezza. And Infocom's entire inner sanctum of designers and writers appear allegorically as the Circle of Enchanters in that game and its predecessor, *Enchanter*. This penchant for alluding to themselves within the games goes back to *Zork I*'s little house, where a wall is described as being "intentionally left blank."

The First Graphic Games
By now the pioneer spirit had sparked a gold rush. From California came the first graphic adventure. Ken Williams and his wife Roberta went into business as On-line Software, which eventually became Sierra On-line. "Ken worked on a mainframe IBM at Financial Decision Systems in downtown Los Angeles," Roberta reminisces. "This was the winter of 1979. Ken would bring back a terminal and work at home sometimes. But he showed me the games that were on this IBM. One was called *Adventure*. I played it with the terminal and printer for hours, long into the night, and was fascinated with it.

"It took me about three months to solve, then I went to our local computer store—and there weren't many of *them* at that time. We'd bought an Apple between the time I started playing *Adventure* and the time I finished it. I'd heard you could get *MicroSoft Adventure* for the Apple. But I also heard that Scott Adams was selling adventure games. I thought, well, here I am, this adventure game addict, and I just have to get more. So I went to the local store and bought a couple of his cassettes, because there weren't any disk drives at that time. And I played a couple of his and wasn't that impressed, at least not compared with *Adventure*. I had a hard time finding more adventure games, and I thought that I couldn't be the only person who liked them. That there must be a market out there for them, and that I could at least do as well as Scott Adams. Which was sort of the beginning of our company, when I saw the need for this kind of program, this kind of game," explains Roberta.

"I decided to use graphics to be different, number one. If you're going to start a company with a single product, it should be different or better than anything else like it. The second reason was that I thought it would be nice to show people where they're at rather than just trying to explain it. *Mystery House* came out in May of 1980, with black and white graphics. I designed and wrote the game and drew the pictures with a graphics tablet, and Ken wrote the program. Then in 1981 we did *Wizard and the Princess* , the first adventure with color graphics."

Enter the Orc: Fantasy Role-playing Games

In basements and bedrooms across the land, a handful of silicon seers sought the same Holy Grail—a computerized counterpart of Dungeons and Dragons. One of them was Robert Clardy, who was working on the AWACS radar project at Boeing Aircraft in Seattle when he bought his first Apple in early 1978. Part of the documentation was a "Red Manual" full of BASIC program listings, and Clardy found himself captivated with the notion of elaborating on an earlier computer game, Gary Shannon's *Dungeon Maze*. By October of 1978 he had constructed more rooms, treasure, elves, dwarves, and magic spells, and quit his job to market the first commercial role-playing game with low-resolution graphics, *Dungeon Campaign*. Designed as a one or two-hour game, it didn't offer the option of saving a game in progress. A different maze was randomly generated for each session.

The Legend of *Ultima*

In Nassau Bay, Texas, Richard Garriott envisioned his own computer role-playing games and even managed to earn high school credits for writing them. "Our school had a teletype terminal tied in to a computer in Houston," says Garriott. To pursue their studies after completing the school's only programming course, he and two other students convinced the faculty to let them organize and run their own class. "All we had to do was have a project; if we could show progress on it, we'd get an A. This was my sophomore year, 1977,

when I started playing fantasy games on paper, like Dungeons and Dragons, Tunnels and Trolls. And I was reading *Lord of the Rings* and C. S. Lewis' *Chronicles of Narnia* as well, and was kind of accosted by all three of these things—computers, the general concept of fantasy, and role-playing games—all at the same time.

"So my project for the last three years of high school was to write fantasy role-playing games on the teletype. They were very simple little dungeon games that would have to reprint the whole thing every time you took a step. I learned a great deal each time I wrote one; then I'd throw it away and write a new one. I just called them number one, number two, and so on. And I was up to 28 when I graduated from high school in 1979.

"I worked in a ComputerLand store that summer, where I discovered the Apple II. And for the first time I thought of putting graphics into the games I'd been writing. I'd seen a low-resolution game called *Escape*, which was like a maze game, and that inspired me to try to figure out how 3-D graphics work. I spent that summer working on 3-D, high-resolution graphics and adapting them to new versions of my fantasy role-playing games—and wrote something that was never intended to be published, *Akalabeth*.

"The owner of the store thought I should publish it. I spent what at the time was a great deal of money for me, $200, going to the print shop and getting some tiny manuals and a cover sheet printed up, and I bought a bunch of zip-loc bags and started selling them at the store in '79. I didn't plan to go national with it, but one of the first five copies made it all the way to the West Coast and into the hands of California Pacific, one of the biggest software publishers back then. A few days later they called and said plane tickets are waiting for me at the airport. I flew to California, signed a piece of paper and they started mailing me money! That was the lucky circumstance that led to me being published."

When Garriott realized what he'd been doing for fun could also be profitable, it occurred to him that he could write a much better game if it were intended for commercial sale—and went to work on one. He called his new game *Ultimatum*. To avoid potential legal problems with a company whose board game had the same name, it was shortened it to *Ultima*. Speaking of names, Garriott publishes

his games under the *nom de plume* Lord British. "It came from a nickname I got while studying computers and mathematics at the University of Oklahoma in the summer after my sophomore year," he explains. "Some people thought that I sounded British because I said 'hello' as opposed to 'hi'. It turns out I was born in Cambridge, England, so the nickname stuck."

Engaging in a bit of real-life role-playing, Garriott donned medieval garb and attended California Pacific's booth at the West Coast Computer Fair for *Ultima*'s 1979 release. "That came about as a result of my activities with the Society for Creative Anachronisms," he says, "which coincided with my exposure to fantasy gaming and fiction. At that show I wore a leather tunic, a small cape, knickers, boots, and I carried a sword and a fillet, which is sort of like a little crown or headband."

(In June, 1979, *Temple of Apshai* became the first of many role-playing games written in the locale that eventually turned into Silicon Valley. After meeting through Dungeons & Dragons sessions, Jon Freeman, Jeff Johnson and Jim Connelley worked from individual apartments in Mountain View, California, to design and program *Apshai* for the TRS-80 Model I.)

The *Wizardry* Saga

In September of

1981, *Wizardry* surfaced in a small town in upstate New York. *Wizardry*'s roots reach back to "circa-1978, maybe '76 or '77," according to co-author Andrew Greenberg. "Cornell University has a week-long study period at the end of classes, and I usually spent this entire time playing Dungeons & Dragons, bridge, poker and Scrabble with friends. But I was feeling particularly bored and wouldn't even play these games. My friends were utterly fed up with me, and one of them shouted, 'Oh Greenberg, why don't you go put D & D on your computer?'"

"I spent 48 hours doodling on the thing, then called my buddies up and invited them over to 'come over and walk through the maze.' Eventually it occurred to me that it would be really neat to have a role-playing game. I'd just sort of been doing this to answer my friend's dare. After scrutinizing D & D and others, I found that none was really appropriate for a computer game. So I sat down and began designing my own. My dorm room at Cornell was literally occupied by friends playing and testing the game. I spent much of the next couple of years sleeping in the room of whoever happened to be playing the game in my room that night.

In early 1981, I was approached by Robert Woodhead, whom I knew from my role as manager of the school's Plato facility. Part of my job was to enforce the trustees' strict rule that we were not to permit game-playing on the system. Robert thought it was his duty in life to play games on the system, and that's how we met. It was basically an incredibly adversarial, confrontational relationship. He hung around the terminal all along and found ways to get around the programs that we set up to keep people from playing games. When he heard that Andy Greenberg, the 'spoilsport and all-around mean guy,' was writing his own game, this just amazed him. He approached me, because he had some ideas along the same lines.

"**R**obert offered to do all the coding to my specifications, so I'd only have to verify his work and do some play-testing. He contributed far more than programming, and I did an awful lot more hacking than I'd intended. By the end it seemed ridiculous not to call him a co-author. What is now *Wizardry* is basically that game, polished for the current market—with a number of changes that were largely suggested by Robert as well as some additions and adaptions that were my own." Greenberg didn't play *Adventure* until 1981

and says *Wizardry* didn't borrow from the classic adventure game: "The whole body of fantasy literature, stories like Tolkien's trilogy, was a more significant influence."

As we step back through the Time Door and re-enter the present, it becomes clear that today's exotic adventure and role-playing games evolved from a father's fairy tale for his children and a generation's fascination with fantasy fiction and traditional role-playing games. Dramatic breakthroughs in presentation and programming have extended the creative borders of these games, which are simultaneously evolving, mutating, and maturing into a high-tech medium for expression. The computers may remain exclusive tools of this planet's master dreamweavers and myth-makers in the next decade, or advanced technology might enable totally computer-illiterate novelists and playwrights to compose interactive art or drama. Either way, the adventure game will someday claim its rightful place alongside literature and cinema as a recognized art form, its subject matter the mythology, fantasy and fiction of the Computer Age.

These solutions and maps may be utilized in many ways, depending on the game and your own inclination. Optimally you'll use them to get past the puzzle or maze that's blocking your path. Answers have been encoded to minimize the possibility of catching the dreaded "Clue Book Syndrome," which spurs adventurers to race through a new clue book and immediately read all the clues, even to games they don't own. A few letters in the code look quite similar and won't be as easy to decode as the others. This may be tedious at times, but makes it even harder for you to cave in to temptation and read a solution from beginning to end, which would only spoil the fun. If in spite of this you still feel an urge to do so, send the book to yourself via fourth class mail: It will be gone for a week or two, during which time you may have developed more discipline.

An effective tactic is to check out the map for rooms you may have overlooked, especially those containing objects. A dotted line means you must solve a puzzle or possess a special item or knowledge in order to reach the adjoining room, while straight lines are unobstructed exits. The maps reflect every location necessary to solve the game, but do not show every inch of every maze in role-playing games like Bard's Tale and Ultima. (If they did, this book could hold only half as many solutions.)

Still stuck? Proceed to the walkthrough, which is divided into a series of locations and things to do there. First glance at the names of the locations to find the path necessary to complete the adventure. (There is often more than one correct path to follow,

and some puzzles will have alternative solutions. These walkthroughs offer just one—but one that has been verified and definitely works.) This will ensure that you're not chasing a "red herring" in the wrong direction. If you're snagged on a particular problem, find the location's section in the solution and decode the step-by-step answers. Don't decode them all at once, though. If the first word translates into a verb such as "put," try to solve the puzzle with that knowledge before decoding more. You might also decode the last word first, which usually yields a noun. When seeking a specific object, look up the coded counterpart of the first letter in its name: for the "k" in "key" you would find the letter j. Then pore over the walkthrough for coded objects beginning with j. This way you don't have to decode each object's entire name and unintentionally find things you'd rather discover on your own.

How to Use this Book

Most solutions to role-playing games refer to numbers on a corresponding dungeon map. With these you should first examine the map of a maze that has you puzzled, then investigate the numbered areas and try to finish it independently. Consult the text portion of the solution only as a last resort, for these are not as heavily encoded as those for text and graphic games. Tips on character development and combat will prove useful for players just setting out as well as to those already involved in the quest. For games with auto-mapping features or grid systems that provide numbers for latitude and longitude, maps are provided only for mazes that are full of spinners, teleports and other confusing elements.

Disk Drive Detectives

ere Sherlock Holmes alive today, Watson would not hear the familiar notes of violin music coming from Holmes' study—the master detective would be too wrapped up in a disk-based mystery like one of these. Since *Mystery House* (the first disk drive detective game) and *Deadline* (the most well-known), this sub-genre of adventures has evolved in subtle ways. Until recently your role was restricted to that of a policeman or private detective assigned or hired to solve a murder. But now you're just as likely to be cast as an ordinary citizen who sets out to solve the crime by interacting with the thugs and suspects.

THE NATURE OF THE CRIMES you're charged with solving has also been expanded far beyond murder: Offenses as wide-ranging as kidnapping and art theft have been the subjects of the latest disk drive detective scenarios. In an unusual text game written by novelist Thomas M. Disch, the mystery revolves around learning your own identity. In another, you're a circus-goer who solves puzzles by walking the tight rope, wearing a clown suit and engaging in other Big Top activities rather than by conducting the customary fingerprinting and interrogation of witnesses and suspects. (Can it be long before we see a game called "Divorce Case Detective," in which your goal is the most common case of the private eye—spying on someone's spouse to obtain evidence of infidelity?) The main mystery that has armchair Sherlocks puzzled, however, is why there aren't as many of these games as there are adventures with fantasy and science fiction themes.

AMNESIA

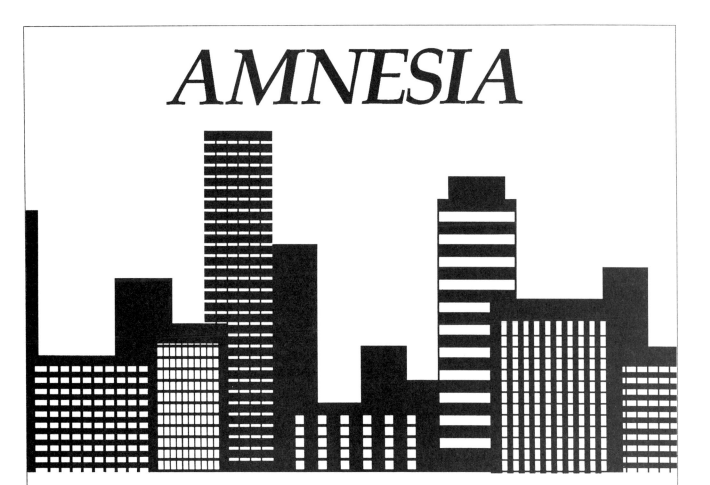

You ou must solve the mystery of your own identity in this all-text story. First you a-wake in a New York hotel without a clue, though plenty of them turn up as you explore the 40,000 locations. Every major street corner in Manhattan, plus the entire subway was pro-grammed into the game. Fortunately you are provided with maps of the streets and subways, so you don't need to draw one (the reason no maps are offered here).

TO REGAIN YOUR MEMORY you must track down old acquaintances and access some word processing files you wrote and hid before losing your memory. True to life in the Big City, survival is a priority. You've got to sustain your energy level by eating and sleeping, or you'll pass out and the police will grab you. (On top of every-thing else, you're wanted for murder!) The boun-tiful prose ranks among the finest to grace a disk and often spills across several screens, for it was penned by science fiction and mystery novelist Thomas M. Disch (who can be found hanging out at the corner of Broome and Thompson.) With a parser that handles complete sentences and mul-tiple commands, *Amnesia* is more articulate than most New York cabbies. It's recommended for those who enjoy reading as much as puzzle-solving.

The Walkthrough

Instead of mapping, make a list of the locations of restaurants and phone booths near the Tenement area. These locations and the Tenement are randomly determined in each new game. When told to go to a location, use the map included with the game to find the shortest subway route. You can transfer to a different train at some stops by saying "Go left/right stairs" or "tunnel."

You will die constantly if you don't sleep and eat regularly. Avoid this by travelling as directly as possible to your destination. Always take the subway nearest the Tenement, and board the E train to 54th Street and 5th Avenue when going to the hotel and the computer store. Use at least two disks for saving games, and do so frequently.

In Hotel Room
Get up. (Answer questions about hair color, etc., in any way.) Get sheet. Wear sheet. Answer phone (when it rings). Yes (to all questions). **Sfbe cjcmf. Sfbe Kpio pof.** (Note password: with God.) Turn on computer. Dial room service. Order (anything).

Eat (food, when it arrives). Turn on TV. Open drapes. Look out window. (These may be done in any order.) Leave. Go to exit. U. Open door. Go right.

The Sauna
Enter sauna. (Type anything.) **Qmfbtf tjs.** Wait (five times). Yes. Open satchel. Yes.

In Hotel Room
Take off clothes. **Xfbs uvy.** Look at **nbudicppl** (note **beesftt**). Wait. Answer phone. Yes. Leave.

In Lobby with Luke
Yes. U. Look. Leave. **ljtt** her. **Op. Op. Zft.** Wait (three times). Leave. Leave. (Go to the **Qsjodfupo dmvc** at West **Gpvsuz uijse** Street and **gjgui** Avenue.) Enter Princeton Club. (Go to area around 10th Avenue between **Uijsuz gjgui** and **Gjguz gjgui** Street and find the Tenement, whose location is randomly determined in each game. When tired, you can sleep here: Enter tenement. N. W. N. N. S. Sleep.)

Save the game, because the locations of restaurants, phone booths and the tenement are determined randomly every time you leave. While looking for it, write down the locations of several phones and restaurants in the vicinity. After completing each of the following sections, you must sleep before continuing. In emergencies, you can sleep in Central Park during the afternoon if you haven't found Bette yet.

Outside Tenement
Walk around the **Ufoui** Avenue area until you meet a black kid. Answer Yes to him. Go to **Uijsuz gpvsui** Street and **Uxfmgui** Avenue and **xbti xjoetijfmet** until you have $15. (This may take several days. Take occasional breaks to eat and sleep. Repeat this if you run out of money.) When you have $15, save the game and go to a phone booth. Use telephone. Deposit coin. Dial (**UUUU**'s number, found in manual).

53rd Street and 5th Avenue.
Enter Sunderland. Go to Front Desk. ask **dmfsl** for **cpy**. **Xjui hpe.** Open box. Get disk. Close box. Leave. Leave. (Between 9 AM and 4:30 PM, go to **Gjguz tjyui** Street and **Nbejtpo** Avenue—make sure you have at least $10.00)

User-Friendly Computer Store
Enter store. Apple. Yes. 1. a **Sjeemf.** F. (Repeat to end of file.) E. 2. **Rvftujpo nbsl.** F. (Repeat to end of file.) E. 3. **Cbmeoftt.** F. (Repeat to end of file.) E. 4. **Pojpo.** F. (Repeat to end of file.) 5. E.

(Go to West **Ojofuffoui** Street and Avenue of the Americas.)

Tiny Tykes Talent Town
Go to brownstone. Ring doorbell. Open door (while buzzer is still buzzing). **Kpio Dbnfspo.** U. Sprinkle. Go to **ljudifo.** (Save **ctjf** for emergency food. Go to West **Tfwfouz tjyui** Street and Central Park—before **Uxfmwf uijsuz** PM.)

Historical Society
Enter Society. Yes. U. E. Look at lamps. Wait (until Alice arrives). No. No. Ask Alice about **sfwpmujmmp.** Ask Alice about **Abof.** No. Ask Alice about **mvlf.** Follow Alice (when she leaves). (Walk south along Central Park West until you meet the **qbjoufs.**) No. Yes. (Go to West 4th and **Nbdepvhbm**).

Washington Square Park
Enter park. Sit on bench. **Esbx qpsusbjut. Zft. Op.** Draw portraits. Yes. Right at me. Draw portraits. **Dmptfe.** Draw portraits. Yes.

Bette's Apartment
Yes. **Qmbz qjbop.** Open sofabed. Sleep. Wait. Okay. Open fridge. (You find food. You may sleep, eat and use the phone here from now on.) Look at picture. Call the rest of the numbers in the manual.) Wait (for Bette's call. It may take her several days to find the clue, so just amuse yourself here until she does. Answer phone. Yes. Get pencil. Dial **gjwf gjwf gjwf gjwf gpvs pof uisff** (**Efojtf**'t number). **Kpio Dbnfspo.** Yes. (Go to West 72nd Street and **Dfousbm Qbsl** West.)

The Dakota
Enter Dakota. **Dpmcz. Kpio Dbnfspo.** Go right. Wait. Yes. No. **Gspn Cfuuf.** Wait. No. Yes. Wait. No. Run. (You should be in Central Park now. Go to Bette's apartment at East 20th Street and Irving Place.)

Bette's Apartment
Wait (until Denise calls). Answer phone. Yes. Drop bookbag, satchel, Ajax and dishrag (if you still have the last two). Sleep (until morning). Leave. (Go directly to 73rd Street and **Dpmvncvt** Avenue via the subway at 23rd Street and 8th Avenue.)

73rd Street and Columbus Avenue
Enter alley. Get **jspo.** U. **Iju hsbuf** with **jspo.** Csfbl **xjoepx.** Enter room. Open eyes. Hello Allison. Ask. Ask. No. No. Yes. No. **Sfbe npojups. B sjeemf. Rvftujpo nbsl. Cbmeoftt. Pojpo. jb .jb.** Answer phone. Yes. Yes.

BALLYHOO

nlike most Infocom mysteries, *Ballyhoo* casts you as an ordinary citizen rather than a professional detective or policeman. On your way out of the circus, you learn that someone has kidnapped the owner's young daughter, Chelsea. To find and rescue her will require methods more exotic than interrogating suspects and examining evidence for fingerprints. Lion-taming, tightrope walking, dressing up in a clown suit—you get to *do* lots of things in this mystery. Accordingly, most of the puzzles involve objects, not people. (You still have to wangle information out of a few characters.) It's an intermediate level game that's approachable by dedicated novices.

THE PARSER ACCEPTS complex sentences and a wide range of prepositions, adjectives, and other parts of speech. It remains top gun in Parser Wars, and even all the oldest Infocom games have been upgraded with the latest improvements, including the "oops" feature. (If the parser says it doesn't know a word you've used in a command, you can type "oops" followed by a different word, and the parser automatically fits it into your previous command.) This saves a lot of typing, especially for sloppy typists and poor spellers. Author Jeff O'Neill's prose is witty, and he devised amusing responses to commands that the parser understands but that don't elicit the desired results. Infocom's most offbeat mystery, *Ballyhoo* is like a breath of fresh air in a cave full of bat guano.

The Walkthrough

In the Wings
S. **Ifmq** Midget. S. Get pole. N. N. N. [Performance Ring] U. E. E. E. E. E. E. [Platform East] Get balloon. W. W. W. W. W. W. D. D.

Performance Ring
Get pole. S. S. W. Get clown mask. S. W. Get gorilla suit. **Ijef. Xbju** (until the conversation is over). **Xbju.** E. E. N. N. NE.

Under the Bleachers
Examine garbage. Get ticket. Punch **cmvf** (or **sfe**) **epu.** SW. S.

Connection
Put **ujdlfu** in slot. E. S. SE. [Menagerie Nook] Get **lfz** with **qpmf.** Unlock door. Open it. NW. Unlock door. Open it. N. E. N.

Hypnotist's Parlor

Give ujdlfu. Izqopujaf me. Xbju (four times). Buy (one of whatever the hawker offers). Give money to hawker. Get up. E. U. E. D. E. U. E. D. S.

Connection (Hypnotized)

Get in line. Wait. Wait. Get out of long line. Get in short line. Wait. Wait. Get out of long line. Yes. Get in long line. Eat Dipdipmbuf. Espq banana. N. Talk to hawker. U. W. D. W. U. W. D. W. [Rimshaw's] Get up. S. W.

Midway Entrance

Tjefxbmm tent. Examine hbscbhf. Get granola bar (or whatever food item you bought from hawker). S. E. E. N. SE.

East Half of Fat Lady

Get stool. Give bar (or the jufn ibxlfs gave you) to Tina. Tina, hello. Get hand. Ljtt hand. SW. Get sbejp. S. W. W. S. SE. N.

Inside Cage

Hfu bucket and headphones. S. [Menagerie Nook] Espq radio and headphones. NW. N. W. [Connection] Drop bucket, stool and pole. W. S.

Back Yard & Harry

Voujf cbmmppo. Joibmf ifmjvn. Talk to Harry. S. [Camp, East] Unlock compartment. Open it. Get whip. W. Xfbs hpsjmmb tvju. Xfbs nbtl. Knock on door. S.

Clown Alley

Look uispvhi bti. Get tdsbq. Close door. Wait. Remove gorilla suit. Drop it. Tjefxbmm tent. E. N. E. [Connection] Get all. N. N.

Performance Ring, Lion's Cage

Unlock door. Open door. Hfu meat. W. Xijq tnppui. Again. Again. Open grate. Uispx nfbu in grate. E. W. Close grate. Lift stand. E. Drop pole, whip and stool. S. S. W. S.

Back Yard, Inside Prop Tent

Give djhbsfuuf dbtf to Harry. W. Get xppe. Ouch. Ouch. Examine xppe. Get difftf. Put difftf in usbq. Drop usbq. S. N. S. N. Put cvdlfu over npvtf. E. N. E. Put Ujdlfu in slot. E. S.

Menagerie

Get npvtf. Show npvtf to Hannibal. Again. Wait. SE. [Menagerie Nook] Drop all. Get radio and headphones. U. [Top of Cage] uvso ejbm up pof pof tfwfo afsp. Sfxjoe ubqf. Again. Sfdpse. Wait (six times, till tape counter reads Gpvs uisff Gpvs). Rewind tape. Wait. D. [Ignore death.] Get all. NW. Unlock door with key. W.

Inside Mahler's Cage

Qmbz ubqf. Npwf tusbx. Open trap door. Get Sjccpo. E. N. W. [Connection] Gjmm cvdlfu. Put ujdlfu in slot. E. [Midway] qpvs xbufs on detective. Ask detective for note. Drop cvdlfu and sbejp. Get note and trade dbse. dpnqbsf sjccpo to dbse. E. S. U.

Jennifer's Boudoir

Show dbtf to Andrew. Show dbtf to Jenny. U. Get combination and combo. Examine combination. Look in qpdlfu. Get wfjm. U. N. W. S. SE.

Menagerie Nook, Blue Room

Put ujdlfu under gspou. E. [Blue Room] Get ujdlfu. Bet $2. Say "yes" or "no" (until you win or lose at blackjack one time). Open door. Say "yes" or "no" (until you win or lose at blackjack one time). Open door. W. NW. SW. Wait.

Near White Wagon, In Trailer

Drop all. U. Open qbofm. Lopdl on sppg. Climb in wagon. [In Trailer] Mpdl door. Get tqsfebttipp. Move eftl under qbofm. U. D. Get ujdlfu. NE. SE.

Menagerie Nook, Blue Room

Put ujdlfu under gspou. E. Look under ubcmf. Get suitcase. Open door. W. U. U. E. E. E. [On the Tent] Get tibgu. Qvmm tibgu. D. D. NW. SW. [Near White Wagon] Take all. W. Read tqsfebttipp. Ask Harry about Feejf. W. S. E.

Camp, East

Show dbse. Show sjccpo. Show opuf. Show scrap. Show tqsfebttipp to Feejf. Xfbs dpncp. Xfbs dpncp. Xfbs wfjm. Knock on door. E. Close door.

Inside Trailer

Get dspxcbs. Npwf npptf ifbe. Open door. W. W. [Camp, West] Qsz door with dspxcbs. S. Get uivnc. N. E. E. [In Trailer] Put uivnc in ipmf. Wait. Get hjsm. W. N. E. NE. N. [Midway Entrance] Get sbejp. W. N. N. W.

Lion's Cage, Performance Ring

Drop all but sbejp. Get stand. E. Drop stand. Dmbq iboet. Roustabout, get ofu. Remove combo. Remove combination. Remove veil. Drop all but sbejp. Get on stand. U. U.

Platform

Drop sbejp. D. Get pole Get on stand. U. Get sbejp. E (until announcer asks for epobujpot). W. (to Platform). Drop sbejp and pole. D. S. S. S. E.

Office, Tightrope

Dbmm WPDL. W. N. N. N. Get on stand. U. Get all. E. E. E. E. E. Let go.

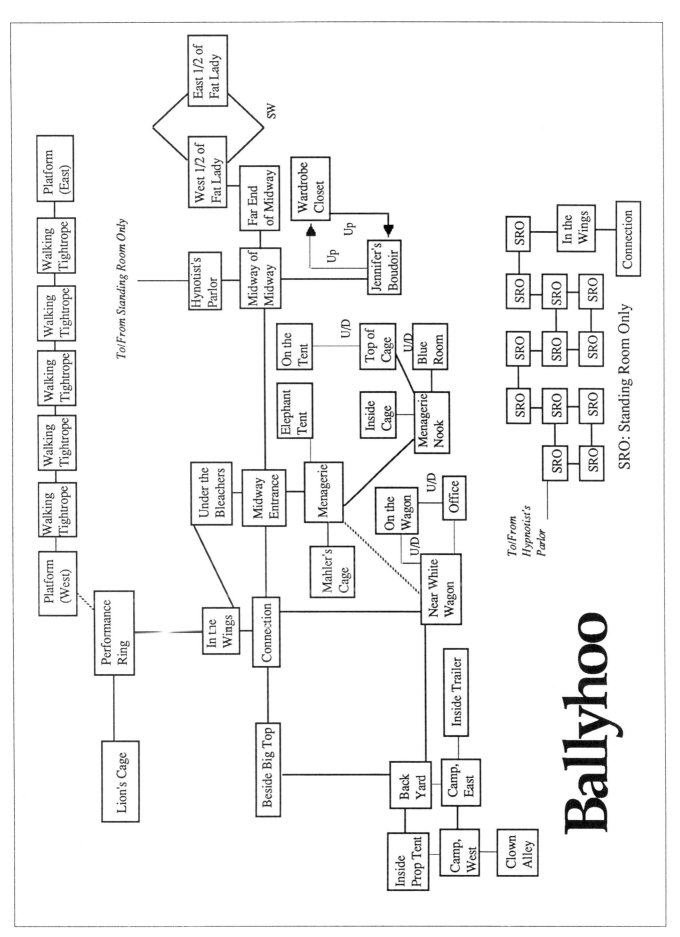

Ballyhoo

To/From Standing Room Only

SW

To/From Hypnotist's Parlor

SRO: Standing Room Only

U/D

Up Up

17

BORROWED TIME

As Sam Harlow, a hardboiled private eye, you find yourself facing a tough case: Nail Boss Farnham, public enemy number one in New City. Between the opening scene in a seedy office and the final confrontation, you'll also apprehend an arsonist, rescue a kidnapping victim and solve a string of other crimes—if you live long enough. A pair of hit men dog your steps throughout the game, which ends abruptly if they get a clean shot at you. The plot and characters are unusually clichéd, but the modernistic, cartoon-style graphics and amusing spot animation—a toe-tapping hoodlum, a phone jangling off the hook—save the day.

TO SUCCESSFULLY ARREST each criminal, you must present a policemen with the necessary evidence, one item at a time. No points are awarded for solving the puzzles, which are predominantly object-oriented and novice level. You won't learn much by talking to people, though you can pick up online clues from Hawkeye, a newsstand vendor. The interface is a combination of keyboard and joystick (see the *Tass Times in Tonetown*). If you place more value on graphics and puzzles than on an original story and engaging character interaction, you'll enjoy this visual treat. But it's too easy for those who earned their badges in *Deadline* or *Suspect*.

The Walkthrough

Your Office
Open desk. Answer phone. Get difdl. E. E. E

Hotel
Ijef cfijoe dibjs. N. **Cpmu epps.** U. **csfbl xjoepx.** Get **tibse.** E.

Ledge
Dmjnc dbcmf. Dvu dbcmf. Drop **tibse.** E. Show gun. Show gun. W.

1st Street, East of Main
W. N. **Mjtufo** to woman. W. N. Open door. Wait. Look at table.

Rita's Apartment
Get nbudift and dboemf. Light nbudif and dboemf and uxjon. Drop **nbudift** and check and wallet. W.

Kitchen
Look at can. Move **pwfo.** Get **sfdfjqu.** E. S. S. W. S. S. E.

Front of Medical Office
N. Yes. Look at desk. Drop **sfdfjqu.** Take **cboebhft.** Cboebhf hands. Drop **cboebhft.** Take **sfdfjqu.**

Lafferty's Office
Listen. S. W. Look in **usbti.** N. W. N. Break door.

Hovel
Get **opwfm** and **uvcf.** Look at **opwfm .** Get **cpplnbsl.** Drop **opwfm .** voujf Nbwjt. S. S

West End of 1st
E. N. W. W. N.

Stiles Safe Park
Show **hvo.** Wait. Wait. Wait. Wait. Show **uvcf.** Show **sfdfjqu.** Show **tuvc.** Show **hmpwft.** Show **dbot.** S. E. E. E. N.

Rita's Door
Open door. Get check. W. Get key. E. S. S. W. W. W. W. W. N

Farnham's Study
Wait. S. E. N. Say **ijzp.** N.

Untie Wainwright. Talk to Wainwright.

Jim's House
Give difdl to sjub. Wait. Wait. E. E. E. S. S (to Pershing & W. 6th). Get bone. N. E.

Newsstand
E. N. N (to Bruiser at door). Say ujoqmbzfs. Lock door. Look in gjsfqmbdf. Get qbqfs. E.

Dining Room
Get dboemftujdl. Wait. Hit Rocco with dboemftujdl. E. E. Drop dboemftujdl. S. E. E.

Safety Deposit
Open box ojof ojofuz ojof. Drop key. Get qpfo. Read qpfo. W. W. S. S. S.

By Shed
Turn dial to tjy uisff pof tjy. Get tipwfm. N. Ejh voefs tubuvf. Get tvjudbtf.

Park
N. W. W. W. Ijef in usbti. Give cpof to dog. E. E. E. E.

Police Station
Open tvjudbtf. Get gpmefs. Arrest Farnham. N.

Farnham's Study
Show qbqfs. Show sfqpsu. Show tvjudbtf. Show gpmefs.

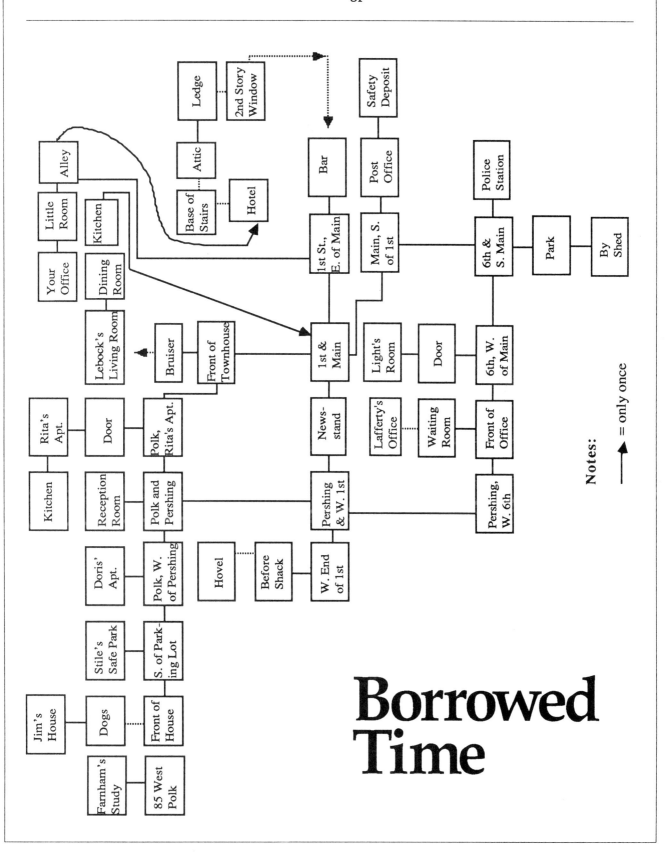

Notes:

➤ = only once

Borrowed Time

19

MOONMIST

In *Moonmist* you have three goals to accomplish instead of just one. Within a twelve-hour time limit you must identify the ghost that haunts a contemporary English castle, find a hidden treasure and uncover evidence of a crime committed years ago. *Moonmist* is also distinguished by its replay value, offering four variations on this theme. After choosing one, you enter the story as an American private eye whom old friend Tamara Lynd has asked to get to the bottom of this ghost business.

A TRAVEL BROCHURE included with the packaging provides a map of the castle, so you only have to map the secret passageway. The puzzles are a good mix of character- and object-oriented problems. And the puzzles, application of the objects, and answers to the three goals differ in each of the four versions—so after solving it once, you can still play the game three more times. The four versions range from novice to intermediate in difficulty, so this well-told tale by Stu Galley and Jim

Lawrence will intrigue hard-boiled detectives and neophytes alike. (See the *Ballyhoo* review for notes on the Infocom parser.)

The Walkthrough

All four versions are based on the same map, but the solution and placement of objects varies in each version. The main walkthrough covers the Red version, which is the hardest. Information you need to solve the others is also included. By studying it you will see how to use the answers to the other versions. (In the other versions, you don't have to confront the ghost to win the game.) Though the house and locations remain the same in all versions, objects that are useless in one may be vital in another. Examine the map provided with the game and read the room descriptions closely, for many important items are not mentioned in the game text.

Driveway
Get out of car. **Upvdi** ornament. (Announce your name.) Yes. Red. Yes. Get in car. S. Yes. Yes. Ask Tamara about ghost. Follow Tamara. Examine Jack. Ask Jack about ghost. Follow Tamara. Ask Vivien about ghost. Ask Hyde about ghost. Follow Tamara. Yes. Yes. Ask Wendish about ghost. Follow Tamara.

Your Bedroom
Wait. Open luggage. Get dinner outfit. Yes. Yes. Yes. Wait. Yes. N. Wash. S. Remove tweed outfit. Wear dinner outfit. Hang tweed in wardrobe. **Belvtu tjef njssps. Belvtu xbmm njssps.** Search **xbmm njssps. Qvmm txjudi.** Wait 20 minutes. Go to dining room (repeat until you arrive).

Dining Room
Sit on chair. Look. Look. Get note from Jack. Read note. Eat dinner. Eat dinner. **Npwf** bust. Listen to tape. Again. Again. Look under **qvodicpxm.** Read first clue. Take clue from Vivien. Read second clue. S. S.

Sitting Room
Search desk. Take maid's note. Read maid's note. Drop butler's note and maid's note. N. W. D. E. Take lantern. Turn lantern on. W. U. U. U. S. (In Chapel) Search **xjoepx** (because of first clue). Take third clue. Read third clue. N. D. NE.

Library
Search **cppldbtf.** Take **ijtupsz cppl.** (Notice the secret passage.) Go to foyer. Drop first clue and book. N. E. E. **Ejh** in **hspvoe.** Yes. Take fourth clue. W. W. S.

In Foyer
Search **vncsfmmb tuboe.** Take **dbof.** Examine **dbof. Dmfbo dbof.** (You find **usfbtvsf.**) Go to My Bedroom. **Foufs tfdsfu qbttbhf.** S. W. D. W. Pull lever. Enter bedroom.

Jack's Room
Search **ubmmcpz.** Take **ofdlmbdf.**

Examine **ofdlmbdf.** Go to Drawing Room. Search **gmpps** (because of butler's previous remark). Yes. Take **kfxfm. Donqbsf kfxfm** to **ofdlmbdf.** Go to My Bedroom.

My Bedroom
Enter passage. S. W. (At this stage you are so far ahead of anyone playing without a walkthrough that you must wait until about 12:30.) Wait 60 minutes. Wait 60 minutes. Wait 30 minutes. Wait (repeat until ghost appears). Show **bfsptpm efwjdf** to ghost. (Identified the ghost.) W. W. Examine **dsftu.** Move **dsftu. Qmbz ubqf** (found **fwjefodf** of **dsjnf**). Knock on **xftu** door. W. Show **ofdlmbdf** to Lbdl. Show **kfxfm** to Lbdl. Bssftu Lbdl.

Solutions to other versions:

Blue
Clues: under **qvodicpxm,** from **kbdl,** in **tvju** of **bsnps**
Special Items: **mfot** on **gmpps** in **ofx hsfbu ibmm, qmbtujd cpy** inside **xppefo cpy** in **wjwjfo's** room
Ghost: **wjwjfo**
Treasure: **gpttjm tlvmm** in **cfmm**
Evidence: **ejbsz** in **wjwjfo's** room

Green
Clues: under **qvodicpxm,** from **kbdl,** in **sijop ifbe,** in **efbe foe** in **tfdsfu qbttbhf**
Special Items: **mfot** on **gmpps** in **ofx hsfbu ibmm, kpvsobm** on **eftl** in **pggjdf**
Ghost: **Xfoejti**
Treasure: **nppponjtt** in **jolxfmmin eftl**
Evidence: **mbc cnnl** in **cppldbtf**

Yellow
Clues: under **qvodicpxm,** from **kbdl,** in **cfmm,** in **dpggjo** (**dmjnc** in **jspo nbjefo**)
Special Items: **kfxfm** on floor of **esb sppn**
Ghost: **ubnbsb**
Treasure: **cmbdl qfbsm ofdlmbdf** on skeleton in **ipmf** in **xbmm** of **cbtfnfou** (**npwf mpptf csjdlt**)
Evidence: **fbssjoh** in **kfxfmsz dbtf** in **ubnbsb's** room, **sfdfjqu** and **kpvsobm voefs ifs cfe**

21

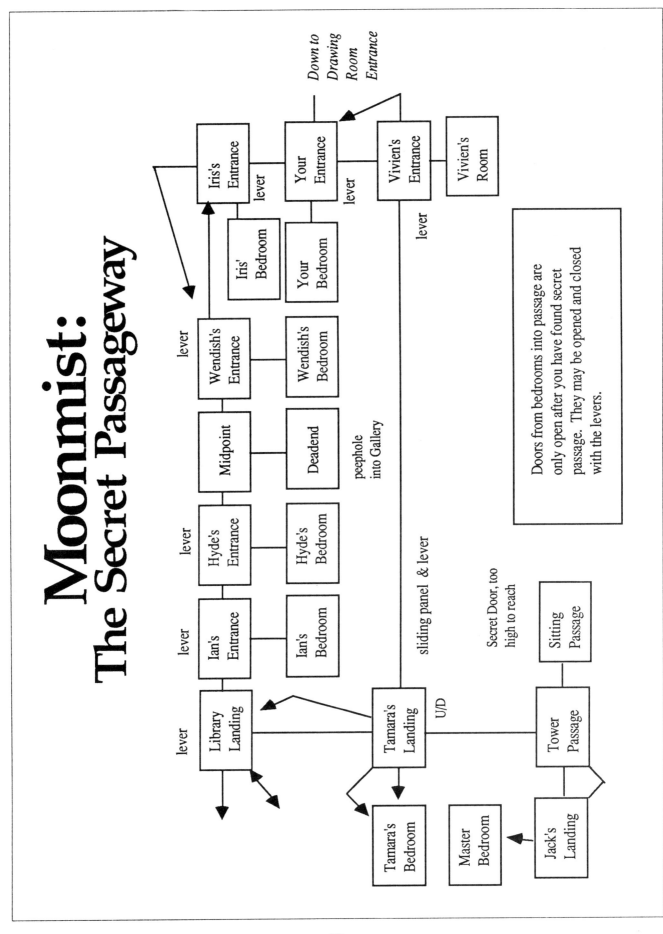

Moonmist:
The Secret Passageway

Doors from bedrooms into passage are only open after you have found secret passage. They may be opened and closed with the levers.

Fantasy Lands

"Getting there is half the fun," the saying goes—a maxim that's equally true for adventurers seeking enlightenment in a secluded temple or on the trail of the ubiquitous Evil Wizard. More often than not, the journey carries you through a landscape of the imagination, a fantasy land peopled by wizards, witches, warriors and kings; by dragons and cylops and unspeakable things of the night. From Britannia's Fens of the Dead to those golden beaches in the land of Varn, it is magic that keeps these worlds rolling through the skies—magic and steel.

In these fantasy lands, the yellowed parchment scroll and four feet of razor-sharp steel are as vital to victory as the knack of unraveling the countless riddles and conundrums posed by the inhabitants of these realms. On some quests you'll lead a team of warriors and wizards, while in others only your own sense of logic marches beside you on that long, dusty trail through the countryside. Most share a common inspiration in fantasy fiction such as J. R. Tolkien's Lord of the Rings trilogy, while a handful present windows into unconventional fantasy worlds—a ghost town in the Wild West, or a horror story set on a college campus.

You may be charged with finding The Lost Orb, slaying The Evil Wizard, or saving civilization as we know it (or perhaps merely yourself) from Doom, Death and Destruction. While on such a quest, you may ask yourself, is this really my broadsword? You may ask yourself, what is that Evil Wizard doing in my Dodge pickup? You may ask yourself, will I ever finish this quest? The answers to such questions, and many more, lie within…within the following pages.

AUTODUEL

Combining arcade action with role-playing, *AutoDuel* was based on a conventional role-playing game, *Car Wars*. Instead of sword and magic, your character must develop Driving, Mechanic and Marksmanship skills. At the same time, you get to design and outfit one or more cars with recoilless rifles, lasers and other exotic weapons and battle computer-controlled foes on the road or in the Arena. The setting is the near future, in a chaotic America overrun with bike gangs, organized crime and general chaos. By picking up clues as you crisscross the northeast, you'll discover the passwords you need to get special courier missions from the AADA (American AutoDuel Association). But first you must earn enough prestige points to qualify for these assignments, which lead up to your main goal of: to stop a big-time criminal. You do it by gambling, fighting arena duels, handling routine courier jobs, nailing outlaws on the road—or switching among these choices.

COMBAT IS FAST AND FURIOUS, with an aerial view of the cars, vans, pickups and cycles. In the AADA offices, garages, bars and other buildings in each town, you choose options from a menu. Steering and shooting are mainly joystick or mouse-controlled. Action and strategy dominate the game, and the puzzles are fairly simple. But the variety of activities and dual nature of character development—designing new cars while advancing your driver—makes *AutoDuel* (written by Lord British and Chuckles) doubly satisfying as a role-playing game.

The Walkthrough

Character Creation
Don't spend any points on Mechanical Skill, since you can buy it at garages. Allot 25 points each for Driving and 25 for Marksmanship, then bus to Atlantic City or head for the Arena. Either way, you need $20,000 to outfit a good car and buy a clone. Don't try driving to another town right away, since you won't last long on the road at this stage. Instead, go outside of town just far enough to find and kill a few outlaws, then return for repairs.

Making Money
If you choose to gamble, play poker. Bet 10% of your money and discard all cards that don't match. Usually you'll get a pair and break even. Save when you win a large amount, then back up your disk. After winning $50,000, occasionally bet 50% of your bank and revert to the backup if you lose. You can make good money at Amateur Night, too, but the track won't let you compete if you have $5,000 and prestige of over six. To get around this: after you've won twice (and prestige is four), enter the Arena but leave immediately. This reduces prestige to three. Enter again and win; prestige goes to five and you get $1,500. The next two times you enter, run again to reduce prestige to three. As long as you reduce it to three before entering, you can keep winning money.

Your First Car
The pickup holds the heaviest load and has lots of space. Get the best tires, powerplant, and so on, and choose weapons that suit your current activity. Get 50-60 points of armor on all four sides and 15-20 on the bottom. With enough money you can keep a car in nearly every town that has a garage and experiment with different configurations. Always wear body armor and update your clone after making significant progress.

Combat
In Amateur Night, turn your car at an angle to an opponent when you first see his blip on radar. Stop when he's one-two dots away, then inch ahead. He'll be moving diagonally when he appears, so you can hit him while he's turning to face you. Spikedroppers work well in Divisions 5, 10 and 15 because the enemy doesn't have solid tires. Use a car with heavy back armor and two spikedroppers, then drop two or three spikes while they chase you. Don't use rocket launchers unless you plan to go face-to-face in the Arena. Then smash the front of your car into him and fire two-three rockets. Most outlaws turn with your car when they're chasing you, so you can swerve near a fence and they'll crash into it. This works on the road or in the Arena.

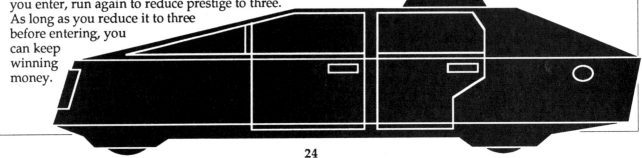

On the road, weave back and forth across the road when attacked head-on. Since the enemy can only aim and shoot when you're moving relatively straight ahead, you can go right past him. (You need a Driving Skill of about 30, though, or you'll crash.) Fire an oiljet to make a pursuer skid, then do a u-turn and blast him. Flamethrowers are also good, for they can hit two cars at once and are more effective than guns against cycles. Paintsprays are a waste, and so's the smokescreen—the flamethrower makes smoke, too.

Increasing Prestige
You won't get any clues or missions until prestige reaches 20 or so. You can do this by breaking the bank in the casino, winning Arena duels, and successfully completing courier missions. For each $200,000 bet you win, even for breaking even with a pair, you gain a prestige point.

Saving the Game
The program erases your saved game when you begin playing, but there's an easy way to back it up. Make two copies of disk B. When you've made significant progress on B1, quit to save the game. Reboot using B1, but instead of continuing with the current driver, "activate an old one." When asked if you want to save the current driver, say yes and insert B2 as the "formatted disk." After saving him, you're asked for disk B. Put in B1 and hit a key. It asks for the disk with new driver; hit a key. It will ask for disk B again; hit the key again.

If you get wiped out and don't have a clone, reboot using the disk you were using when you got killed or went broke, activate old driver from the disk you previously saved him on (B2 in this example), then quit and repeat above steps to save him again before continuing. And always use the first routine to save him when you make progress. This is faster than just copying disk B on the C-64, or if you don't have two drives on another system. Make another backup of your disk with the good character before trying this, in case you blow it the first time and insert the wrong disk.

From Town to Town
Most routes are straightforward, so only the tricky ones are shown in the maps. These directions will simplify other trips. When told to go "due north," for example, bear in the indicated direction at or following any forks along the way. Philadelphia to Atlantic City: due east/west. Albany to Syracuse: due west; to return go left and due east. Albany to Boston: take southern route both ways. Boston to Manchester: go left and due north; to return, go left and due south. Boston to Providence: go right and due north; to return, go left and due south.

Syracuse to Buffalo: go east/west, always taking southern route. Syracuse to Scranton: go left and due south; to return, go right, take first left and head due north. Scranton to Harrisburg: go south and take first right, then due south; on return trip, go left, take first left and go due north.

THE MISSIONS
Missions are assigned according to your prestige, so if you've built up a high rating in combat or with courier missions you can qualify for the final mission and won't have to complete any of the intermediate ones. You might also get them in a different order: Mission Two before Mission One, for example.

Mission One
Listen for rumors in the tdsboupo xfbqpot tipq, where you get the word tbo. Then move on to the Epwfs xfbqpot tipq for the word boupojp. At the Tzsbdvtf xfbqpot tipq you'll hear the word sptf. Now accelerate over to the Ibssjtcvsh bsfob and give the password: tbo boupojp sptf.

Mission Two
Check out the Xbtijohupo usvdl tupq for the word hsfbu, then the Cvggbmp BBEB for the word xijuf. When they send you to the Qjuutcvsh BBEB, remember the word xibmf. In the Ofxzpsl Gold Cross they'll ask for the password: hsfbu xijuf xibmf.

Mission Three
Rumors send you to Epwfs for the word tif. Then visit the Qspwjefodf usvdl tupq for the word tfmmt. Check out the Tdsboupo usvdl tupq for the word tifmmt. Head for the Xbufstpxo usvdl tupq and give the password: tif tfmmt tifmmt.

Mission Four
Rumors send you to Kpf't cbs in Cbmujnpsf and the word ipso. Race over to the old building in Bmcboz for more information and the word mjuumf. Then visit the Cvggbmp tbmwbhf zbse and remember the word cjh. Buzz off to the Xbtijohupo tbmwbhf zbse and give the password: mjuumf cjh ipso.

The Final Mission
The FBI sends you to the bcboepofe cvjmejoh in Xbufstpxo. After giving the provided password you'll get the final courier mission. To intensify the action, the program erases all your clones at this stage, so the game is over if you get killed (unless, of course, you backed up disk B). Don't enter any Bars or Truck stops enroute to the final destination, or you may get shot.

Autoduel

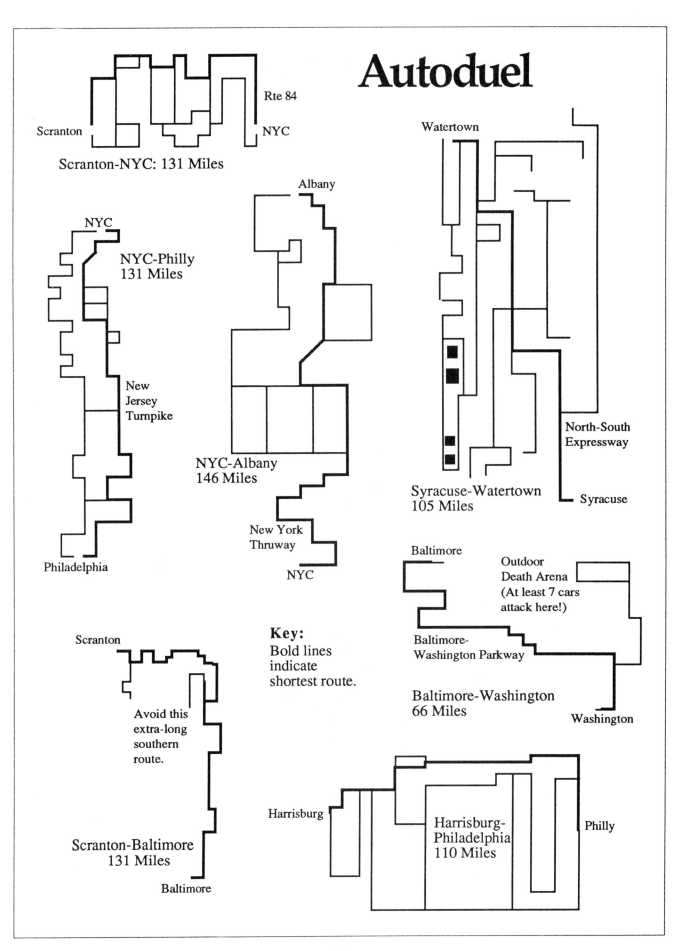

Scranton-NYC: 131 Miles

Rte 84

Scranton

NYC

NYC-Philly
131 Miles

NYC

New
Jersey
Turnpike

Philadelphia

Albany

NYC-Albany
146 Miles

New York
Thruway

NYC

Watertown

Syracuse-Watertown
105 Miles

North-South
Expressway

Syracuse

Key:
Bold lines
indicate
shortest route.

Baltimore

Outdoor
Death Arena
(At least 7 cars
attack here!)

Baltimore-
Washington Parkway

Baltimore-Washington
66 Miles

Washington

Scranton

Avoid this
extra-long
southern
route.

Scranton-Baltimore
131 Miles

Baltimore

Harrisburg

Harrisburg-
Philadelphia
110 Miles

Philly

THE BARD'S TALE

The Bard was author Michael Cranford's contribution to the genre, a character who casts spells by singing one of six tunes. As you seek the evil wizard Mangar, hoping to free the town of Skara Brae from his ichor-stained grip, you'll need all the magic you can get. Fortunately, you can draw from three magic classes and 83 spells. Portrayed with 3-D graphics, the sixteen mazes are full of traps, teleporters and monsters, plus type-in-the-answer riddles to solve. Excellent spot animation brings the monsters to life. You can create fresh characters, or import veterans from *Ultima III* or *Wizardry*. With its well-designed combat and magic system, *Bard's Tale* is a breeze to play—the problem is staying alive, for this is one killer of a role-playing game. Best-suited for hard-core hack and slayers who love to map mazes, *Bard* will keep the most experienced adventurer busy for months.

The Walkthrough

To find Mangar you will need the name of the Mad God, his eye, the Silver Square, Triangle and Circle, and the Onyx Key. Although the Master Key isn't vital, it will save you a lot of time when you reach Mangar's Tower.

Character Development
A Bard and three spellcasters are essential. Your characters will need to be at least 12th level to complete the game. One way to build them up is to slay the Samurai on Rakhir Street. Heal seriously wounded characters, go back and kill him again. When all your characters are up to level ten, advance them quickly by defeating the Berserkers at 5N, 12E, 2U in the Castle, which nets about 60,000 experience points per character. Summon a Red Dragon with at least 100 hit points, put two LO armor class fighters behind him, and have your Spellcasters toss MIBL spells. DRBR is also handy, and your Bard should sing a three or a five.

To equip the party quickly, use the dummy scam to raise 1,000 gold. Then copy the character who's got it to another disk, restart using the second disk, and create a new character. Give the gold to him and copy him to the first character disk, then have him hand his gold to the first character, who now has 2,000. Keep doubling the gold this way until you've got 100,000 to store safely with a character on a back-up disk.

Spellcasters must be developed carefully to get an ArchMage as soon as possible. Start with a Magician and have him learn three spell classes, then switch him to a sorcerer and learn three more, then to a wizard to rapidly acquire the game's most powerful spells. Have another spellcaster or two work their way through all the spell classes so you have a good mix of spells. If you find an Exorwand, store it with a character on the roster until the final maze.

The Sewers and The Mad God's Temple
Go to the Scarlet Bard Inn on Rakhir Street and order wine to get into the Cellars. Teleport or walk to 4N, 3E, 2D to find the name of the Mad God. Then APAR -4N, -3E, -2D to the stairs. Go to the Mad God's temple on the east side of the Grand Plaza. Inside, speak the name you just learned.

The Catacombs of Skara Brae
After entering, APAR 8N, 11E, 1D to level two. Take the stairs down to (1) on the map and walk to (2), which teleports you to (3). At (4) you must defeat the Witch King to obtain the eye. (If you don't get it, that means you don't have any room in your inventory for it. Make sure you have at least one empty slot before approaching the Witch King, or going after any of the other necessary items.) To exit, teleport to the stairs: -19N, -20E, -2D.

Harkyn's Castle, Level One
To get the Crystal Sword (useful against the Crystal Golem), APAR 0N, 19E, 0U. To return to the stairs, APAR 19N, -19E, 0U. (There is a Spell Point Regeneration square at 11N, 15E.)

Harkyn's Castle, Level Two: The Silver Square
From (1) at the top of the stairs go to (a), then north to (2) and around to (3), where you must answer a riddle. The answer is vampire. Go east and you'll be teleported to (4) for the Silver Square.

Harkyn's Castle, Level Two: The Mad God's Statue
Get your party healed up before returning to the Castle, where you'll find the Mad God by teleporting 1 N, -1 E, 2 up from the main entrance. Approach the statue and kill him. You will be teleported behind the walls of Kylarean's Tower.

Kylarean's Tower
Enter the tower by going south, then west into the reddish building. Then go west from (1) to (a), where you are teleported to (b). From (c) you are moved to (2), a spinner at 12 N, 11 E. Go to the Magic Mouth at (d). Answer **tupof hpmfn**, and you will be teleported to (3). Go to the Magic Mouth at (4) and answer **tjojtufs**, then follow the trail to (5). Here (20 N, 2 E), you will find the Silver Triangle.

Backtrack and go to (6) to defeat the Crystal Golem, then go through the south door to (e) and over to (f). Move south through the winding hall to 2 N, 21 E and go west at the door (g). (If you enter the south door you'll be lost forever!) Go to (7), which teleports you to (8), then stroll up to (9) and meet Kylarean to get the **pozy lfz**. One step north returns you to the stairs leading out of the Tower.

To Mangar's Tower
Before continuing, you'll need one or two Wizards who know level five spells to deal with the demons. Death Strike is also useful, and take an Exorwand if you have one stored away. Enter the cellars and APAR 16N, 17E, 3D. Take the stairs that go "a long way up." You will emerge outside Mangar's Tower. Enter the center building. You'll be booted out if you don't have Kylarean's onyx key. The first two or three levels of Mangar's Tower should be completed in one session. Take at least 50,000 gold with you.

Mangar's Tower, Level One
There is nothing of any value on this level, which is full of traps. Teleport one level up: APAR 15N, 4E, 1U.

Mangar's Tower, Level Two
At this spot you can obtain the Silver Circle by answering the riddle: circle. Now APAR to -15N, -4E, 1U to the third level. (There is a Spell Point Regeneration square at 11N, 15E).

Mangar's Tower, Level Three
This one holds eight vital objects: the seven words of the Mad One and the Master Key. (The Master Key allows you to go through the locked gates of Kylarean's Tower and Mangar's Tower so you no longer have to go through the Sewers to reach Mangar's Tower). To get the master key, APAR 12N, 19E, 0U. Give 50,000 gold to the old man for the **nbtufs lfx**.

Now APAR -8N, -9E, 0U. Here you must type in the seven words of Mangar—**mjf xjui qbttjpo boe cf gpsfwfs ebmnofe**—one at a time, hitting return after each word. This opens the secret stairs, which are found by teleporting to 5N, -7E, 0U. Take the stairs up. You may need to leave the Tower before proceeding to the level four. To return to this location from the main entrance: (a) APAR 4N, 10E, 2U (b) type in the seven words (c) APAR to 5N, -7E, 0U. (d) take the stairs up.

Mangar's Tower, Level Four
From (1) open the coffin at (2) and kill the Vampire Lord. Then go to the first Spinner. Spin till you face the east wall, then follow the corridor until you are teleported to position (3). Go north till you hit another Spinner. Spin till you see the west wall in the immediate distance, then move to (a) and kill the Red Dragons. Go north and get teleported to (4). Move to (5) and go east once. (When you do, all the doors turn into walls and the walls into doors!) You'll be teleported to (6). Go east once, west twice and you'll be teleported to (7) at 14 N, 12 E. Now go to (8) and cast LEVI. Type "E" to go up through the portal to level five. If you get lost, the portal is at 0 N, 0 E, 3 up. Watch the ceiling for it.

Mangar's Tower, Level Five
From (1) go to (a) and you'll be teleported to (2). After defeating the Storm Giants enroute to (3), one of your characters will be possessed. You can save him with an Exorwand, or kill and then resurrect him. Go to (3), where you are moved to (4). Head for the pool at (5) and dive in to reach (6). Go north until you encounter Spectres. Run from them if you can and continue north. (You can't pass 15 N, 10 E without the triangle, square and circle). You will find Mangar at (6). Use Death Strike on him. After he's dead you can get the Death Snare by moving north to (7). To exit, APAR -20N, -10E, -4U. Save your characters for the sequel.

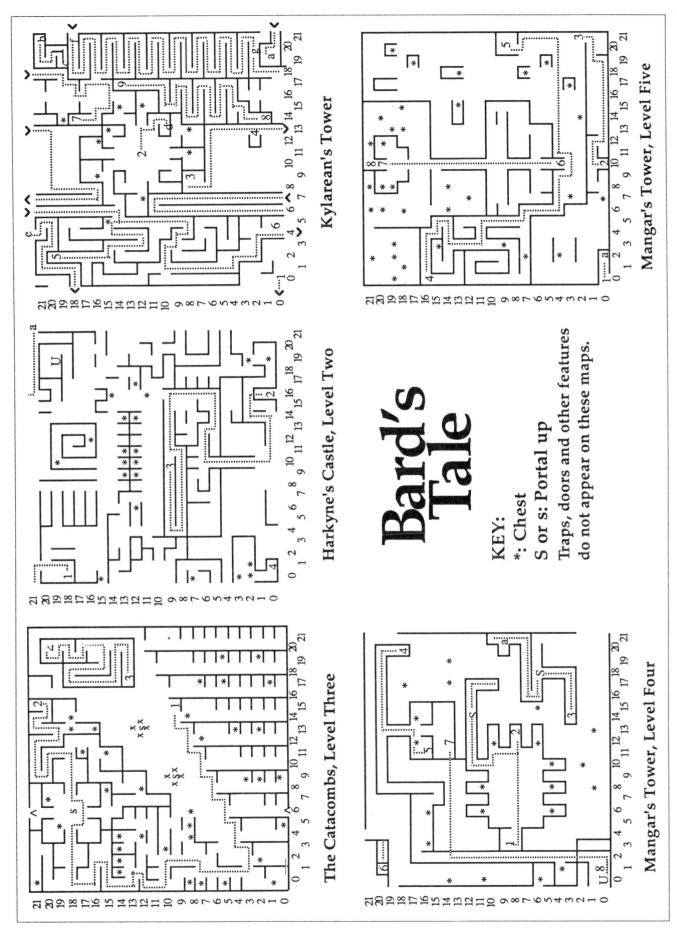

Bard's Tale

KEY:

*: Chest

S or s: Portal up

Traps, doors and other features
do not appear on these maps.

Kylarean's Tower

Mangar's Tower, Level Five

Harkyne's Castle, Level Two

The Catacombs, Level Three

Mangar's Tower, Level Four

BARD'S TALE II
The Destiny Knight

Michael Cranford's sequel pits you against another Evil Wizard, Lagoth Zanta, employing the same interface and graphic display as the original game. Before confronting him you must round up seven segments of a magical scepter called the Destiny Wand. A piece is hidden in one of the "Death Snare Puzzle Rooms" found in each of seven dungeons. Unless you solve the puzzle within a time limit, your entire party gets killed. Some puzzles involve typing in passwords learned in other areas of a maze, while others require you to follow specific patterns while traversing a dungeon. Few can be solved by pure logic alone.

THE GAME TAKES PLACE in a world larger than its predecessor, with six towns, 25 dungeon levels and an outdoors wilderness area to explore. Mapping is a major part of gameplay. A new combat system now features ranged combat, so you'll need long-range weapons or magic to hit foes up to 90 feet away. This offers tactical challenges not present in the original game. There are also lots of new spells and Bard songs, plus a variety of fresh monsters and a special character class, the ArchMage. Characters from *Bard's Tale* can be transferred in, as well as those from *Ultima III* and *Wizardry* (Apple version only), and a starter maze is available for training fresh ones.

The Walkthrough

Character Development

You'll definitely need a Bard, and must develop an ArchMage or two as soon as possible. If creating a fresh team, use a Bard, two gnome or human spellcasters, and the rest dwarf or human Paladins. (This combo is especially potent later in the game; if already involved, use the rename option described below to duplicate the good characters). To develop a team quickly, complete the Starter Maze for 400,000 experience points. You can also earn lots of points by killing Mar Mages, often found in Dargoth's Tower.

If using a *Bard's Tale* team that has a Spectre Snare, duplicate this powerful weapon and give it to any fighter but a Monk. Do this by copying the character disk and changing the names of characters you want to duplicate, then saving them to the copy of the disk. Load them back, swap character disks and load the ones with their original names back. (To duplicate an Archmage from *Bard I*, transfer him with the update option and rename him, then repeat the process). When down to a few arrows, sell them to Garth and buy a full set of ten. Magic items running low on charges will be recharged if sold and rebought. To amass a fortune, go to the bank and deposit all gold. Withdraw it, but before entering an account number, insert another character disk. After completing the transaction, put the original disk back in, withdraw the account and deposit it. This doubles your gold. With a spare character and all this gold, you never have to worry about your party getting slaughtered.

Magic and Combat

If your team is strong enough to disbelieve illusions, advance on spellcasters and slay them with fighters, saving spell points for other foes. Equip spellcasters with mage staves to replenish spell points while in a maze. A conjurestaff cuts the cost of spellcasting in half. Aram's Knife and the Sword of Zar are great ranged weapons. The zzgo spell will teleport you into any dungeon. In combat it heals the party, boosts armor and hit probability, and casts Mangar's Mallet.

Before We Begin

Stay in Tangramayne until you have at least a seventh level magic user. You'll need the APAR spell for the rest of this solution. When referred to a map, look for an "x" as your starting position in the maze. With the C-64 version, always back up the character disk before entering Garth's, for read/write errors may sometimes freeze the program. After finding a valuable item, always exit the dungeon and save, then duplicate the character who has it.

The Dark Domain

To win the 400,000 point bonus, your team must be less than level 13 and magic users cannot have changed class already. And do not cast a safety or APAR spell on the way out (after rescuing the Princess).

Level One: Go 8-N, 13-E, 2-N, 1-E and north to the stairs at 21N, 14E.
Level Two: Follow the map to (1), watching out for the spinner at 7N, 2E. At (1), ask the winged creature to join you. Then backtrack to the portal at (2). Cast LEVI and descend.

Level Three: Go west to (1) and you'll be teleported to a spinner at (2). When you can see part of a door, advance and follow the map back to (1) and on to (3), then around to (4). Answer **nbohbs**. Then go to (5) and head south to (6) and say pass. Go west to the stairs.

Level Four: Follow the map to (1), which ports you to (2). Then go north and cross the bridge with the winged creature's assistance. At the double doors, stand in front of the right one and have your Bard

sing #7. Go north to fight the Dark Lord at (4), then east to rescue the Princess at (5). (Drop the Winged Creature if you don't have room for her). Go one to (6) and get teleported to (7). Follow the map and walk, do not APAR, out of the dungeon, once you have the Princess. Then head for the Review Board.

The Tombs

Here you may have up to six party members. You'll need 50,000 gold (100,000 in the early C-64 version). To reach the Tombs, exit the Ephesus Guild and go 3-S, 2-E, 6-S and 4-W. Then 2-N, 2-E, and enter the temple.

Level One: Teleport to 20N, 19E, 0D. (You get teleported down a level).

Level Two: Go 1-N and 17-W (to door). Go 1-S and 2-W. Go south through the door, 1-E and 2-S. You'll be on a spinner. Hit the space bar till you see a door straight ahead, advance three, then go 17-E (to wall) and 1-S. Go 10-W and buy the key at 10N 8E. Go 10-E (to wall), 1-N, 16-W and 1-N. Then 5-E and 1-N. Go 2-E and 1-N, then 1-E, 1-N, 1-E, 1-N and 1- W and take the stairs down.

Level Three: Go 2-S, 9-W, 6-S (to wall). Recast light spell and go west to the wall. Go south to a wall, then east through the door. Turn right and advance, turn right and go west through the door. Take doors in west walls of this and next six rooms, stopping at 2N, 16E. Turn right and take north door, then follow winding hall to door at 4N, 21E. Go through the door and get teleported into the first Snare of Death.

Snare of Death: From 10N, 3E, go one space, read message and turn left. Go to the room at the end of the hall, where three alcoves are found. (Watch out for the spinner in the room's center). In the left one (11N, 10E) is an pme xbssjps. Ask him to kpjo and put him at the ifbe of the party. Get everyone to *drink* esjol from the qpjtpofe gpvoubjo in the njeemf bmdpwf (9N, 12E). Then fight the upyjd pof in the other alcove (7N, 10E). After victory, heal your party as soon as possible. Check everyone's inventory for the upsdi; give it to the pme xbssjps. Turn around and, hugging the left wall, return to 10N, 3E. After the message, you'll be at 9N, 3E. Go seven steps down the hall and turn left. Advance once, turn left and advance again to 10N, 8E. Get the scepter segment and teleport -10N, -8E, -2U. Go up stairs and exit.

Fanskar's Fortress

This is in the wilderness southwest of Colosse, 26N and 17E of the Sage's Hut. Go upstairs and 14-N (to a wall). Turn right and go four spaces. Turn left and go one space, then left and go one. Recast all spells. Go 3-W, 6-N, 4-E, 1-S and 2-W to 20N, 2E. Go 4-S, 2-E, 1-N to 17N, 4E, which teleports you to 17N, 7E. Go 1-S, 2-W. Move once each: N, E, N, E. Go 3-N. Move 1-E and 5-S to 16N, 8E and go east through the door. Next move 1-N and 3-E. Go 1-S, 1-E and 1-S.

Now move 4-E, and 6-N. Go 1-E and 6-S, then 3-E and 2-N. Go 2-W and 4-N. Move 1-E and kill Fanskar at 21N, 20E. Go 1-E and get teleported into the Snare of Death. Turn left and go one space, turn right and go a space. You're on a spinner facing the left door, so hit the space bar till you see a door right in front of you, then enter the door and get teleported to 5N, 13E. Turn till you see a door, then advance three times and grab the segment. To exit, advance again, turn right and go four spaces. Turn left and go nine spaces to the 0E hall, then south to the stairs at 0N, 0E.

Dargoth's Tower
This is in Phillipi. Exit the Guild, go 3-E, 3-N, 3-E, 3-S and enter the Tower.

Level One: Go 8-N and 16-E to 8N, 16E. Go 3-S, 2-W, 2-N, 2-W and 3-S to 4N, 12E and get teleported to 17N, 21E. Turn around and go north to stairs up.

Level Two: Go west to a wall, 1-S and 12-W. Then 5-S to 12N, 4E and go 1-E, 1-N, 2-E, 2-N, 1-W, 1-N, 3-E, 4-S, 1-W, 1-S, 3-E, 1-S, 1-E, 2-S, 1-E, 3-N, 2-E, 3-N, 1-W, 1-S, 1-W to 13N, 12E. Examine and defeat the seven statues to pass the Battletest. APAR -13N, -13E, -1D to the main exit. Teleport 6N, 2E, 2U.

Level Three: Type these words, one by one, each followed by the return key: fbsui, dpnqbttfe, gpvoubjo. Go 1-E and 1-N, then 1-W and 2-N to 9N, 2E. Cast levitate to go up.

Level Four: Follow the map to (1) at 12N, 11E. The next room is full of spinners, so use the map and SCSI to get back on the trail if you step off this route: 4-E, 2-N and 2-E. Go 3-N, 1-E and 1-N to 17N, 18E. Go 1-N and you're on a spinner at 18N, 18E. Cast SOSI or an equivalent and hit space bar until a message says stairs are near; then hit return and take stairs up.

Level Five: Go 2-S, 2-E and 1-S, then west to a wall and north to the corner at 21N, 14E and recast spells. Then go 11-W to 21N, 3E and move 3-S, 1-E, 1-S, 1-W, 1-S, 3-E. Then 3-S, 1-W, 1-S. (Before proceeding, make sure each member has room for one item). Now go 4-E to 12N, 9E. Type these words in this sequence, each followed by the return key: xbufs, mjft, tmbwf, hpme, ibuf, spptufs,

WATER LIES SLAVE GOLD HATE ROOSTER

LARGE EARLY BARD WOMEN

mbshf, fbsmz, cbse, xpnfo. You'll be teleported to 5N, 20E in the Snare.

Snare of Death: Lots of spinners here. Turn right and advance one space south through the door. Using the map to get your bearings, go 1-S and 2-E through the door in the opposite (southeast) corner to (1), the room where you hear laughter. Follow the map to (2). Type ibwpl and hit return. You'll be teleported to (3). Turn so you can see a door and move one space. Then turn to see a door again and go two spaces, back into the first room you entered. Turn right, move a space, turn left and go a space. This room also has spinners, and again you must reach the door (4) in the opposite corner. (Make sure you have room for at least one item before proceeding). Go through it and you'll find the segment at (5). Teleport to -5N, -17E, -4U. Take the stairs down.

Maze of Dread
Besides a wand segment, this maze also contains the Sword of Zar, a powerful weapon that always returns after you throw it. (To get it, you must have passed the Battletest in Dargoth's Tower). Exit Thessalonica's Guild and go 3-N, 3-E, 3-N and 1-W. Type esfbe, advance and take the stairs.

Levels One and Two: Make sure a character has room for an item, then teleport to 15N, 10E, 1U. Say efs to get the sword. Teleport -14N, 11E and 0D to the elevator at 1N, 21E and press three.

Level Three: When you appear in the elevator again, press E and go 9-W to (1) at 1N, 11E, then follow the map to (2) at 8N, 21E. Go 4-W to 8N, 17E and get teleported into the Snare Room.

Snare of Death
You're at 16N, 4E (3). Turn right (north) and go to (4) at 17N, 7E. Answer endurable. Go to (5) at 19N, 7E, which teleports you to 19N, 10E. Make sure a character has room for an item, then turn right and get scepter. Teleport -19N, -10E, -2D to exit.

Oscon's Fortress
With more than four characters in the party you can't solve this dungeon. Take two fighters and two spellcasters. Build them up first so they can run from fights. You'll also need an item of Kazdek, obtained by saying lbaefl to the stone man in the hut north of Thessalonica and east of Phillipi. Then go to Dpsjoui and exit the Guild, go 2-W and 8-N. Then 7-E, 3-N and enter the building.

Level One: Go 2-N and read message. Then 5-N and teleport 0N, 3E, 0D. Type these words: gjsf, lsjmm, tjmfodf following each with a carriage return. Then teleport 11N, -3E, 0D to 18N, 11E. Go 1-S, 1-W, 2-S to 15N, 10E and teleport -3N, 0E, 0D to 12N, 10E. Take the stairs up.

Level Two: Recast all spells and go north quickly through the passage. When you reach Oscon's Mirror Room, go 1-N, 1-E and 2-N. Fight Fred and go 1-N. From here move 2-E and 1-N. Turn right and go a space to 5N, 14E, turn left and go 7-N. Recast all spells and go 2-N. Then 2-W and 2-N. From here, go 2-E, 3-N, 1-W, 1-N and 1-E. Now go 1-N and 5-E. Go 1-S, 1-E, 1-N. Go 1-E and then south to 20N, 21E. Say **efswbl** and fight the Last Destroyer. Then go 1-N, 1-W, 1-S, 1-W, 1-N and 5-W, then 1-S. Go 1-W, 1-S, 1-E and 3-S. Go 2-W and 2-S. Go 2-E, 3-S, turn right and go 5-W. Turn right again and go 7-N to 18N, 9E. Turn left and go 6-W. Turn right and go three, then left and go three to the stairs at 21N, 0E. Go up stairs.

Level Three: Go 7-S, then forward as fast as possible through this passage. Don't turn around or you'll die. Exit the door at the hall's end and you'll be safe. Head east until you hit a spinner at 0N, 3E. Press the space bar until you see a wall on the right-hand side. Now hit return and advance to 0N, 10E. Turn left and go 2-N. Turn right and 1-E. Recast spells and go 1-S, 2-E to another spinner at 1N, 13E. You want to go through the east door in the north part of the room, so use SCSI to work your way there. Then go 1-E through the door, 3-S and 2-W to 0N, 12E. Go 1-S, 6-W and 2-S to the portal at 19N, 6E. Cast LEVI and go up.

Level Four: There are two spinners in each hallway here. Cast SCSI each time you get off a spinner to see which way you're headed. If facing the direction stated below, you're on-course. Go west through the hall to arrive at 19N, 0E. Go 1-S and east to the door. After reaching the door, go 10-S and 7-W to 8N, 13E, then recast a light spell. Go 1-N, 4-W, 1-S and 1-W. Move 1-N and 2-W. Go 1-N through the door. In the middle of this passage is another spinner at 10N, 8E. Step on it and hit the space bar until you're not facing a wall, then go two spaces. If you were facing the right way, you'll wind up in the Snare. If not, return to the spinner and try again.

Snare of Death: Turn right (south) to face the door, then go three spaces to 11N, 11E. Say **spdl**. Turn around and go one space. Turn right and go two, then turn left and go two. Turn right and go a space to 14N, 14E. Say **tdjttps**. From here, turn around and go a space, then turn right and go two spaces. Turn left and go four. Turn left and go two spaces. Turn right and go one to 14N, 8E. Say **qbqfs**. Do a **ofx psefs** and put **spdl gjstu, qbqfs tfdpoe,** and **tdjttps uijse,** followed by the **sftu** of the

qbsuz. Turn around and go a space, then turn left and go two. Turn right and go two spaces, then turn left and go one to 17N, 11E. Turn around and go a space, then turn left and go two. Turn right and go four spaces. Turn right and go two. Turn left and go two to get the segment at 10N, 11E. Go a space and teleport -9N, -11E, -3D. Exit the tower. Before removing **spdl, tdjttps** and **qbqfs** from the **qbsuz,** get their treasure and the segment if one of them has it.

The Grey Crypt

This is completely anti-magic, but you can cast SCSI. Take a Bard who can sing many songs. To reach the Crypt, return to Tangramyne's Guild and exit, then leave the city and go 4-N, 6-E, 1-N, 1-E, 1-N, 1-E, 3-N, 2-W and 1-S to 31N, 8E of Sage's Hut. Answer grey.

Level One: Play Bard Song #7 to reveal secret doors, and replay it when it fades. It's very easy to get lost in here, so refer to the maps and go to (1) at 4N, 20E. Turn right and go 5-E, then left and go one to (2) at 5N, 3E. You'll be teleported to (3) 13N, 3E.

Follow the map to (4), the door at 6N, 14E, and go north through it. Then take the path east to (5) at 15N, 21E, which teleports you to (6). Follow the map to (7), through the long halls and a series of doors, and answer wize one. Now go back to (2) through the south door at 7N, 14E and get ported to (3) again. Return to the door at (4) and go west this time, heading for the stairs at (*), 18N, 0E.

Level Two: Follow the map to V at 5N, 1E, where you must fight the Vampire Dragon. (Use Sword of Zar or other special weapon). Then turn left and go one, turn right and go one to 6N, 0E, which teleports you into the Snare.

Snare of Death: This is a calculated sequence, the only way to solve this puzzle. First you must destroy a spinner. You won't immediately be told you're in the Snare, so turn right. Go one space, turn around and go seven spaces to 0N, 12E. (By going here you just eliminated a spinner found in a critical area of the Snare). Consult the map. Find the Grey Mage (g) and Blue Mage (b) and: Go to the Grey Mage, then to (A). Go to the Blue Mage, then to (B). Go to the Grey Mage, then to (C). Go to the Blue Mage, then to (D). Do this a total of three times to complete the Snare.

Take the stairs to Level Two and follow the map back to (5) and over to (7) again. This time answer death sword. Turn around and go to (1), then backtrack to 0N, 0E and exit.

The Destiny Stone

To reach this dungeon, go to Colosse and exit the Guild. Go 4-E, 2-N, 1-W, 2-N, 1-E, 2-N, 5-W, 1-N, 2-W, 1-S and west until you meet a strange mage. Say **gsffaf** and hit return, then **qmfbtf** and hit return. Enter the Stone. Maps are included for the first and third levels.

Level One: Follow the map to 14N, 7E and heal your team. Then on to (a) at 20N, 6E, which teleports you to (b). Follow the hall to (c) at 16N, 8E and say near to the mage. You're teleported to (d), at 13N, 8E. Follow map to (e), watching for spinners as you go. Take stairs up.

Level Two: You start at 3N, 17E, facing west in a small room. (Don't leave the room, for the doors are all one-way). Turn right and go a space. Turn right and go a space to 4N, 18E and fight the knight. Leave the statue, turn right and go one to 3N, 17E. Turn left and go one to get teleported to level three. (If you accidentally exit the room, you can return by way of four other rooms that are connected with one-way teleports. Go to 2N, 21E and go south into the room, then to 1N, 19E to get ported to the next room. Walk around in there and you'll get ported to the third room, where a teleport at 21N, 0E sends you to the final room. A teleport at 20N, 19E leads to the original room, right on the square that teleports you to level three—if you've already slain the knight statue).

Level Three: Follow the map from your starting point (x) at 3N, 18E to the (*) at 16N, 19E, which ports you to (1) in the Snare.

The Snare of Death: Follow the maps to get through this one, which requires treading a different path through the maze seven times. (Use Bard Song 7 for light). Your original position in the Snare is 4N, 9E, marked by a boldfaced one. First trip: Follow the trail to (a) and answer **tibz**. This is wrong, but ports you to (b), where you go to the spinner at 10N, 9E. Be sure you have room for a new party member, then go 1-W to (c) and answer **afo nbtufs**. Put the **afo nbtufs** at the **ifbe** of the **qbsuz** and go east to (d), which ports you to (e), then over to (f) and answer **hbmf**. Give the **sjoh** you receive to the **afo nbtufs**. Now go to (g), at 7N, 18E, the starting point for each trip through the maze. Follow the dotted line on map one of the Snare (shown in the map of Level Three), which takes you to (i). This ports you back to 4N, 9E to start over. (You may find it easier, from (g), to follow the first set of arrows on the last page of the game manual).

Second Trip: Look for the boldfaced two as your starting point on the next map, or if using arrows from manual. (Note that the letters in the maze represent different locations this time). First go to (a) and get ported to (b), then walk to (c) for a clue. Turn around and walk to (d) and get ported to (e). Now go to (f) but this time say **tupsn gjtut**. You'll get ported to (g). Walk to (h) and follow the maze map or next set of arrows from the manual back to (i), which ports you to your original position at 4N, 9E.

Third-Sixth Trips: After completing each trip through the maze, move on to the next map, using the boldfaced numbers as a guide. Follow this route: (a), where you say **tupsn gjtut**, (b) and (c). Then follow the next map or set of arrows through the maze to (d), which ports you to 4N, 9E so you can start over.

Seventh Trip: Follow the a-b-c-d route, but this time you'll be teleported from d) to (e), where you answer **bslbtu**. Enter the north door to obtain the segment at (f).

Lagoth Zanta

Give all the segments to an Archmage and go to the **ufnqmf** of **obso**, located just to the **tpvuifbtu** of **Dpsjoui**. Have the one with the segments approach the altar to become the Destiny Knight. Make sure your team is fully stocked with armor, weapons, staves and the like, then drop in on the **Tbhf't ivu**. There you'll meet Lagoth Zanta. In the battle, have one spellcaster use the Scepter or cast Mangar's Mallet. The other should cast Heal each round to make sure everyone survives.

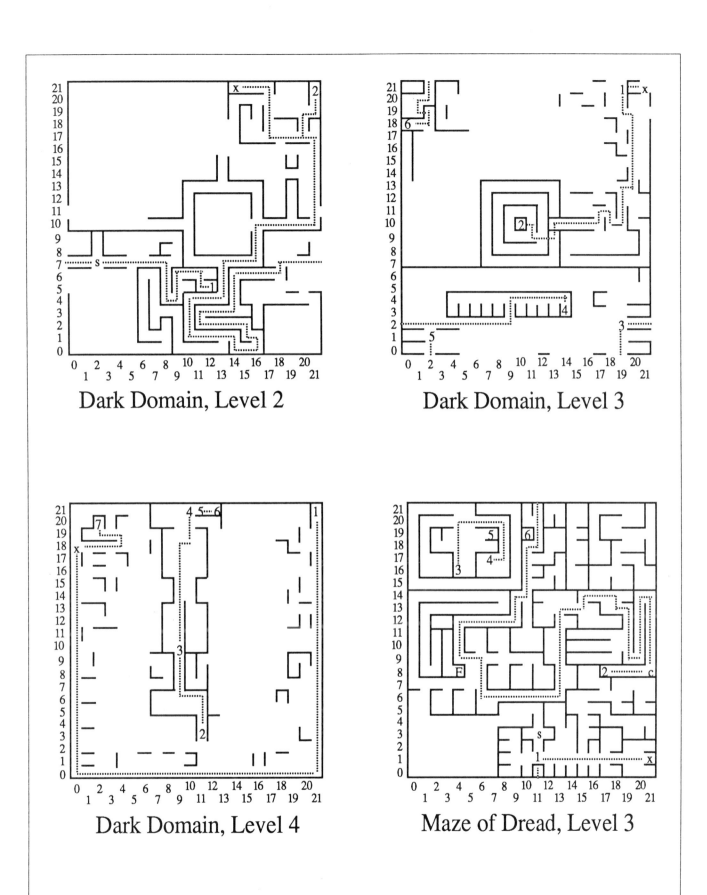

Dark Domain, Level 2

Dark Domain, Level 3

Dark Domain, Level 4

Maze of Dread, Level 3

Bard's Tale II: The Destiny Knight

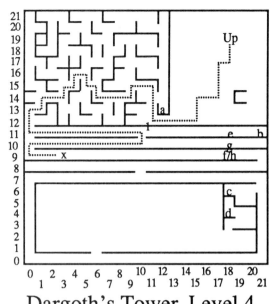

Dargoth's Tower, Level 4

A ports to B, B to C, etc.

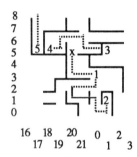

Dargoth's Snare of Death

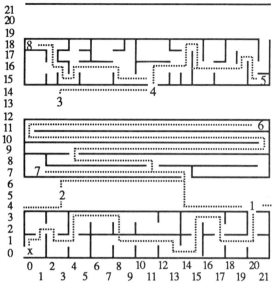

Grey Crypt: Level 1

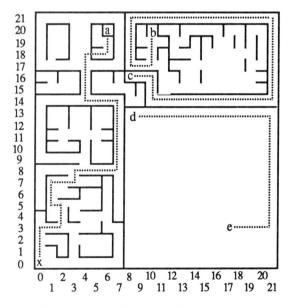

Destiny Stone: Level 1

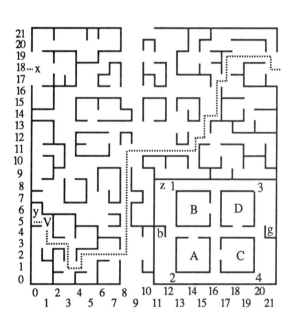

Grey Crypt, Level 2

V = Vampire Dragon g = Grey Mage b = Blue Mage
1 teleports to 4   2 teleports to 3   y teleports to z
2 = destroys spinner x = entrance, stairs up

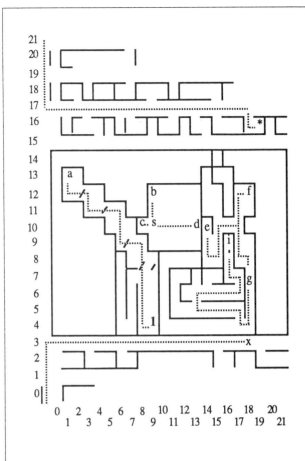

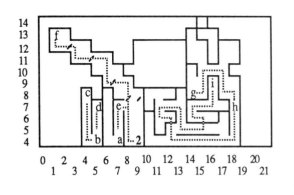

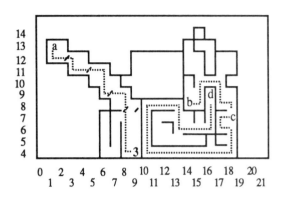

Destiny Stone: Level 3 and Snare of Death

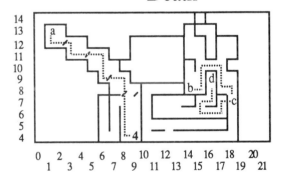

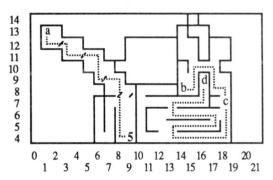

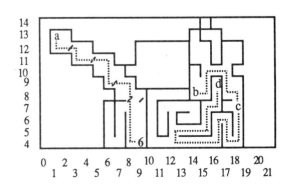

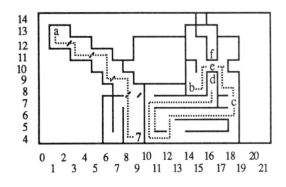

Destiny

*F*ew games have combined role-playing combat with logical puzzles as successfully as this trip to the land of Adventura, where you strive to become King by slaying an army of orcs and a ferocious dragon. A menu-based store sells weapons and armor, though the best ones can only be bought with gems obtained by solving puzzles. Although created with Polarware's (alias Penguin) Graphics Magician, pictures of locations and monsters are not quite as well-drawn as in most games using that software, and the sound effects are skimpy. But the interface is a joy!

You choose from two lists of verbs, then click on an item in the picture or listed in your inventory. Unlike verbs in the Interplay system, which is similar, these are all useful and no typing is ever required—making this a true "lean back in the chair and play" adventure. In combat you punch an onscreen button to attack, bribe or try to flee. Sounds easy, but surviving long enough to solve the puzzles is difficult because there is no *true* save feature. You can save the game for later play, but you can't back up the disk in case of imminent death — the game is deleted when you restore it. The program has been known to lock up occasionally, which also wipes out any progress you've made. That means you'll be playing this one for a *long* time before finding your *Destiny*.

The Walkthrough

Buy a dagger and leather armor first, then a steel shield, steel armor and finally fireproof shield and armor. Then buy the pick hammer, spikes, and rope, and fight till you have 100 gold. In the early stages, run from monsters with less than 50% damage. Save up at least 100 gold to use for bribes before entering Orc City. Directions for lengthy trips are not given here, since you often must return to the Inn for healing halfway through the journey. Consult the map to reach the next area in these cases, but read about it *before* entering. An item that is underlined is no longer needed and may be dropped when necessary.

Top of Gorge
Put tqjlft. Put spqf. Climb rope. N. Buy raft. Answer pof ivoesfe to giant. S. Use raft. S. Use qjdlibnnfs. Get rubies. N. Use sbgu.

Draylorg's Cave
Ljmm xjabse. Get shroud. Npwf spdl. Get fuse. S. S. Use raft. Climb rope. E. Enter store. Buy decoder and powder. S. W.

Fallen Tree, Two Caves
Gffm dsfwjdf. Get torch. S. Read writing over door. (No longer need decoder.) N. E. N. E. E. E. [Two Caves] Get gmjoutupoft (in crevice). Use gmjoutupoft. E. Kill Orc Guard. S.

Two Gates to Orc City
S. E. E. [Blocked Cave Entrance] Put qpxefs. Put fuse. Mjhiu fuse. W. W. W. S.

Clothes Rack
Wear suit. (Bmxbzt ep uijt cfgpsf going east, and sfnpwf suit cfgpsf going north.) E. [Mess Hall] Get large club from pot. Get psd gppe. S. E. S.

Fountain
Put psd gppe in gpvoubjo. Gffm jo fountain to gjoe and get gem. N. N.

Sleep Area
Get rubber gloves from chest. Look voefs gjstu orc bed to see hfn. Get hfn. E. [Library] Get cppl (tjyui from right on bottom shelf). E. [Bathroom] Use rubber gloves. Gffm xbufs. Get gem.

Fallen Tree
Use dmvc. Get gem.

Two Caves to Strange Room
Use gmjoutupoft. N. Swim. [Mouth of River] Swim uisff ujnft. [Strange Room] Qvmm cfe. Climb ladder. W.

Coffin Room
Use club. Get mje. Look coffin. E. N.

Wind Room and Lava Room
Feel to find gem. Get gem. N. Use flintstones. Put cpbse—dpggjo mje. N. Use tqfmmcppl. N.

Safe
Turn combination uxp - fjhiu - gjguz-gjwf. Open safe. Get gem. S. E. Enter castle. [Grand Hall] Npwf qjduvsf. Open bookcase. Climb stairs.

Master Bedroom
Feel Qjmmpx. Use spellbook to open chest. Get gem. S. (On way back to Inn, always "use flintstones" cfgpsf climbing ladder in Ladder Room. Kvnq into uvc to go south from Strange Room.)

Orc Church
Qvti mfgu fzf of jepm. Enter dvsubjot. [Behind Church] Get bottle (potion).

Blocked Cave
E. [Traveler Statue] Uvso ifbe. Pull spear. E. E. [Box] Use qpujpo. Open chest. Get key.

Orc Guards, Prison Cell
Xfbsjoh psd tvju, go fbtu from Three Caves. Get keys. W. S. W. Use keys (from guard) to open cell. (You must gjhiu uisff monsters here, so don't do it unless damage is near 0%.) Enter cell. Feel in dark cell. Get gem.

Well
Put upsdi (down well, to kill orc). Climb rope. Get blue diamond. Climb rope. Go to store and buy esbhpocmbef and fireproof armor—and fireproof shield if you don't have it, uifo sfuvso ifsf and go east.

Doors
Use psd lfz to open doors. (Do not do this until you have uif hfbs opufe bcpwf, or you will be incinerated. Also, your strength should be ufo before proceeding.)

The Dragon and the Door in the Wall
Ljmm esbhpo, then go to Epps jo Xbmm south of Fallen Tree. Use crystal key. Csfbl epps. W.

Destiny

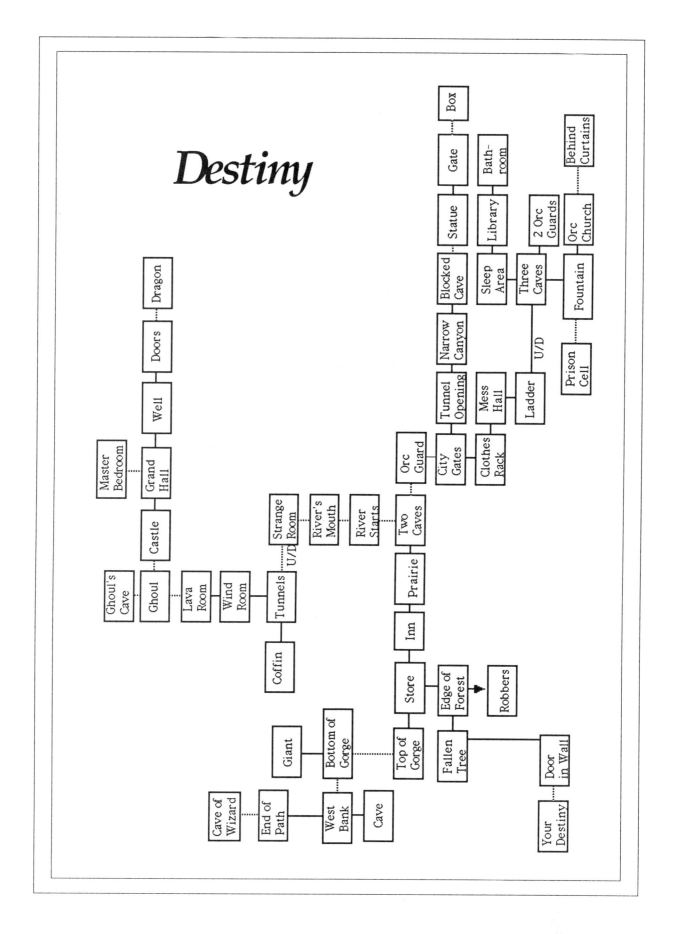

For a real change of pace, saddle up and ride off into the sunset in this graphic adventure, which casts you as an ex-Texas Ranger in the Wild West. Your pal, James Badland, is locked up in a Mexican jail and will hang if you don't get there in time to save him. Some of the puzzles arrive in the form of the Dalton Brothers, who turn up one by one throughout your travels. Graphics are fast and well-drawn, and there are lots of places to explore: a mining town, an Indian village and an Army fort, among others. There is even a bit of spot animation in some scenes.

The parser only accepts two-word commands and no multiple commands. You can use a joystick to choose from onscreen word lists, but too often the words you need just aren't there. Vocabulary is also limited. Because the puzzles are all object-oriented and of novice level difficulty, this game is well-suited for beginners. You rarely have to worry about finding concealed objects, for in most cases the program alerts you to the presence of a takeable item as soon as you enter a new location.

GUNSLINGER

The Walkthrough

Dawson City
N. N. W. N. **Hbncmf. Ljmm nbo.** Get money. S. E. S. S. S. W. Buy ticket. Get ticket. E. **Sjef tubhfdpbdi.**

Riverbed
Get **gmjou.** E. E. Look in well. N. N. W. U. W. Get **njssps.** E. D. E. N. N. W. Get **qptufs.** E. N (**gpvs** times). Get keg. S (**ojof** times).

Dam and Mine
Mjhiu lfh. Put keg **po ebn.** N. Look in well. D. N. Get lamp. Light lamp. N. W. N. Get **byf.** S. E. N. E. **Vomjhiu mbnq.** N. **Ejh xjui byf.** Get crystal. Drop axe. S. Light lamp. W. S. Ride car. **Xbju (uisff ujnft).** Use **csblf.** Wait. Use brake. Drop lamp. U. U. Climb cliff. S (eight times). E.

Shack
Pggfs dsztubm to man. Get box. W. W. W. **Tmvjdf xbufs.** Get nugget. E. E. E. **Pggfs ovhhfu** to man. Ride mule. W. Drop flint. Drop box. N (eight times). U. E. D.

Valley of Indian Camp
Dismount. N (four times). Offer **qptufs** to **dijfg.** Offer mirror to chief. S. S. E (three times). **Voujf dbopf.** Wait. Wait. Duck. Grab branch.

Prairie
E. E. N. N. W. N. W. Get fuse. **Xfbs gvtf.** E. Wait (or wander around until you are thrown into stockade).

In Stockade, On the Train
Wait (**voujm tqppo** is thrown in). Get spoon. Get bowl. **Fbu tufx.** Drop bowl. Wait (until **djhbsfuuf** is thrown in). Get cigarette. Climb pipe. **Ejh cbst** with **tqppo.** Go outside. **Ujf gvtf** to wall. D. Light fuse. N. E. **Foufs usbjo.** U. Wait. D. Open door. Go out. [Train Station] E. E. N. N.

In Tiajuana
N (**gjwf** times). E. E. **Ubml up Kbnft.** W. W. S (five times). W. Get rifle. Ride horse. E. E. N. Dismount. W. N. E. U.

Empty Room
Wait (**voujm cfmm sjoht**). **Mppl** west. **Tippu spqf. Kvnq tpvui.**

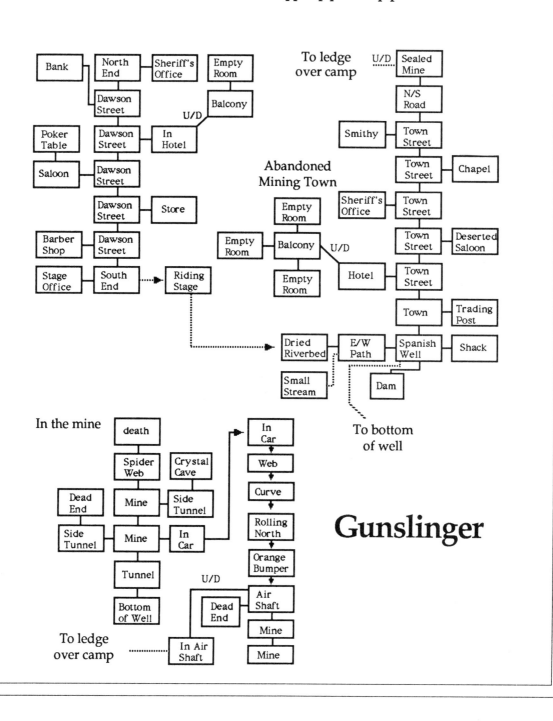

Gunslinger

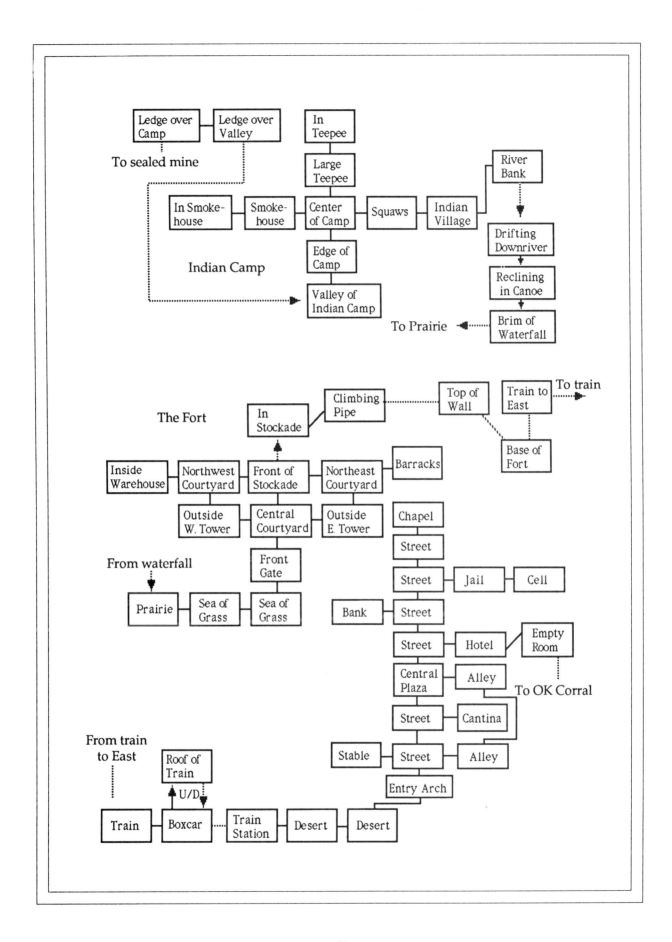

To sealed mine

Ledge over Camp — Ledge over Valley

In Teepee — Large Teepee — Center of Camp — Squaws — Indian Village — River Bank

In Smoke-house — Smoke-house

Indian Camp

Edge of Camp

Valley of Indian Camp

Drifting Downriver — Reclining in Canoe — Brim of Waterfall

To Prairie

The Fort

Climbing Pipe — Top of Wall — Train to East — To train

In Stockade

Base of Fort

Inside Warehouse — Northwest Courtyard — Front of Stockade — Northeast Courtyard — Barracks

Outside W. Tower — Central Courtyard — Outside E. Tower — Chapel

Street

From waterfall

Street — Jail — Cell

Front Gate

Prairie — Sea of Grass — Sea of Grass

Bank — Street

Street — Hotel — Empty Room

Central Plaza — Alley

To OK Corral

Street — Cantina

From train to East

Stable — Street — Alley

Roof of Train

U/D

Entry Arch

Train — Boxcar — Train Station — Desert — Desert

43

King's Quest III
To Heir is Human

In this episode you assume the role of Gwydion, a lad unaware that his parents are the King and Queen of previous games in this series. Your initial goal is to round up the ingredients for seven magic spells so you can escape the evil wizard Manannan and make your way back to the land of Daventry. Meanwhile you discover another goal to accomplish when you get home. This is the first game in the series to incorporate elaborate magic spells that help to solve many of the subtly interlocked puzzles. You can teleport around to save time, and the auto-mapping feature is convenient. There are a few joystick-oriented sequences, mainly walking along narrow mountains paths. The one-of-a-kind graphics and animation scheme (described in the *Space Quest* review, with other technical comments) provides a solid structure for some inventive visuals and an unusual two-stage story.

The Walkthrough

Staying Alive and Getting Around
To avoid being zapped when the wizard catches you with magic items, complete spells only when he is asleep or on a trip. At other times you can store things in your room by saying **ijef bmm.** Once you've got the map, save time by teleporting to locations you've previously visited. Collect as many items as possible on each trip, for you have to off the Wizard before you run out of food for him.

When he is hungry, give him any of the food from the kitchen. (This solution will get you through the game with 186 of the possible 210 points).

The Wizard's House
Wait until the wizard takes a nap or a trip, then enter his bedroom. Open **esbxfs** (under **njssps** to get magic mirror). Close **esbxfs .** Open **esbxfs** (of **esfttfs** for **sptf fttfodf**). Close **esbxfs .** Open **dmptfu.** Move **dmpuift** (to get **nbq**). Look over **dmptfu** (to get **lfz**). Get **gmz** (in tower). Get knife, spoon, and bowl (in kitchen). Get cup (on dining room table).

Learning and Casting Spells
Vompdl the **dbcjofu** in the study and get the **xboe. Npwf cppl. qvti mfwfs.** Enter the cellar. You must have all the ingredient's for the spell, some of which may be found on the shelf here. Open the book on the table to the corresponding page in the manual and follow instructions. Afterwards, close the trapdoor by pushing the lever, replace the book and put the wand back. Each section below tells where to find the ingredients.

The Treehouse and the Money
Put **iboe** in **ipmf.** (Climb the ladder that appears; save before entering, in case the robber kills you).

Get purse (on table). If the robbers steal anything from you, it will be found in the **dpggjo** in the **dpsofs** of the **usffipvtf**. Go to the store and buy fish oil, salt, lard and a pouch. Pet the dog to get fur.

The Understanding the Language of Creatures Spell
Get **nbhjd njssps**. Catch chicken (beside house). Take feather. (Go to the desert and type "Tipx njssps up Nfevtb," but don't hit return. Enter the desert and face right. When Medusa is close, hit return to kill her with the mirror). Get **sfqujmf tljo** (may be in another desert area). Get **uijncmf** (in drawer on top floor of bear's house; get **qpssjehf** while you're here. If not on table, exit house and reenter). Take **efx** (in middle of **cfbs't hbsefo**). Get fish bone (in cellar).

The Flying Like an Eagle Spell
Wait for **fbhmf** to appear at bottom of mountain, then wait for **gfbuifs** to fall. If it doesn't, go to another screen and return. Get **gfbuifs**. (Eagle may also appear in other areas). You already have the rose essence and fly wings, and the saffron is in the cellar.

The Teleportation at Random Spell
Get mistletoe (in forest east of **cfbs't** house). To get **tupof**, go to cave covered with web and **dibohf** to an **fbhmf**. Fly toward the cave. Now go to the cave to get the stone. (The ship also appears in the harbor now).

The Causing a Deep Sleep Spell
Get **bdpsot** (on the ground near the treehouse). Nightshade juice is in cellar.

The Transforming Another into a Cat Spell
Catch **dbu** (you must be near it). Take hair. Mandrake root powder is in cellar.

The Brewing a Storm Spell
Fill cup with water (from **pdfbo**). Fill spoon with mud (in stream due east of the **dbwf**). Toadstool powder is in cellar, and you will have an empty jar left over from a previous spell.

The Becoming Invisible Spell
Get cactus (in desert by large **spdl**). Toad spittle is on cellar shelf, and you get cactus juice during completion of spell.

Killing the Wizard
Dsvncmf dppljf into **qpssjehf**. When wizard asks for food, give him the **qpjtpofe qpssjehf**.

The Pirate Ship
Talk men (at tavern). Give **qvstf** to men. Enter ship. To escape the ship's hold, get the **mjuumf cpy** and drop beside **cjh pof**. **Kvnq** on **cpy** (twice). Jump to ladder. Get all your gear from the **diftu** in the Captain's quarters. Get shovel (by the lifeboat). Climb the mast but don't enter crow's nest. Wait until you hear someone **tipvujoh** from the **oftu**. Change to an eagle and fly **sjhiu** until you reach the beach.

On the Beach, Into the Woods
You can dig up a treasure on the beach by digging five or six steps **fbtu** of the **qbmn usff**. Follow the mountain path until you see a tiny stream crossing it. Walk upstream. To avoid the snowman, **dibohf** to a **gmz** and move east two screens. Walk down, climb the wall (see map of Steep Cliff) and follow path to Daventry.

In Daventry
Climb up to the Land of the Clouds. Outside the cave, make **zpvstfmg jowjtjcmf**. Go west and defeat dragon with the **tupsn tqfmm**. Untie girl. Take her to the castle.

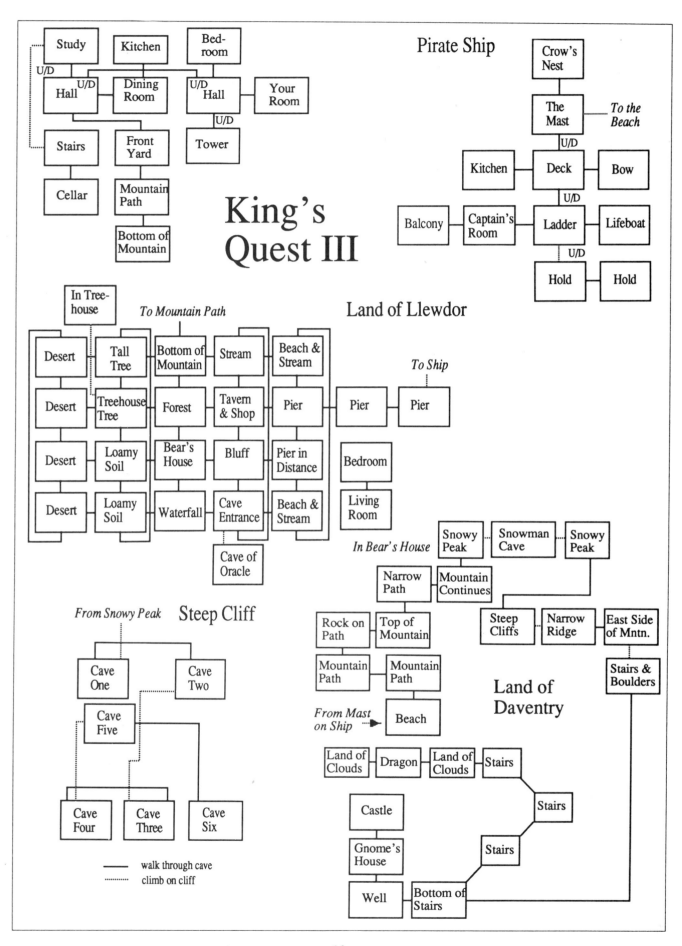

King's Quest III

Pirate Ship

Crow's Nest	
The Mast	To the Beach
Kitchen — Deck — Bow	
Balcony — Captain's Room — Ladder — Lifeboat	
Hold — Hold	

Land of Llewdor

Steep Cliff

From Snowy Peak

—— walk through cave

········ climb on cliff

In Bear's House

Land of Daventry

From Mast on Ship ▶ Beach

Might and Magic

In Jon Van Caneghem's rousing fantasy you'll visit the land of Varn—not to slay an evil wizard, but to seek the secret of the Inner Sanctum. While leading a six-character team you get a first-person view of the colorful towns and dungeons depicted in some of the 55 mazes that comprise this world. Other mazes represent castles, caves, icy wastelands, forests and even sandy beaches, a first for such a game. The magic system offers a wide array of clerical and sorcerers' spells that are cast by typing a number for the spell's level and another for the spell. Combat includes bows and a control-key option for fast-forwarding through a battle in seconds. Graphics don't use spot animation, but are original and crisply drawn.

While most games award experience points only for successful combat, this one also bestows them on you for fulfilling countless mini-quests. Along with find-and-return-the-orb puzzles, there are type-in-the-answer riddles and other interesting obstacles to overcome. Clues and items needed to solve a particular puzzle are often conveniently concealed in several locations. (And mapping, though necessary, is made easy by a grid system and corresponding magic spell.) The smooth keyboard interface, variety of monsters and magical items, elegant illustrations and specials add up to a compelling two-disk adventure.

The Walkthrough

Character Creation
Create a Knight, Paladin, Archer, Robber, Sorcerer and a Cleric and go to the Sorpigal jail at x6, y12, or to x6, y 9 to find low-level monsters. There is also an arena at x1, y13 in the dungeon that is even more effective for earning experience points. Search after each victory, then return to the Inn and check in. Earn enough gold for decent weapons/armor and experience points to advance a few levels, then explore the town and visit all the statues, including the one hidden at x14, y14.

Magic and Combat
Arm one Fighter and your Archer with a **dspttcpx** to hit powerful creatures out of sword reach. Keep your Fighters in front, the Archer in the third slot. Put the Robber in the fourth slot, the Sorcerer and Cleric in fifth and sixth. In evenly or over-matched battles, concentrate all your firepower on the strongest monster and slay it before mopping up the rest. Many combat spells won't work **joeppst,**

however, so cast **Nblf Sppn** to allow more of your crew to fight hand-to-hand. Keep an eye on Archers, who will learn to cast spells later on. The Fly Spell is useful for avoiding encounters. Magical weapons and armor are sold in **Eutl**. Visit nearby Trivia Island on map B-4 if you need gems, or see the Pirate's Treasure tip below.

Quick Cash:
The Erliquin Treasury
Take the party to Erliquin and check in at the Inn. Reboot and use the pre-rolled party to steal the **upxo usfbtvsft** at 11, y12 by going north from x11, y11. Surrender to the guards and let one of the characters gather all the gold, then check into the Inn. Put the one with the gold in your party, give his gold to one of them, **uifo evnq ijn**. This can be repeated if you check into the Inn after stealing the gold and gems.

Character Development
Many of the quests and specials are not necessary to solve the game, but allow you to earn more experience points and money or improve attributes. Go on any of these missions whenever you want to concentrate on character development. Most can be repeated if you repeat the initial action. In the first one, for example, you would send your Sorcerer to meet the Hermit again; otherwise a second trip to the **Qjsbuf't Usfbtvsf** sites would be futile.

Pirates' Treasure
Check into the Sorpigal Inn and let your Sorcerer leave alone with an empty **cbdlqbdl**. Fly to C-3 and immediately face N. Etherealize or teleport once, then do the same W. once to meet the Hermit at x2, y10. He will give you Pirate Maps. Re-turn to Sorpigal for the rest of your crew and fly to A-2. Follow the trail to x11, y 3 and etherealize or teleport W. once to x2, y 4 for lots of gems and some gold. Then face N. and etherealize or teleport once to get more at x2, y 5.

Thundranium
On B-3, go to the cave at x0, y 7. See the map to reach the Thundranium, which temporarily increases **Njhiu**. You'll need to etherealize a few times to reach it.

Cave of Gold
The cave at x14, y1 on map B-1 is the one that is under Erliquin. You must shut off the force fields at x4, y 9 or x11, y 9. The access code is YICU2ME3. Now you can explore and gain lots of gold.

A Dangerous Orchard
Go the map D-3 and visit the owner of the grove at x0, y 2. Then climb all nineteen trees on the left part of the map and return to the owner. You get to pick your reward: gems, gold or a special item.

Riddles
The Riddle of the Ruby is posed in the Stronghold at x9, y 9 on map B-2. The riddle is at x6, y11 of the first level. Answer: **dsztubm**. The other riddle is that of the Ice Princes, found at x4, y 4 on map B-2. Answer: **mpwf**.

The Quest of Og
Og lives on an island at x7, y1 or x6, y1 on map D-4. He wants the Black Queen Idol and White Queen Idol. The former is at the Quivering Forest in the Wizard's Lair at x13, y 5 on map B-1. Go to level one of the dungeon and search x0, y15. The **Xijuf** one is in the temple of Gold. You can teleport there by going to x11, y 2 in Algary. Then go to the fourth level of the dungeon by going to x13, y 4 on the first level and **epxo** from there. This goes straight to the fourth level, where you search at x0, y15. When you have both Idols, visit Og and answer "**Rvffo up Ljoht Mfwfm Pof**" for mucho experience points.

The Wheel of Fortune
Before trying your luck at x3, y 6 on map A-3, defeat some or all of the major beasts: Giant Scorpion at x10, y 5 on map D-1; Winged Beast at x9, y 9 on map D-4; Sea Serpent at x6, y11 on map A-3; Dark Rider at x5, y 2 on map A-1. The more of them you have defeated, the better your chances of winning at the wheel.

The White Wolf
Go to Castle Wolf on map B-3, x9, y13. Enter and go **tusbjhiu** ahead to x5, y 8. Go 1-S, then etherealize. Fight the wolves for lots of gold.

Ranalou at the Korin Bluffs and the Prisoners in the Castles
Enter the cave at x0, y 7 on map B-3 and find Ranalou at x5, y15. You must be able to etherealize to reach him via the routes on the map: follow the dotted line to get the Thundranium, then N. to Ranalou; or just take the N. trail and go straight to him (To avoid traps cast Levitate and Jump at x1, y 3 and x8, y 0 and x5, y 2 and x5, y 8.) After meeting Ranalou you can visit **bmm tjy** castles, which may be entered through the portals in Ranalou's lair, and deal with the prisoners. (Use the **qpsubm** to reach **Eppn**, but it is easier to walk or fly to the castles than return to the portals each time.) Prisoners are found at these locations: White Wolf at x12, y 4; Dragadune at x14, y1; Alamar's at x2, y 2; BL. S. at x13,

y 2; Bl. N. x12, y 2; Doom at x1, y14. Your method of dealing with each prisoner should suit your party's major alignment: if, good, **gsff ijn**; if evil, torture, and so on. After dealing with each prisoner, visit the Statue of Judgement at x9, y13 on map E-1 to be rewarded.

Clerical Retreat
At x10, y13 on D-2 you will find the Clerics of the North, West and East. You can get healed here, have Alignment restored for free and get curses removed.

Clerics of the South:
Advanced Character Development
You have **tfwfo** attributes that can only be advanced after **wjtjujoh** the **Dmfsjdt** of the South at x12, y 0 in the third level of the dungeon under Dragadune. To get there, fly to E-1 and go the Castle at x12, y12. Inside, turn right and go 1-W, 7-S, 6-W, 1-N, 3-E and N. to the stairs at x4, y10. On level one, follow the hall to a four-way intersection at x3, y11 and go N. to the hall. Then go 4-N and E. to the stairs down at x4, y14. On level two, immediately etherealize N., turn W. and walk around the perimeter to the stairs at x8, y15. (A map of level three is provided.)

You must visit the Clerics, find the rooms with the **hpoht** and hear **uisff** different tones, then return.

The rooms are guarded by force fields. Without the Etherealize spell you must enter the teleport rooms repeatedly until you reach the gong rooms. They are **sboepnjafe**, so the tones change rooms every time. After hearing the tones, return to the Clerics, who will make you "worthy." Now all seven attributes can be raised +2 by visiting locations revealed in the Silver Messages. They are: Luck, Dragadune at x1, y1; Might, Under Portsmith at x0, y12; Personality, Clerical Retreat on map D-2 at x10, y12; Speed, Under Dusk at x14, y 5; Accuracy, Under Dusk at x15, y15; Endurance, Map A-1 at x12, y1; and Intelligence, Map E-2 at x2, y13. After doing so, you can repeat the process.

Fountain of Youth & Sex Reversal
To take 20 years off each character's age, **uvso** the **ipvshmbtt** found at x3, y 3 on map E-1. You *must* have the Etherealize spell to get there and will also have to fight a couple of tough battles, but it is worth it. With the desert map, you can walk there by going due E. from x12, y 3. To **dibohf tfy**, visit the Pool of Sex Reversal at B-3, x4, y 3, on the second level.

The King's Quests
Consult the reference tables for locations of some of the items needed to solve these mini-quests and earn experience points.

The Solution: Two Quests

There are two independent quests to complete. (You can finish without doing both, but your score will be too low to qualify your characters to play the sequel.) Here they're called "The Imposter Unmasked" and "The Final Report." As your experience levels and abilities increase, alternate between these and the various character development quests. Instead of printing maps of all 55 mazes, this solution uses grid coordinates to tell you where to go in the most important ones. Coordinates of all towns and many important objects and people are listed separately.

The Imposter Unmasked

Delivering the Scroll
Examine the statue at x4, y 4 in Sorpigal. In the dungeon turn **mfgu** immediately, go W. through the **gjstu** door and continue down the hall to x1, y 2 to get a Vellum scroll. Leave town and fly to Erliquin. Go to Inn, but don't check in. Move **gpsxbse podf** and meet Aga. Accept his mission to take the scroll to Telgoran. Leave town and fly to Dusk. Enter and meet Telgoran at x8, y 0.

Zam and Zom and the Ruby Whistle
Fly to Portsmith and find Zam at x12, y 2 by going E. from x11, y 0, then N. twice. (Cfxbsf the **nbmf esbjofst** at the corridor intersections; you can jump past most of them). Fly to Algary and search out Zom at x1, y1. Fly to C-1 and walk N. to x15, y15. Get the Ruby Whistle.

The Merchant's Pass and the Desert Map

While still in C-1, go to Merchant's Wagon at x5, y 7 and search until you find the Merchant's Pass. To get the map, visit **Mpse Ljmcvso** on map C-3 at x6, y14: Fly to C-2 and walk S. along y12 to x12, y15 on C-3. Turn right and go to x4, y14, then move 1-S, 1-E, 2-S and 1-E. Go 3-N to reach Kilburn. (If low on food in the desert, nomads at D-1, x10, y13, will trade you cactus nectar for item A in your first character's backpack. Make sure he doesn't have anything valuable in that slot.)

The Aliens

Fly to E-2 and go 3-N. **Kvnq**, move 3-W and 2-S to x8, y 3. Turn right and follow the path to x3, y 4. Move 5-N and jump to x3, y11. Be friendly.

The Gold Key and the Dog

Fly to B-3 and go to x14, y10. **Ufmfqpsu** 4-E to x14, y 2. Blow the Ruby Whistle **uxjdf** and enter the Minotaur's Den. Go 4-W, 4-N, 3-W and descend the stairs. Move 1-W, 7-S and 2-W through the door. Follow hall to the Dog at x3, y 4. After getting points from the Dog, search for the Gold Key. Exit the Den and go 3-W, 2-S to leave the Enchanted Forest. Or from the Den, cast town portal to a city.

The Eye of Goros

Fly to B-1. Go to x0, y 7. Enter A-1 by going W., then follow path to x10, y 0. Go W. to x0, y 0, due N. to x0, y11, and 3-W to x3, y11. Move 2-N, 1-E, 2-S. Follow the trail in the mountains to the **tfdsfu fousbodf** to Castle Doom at x7, y14. Enter, turn right and follow the hall to x7, y 5. Jump and continue to x8, y10. Jump, go to x5, y 6, face E. and jump. Follow hall to captive King at x7, y 8. Take the Eye of Goros and port to a town, or return to the secret entrance and exit.

The King's Pass and the Silver Key

Fly to A-2 and go S. to x11, y 3. Etherealize and go W. to x0, y 6. Move N. to x0, y15. Accept King's Pass from the Druid Percella. The **Tjmwfs Lfz** is needed in many dungeons. To get it, fly to B-1 and go S. from x6, y10. Follow the trail to x4, y 6 and go N.

The False King and the Soul Maze

Fly to E-3. After expulsion by the Lion Statue, go to x9, y 2 for the password. Go to x12, y 6 and give password. Move 1-N and 2-W to Castle Alamar. Enter and proceed 12-E to King Alamar. You will be cast into the Soul Maze at location x6, y 0. Complete the partially revealed map to learn the imposter's true identity, **Tifmufn**. Report name to Questioner at x6, y 0. Exit Soul Maze.

The Final Report

The Coral Key

Go to the Gypsy in C-2 and x9, y11. Have fortunes read for each character and record them. Fly to A-4. Cast "**xbml po xbufs**" and go 7-S, 7-W, then follow trail W. and S. to Hooded Figure at x4, y 6. Answer his questions with **dpmpst** from the Gypsy to get the Coral Key.

The Key Card

Fly to C-4. Go 2-S and 2-E. Cast "walk on water" and go 9-S. Fight crazed natives at x7, y 4, then proceed 2-S and enter Coral Cave. Step 2-S, 1-W and set Stabilization Dial #1 to B. Go 2-E and set Stabilization Dial # 2 to J. From x7, y 3, go 2-S, 3-W, 1-S and 2-W to x2, y 0, which teleports you to x0, y 5. Answer Volcano God's riddle with gala to get Key Card.

The Diamond Key
Fly to B-1 and march S. and E. to x7,y 3. Move 2-W and go S. into B-2. Go S. and W. to x2, y 2, then 1-N and etherealize. Turn right and move forward twice to Ice Princess at x4, y 4. Answer her riddle with **mpwf** to get the Diamond Key.

The Astral Maze and the Inner Sanctum
Fly to E-3. After being ejected by the Lion, move forward once, turn right and go to x1, y 3, then move N. to the Diamond Door. Use key to reach Astral Plane. Follow map to any of the five astral projectors and etherealize to enter it. This shoots you back to Sorpigal. Return and enter each of these doors, then insert the Key Card in the door at x8, y 5 and move 2-N, 1-E to get your rating. Rest at Inn and leave town. Fly to B-1. Proceed to "Gates to Another World" at x4, y15. Enter the Gates.

Reference Table of Key Locations

Towns			*Structures and Caves*			
Dusk	E-1	x9, y11	Wizard's Lair	B-1	x13,y 5	2
Erliquin	B-1	x13, y 0	Raven's Lair	B-2	x9,y 9	2
Portsmith	B-3	x3, y 3	Medusa's Cave	B-2	x8, y 4	1
Sorpigal	C-2	x10, y10	Castle White			
Algary	D-4	x7, y 7	Wolf	B-3	x9, y13	1
			Crazed Wizard			
Castles			Cave	C-2	x 15, y11	1
Dragadune	E-1	x12, y12				
King Alamar's	E-3	x14, y 7	Polyhedron			
Doom	A-1	x7, y14	Cave	D-3	x 7, y12	1
Blackridge N.	B-1	x14, y10	Building of			
Blackridge S.	B-1	x11, y 2	Gold	E-4	x10, y 5	
White Wolf	B-3	x9, y13				

People, Creatures and Things

Name	Sector	Surface	Interior	Level
Dark Rider	A-1	x5, y 2		
Red Dragon Lord	A-2	x11, y3		
Inspectron	B-1	x14, y10	x7, y 4	1
Wizard Orkim	B-1	x13, y 5	x12, y12	1
Lord Hacker	B-1	x11,y 2	x11, y 7	1
Agar	B-1	x13, y1	x4, y 3	1
Lord Archer	B-2	x9, y 9	x14, y1	2
Medusa	B-2	x8, y 4	x15, y 4	1
Lord Ironfist	B-3	x9, y13	x1, y 8	1
Grey Minotaur	B-3	x14, y 2	x8, y14	2
Gypsy	C-2	x9, y11		
Wizard	C-2	x10, y10	x1, y1	1
Crazed Wizard	C-2	x15, y11	x2, y15	2

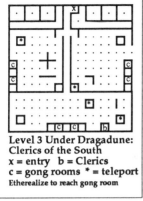

Level 3 Under Dragadune:
Clerics of the South
x = entry   b = Clerics
c = gong rooms * = teleport
Etherealize to reach gong room

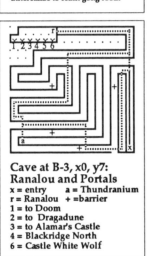

Cave at B-3, x0, y7:
Ranalou and Portals
x = entry   a = Thundranium
r = Ranalou   + = barrier
1 = to Doom
2 = to Dragadune
3 = to Alamar's Castle
4 = Blackridge North
6 = Castle White Wolf

Name	Sector	Surface	Interior	Level
Hermit	C-3	x2, y10		
Lord Archer	B-2	x9, y 9	x14, y1	2
Wyvern's Eye	C-3	x7, y 7		
Virgin	C-4	x7, y 2	x5, y 0	1
Blithe's Peak	B-3	x9, y 6		
Minotaur's Den	B-3	x14, y 2		
Shrine of Okzar	E-1	x9, y11	x0, y15	2
Medusa Head	B-2	x8, y 4	x15, y 4	1
Raven's Lair	B-2	x9, y 9		2
Fabled Fountain of Dragadune	E-1	x12, y12	x13, y15	1
Secret of Portsmith	B-3	x4, y 3	x11, y 8	1
Jolly Raven	C-4	x8, y13		
Pirate Ghost Ship	B-4	x8, y 7		
Trivia Island	B-4	x8, y 2		

Character Development Sites

Pool of Wisdom	D-2	x10, y12		
Prism of Precision	E-1	x9, y11	x15, y15	2
Flame of Agility	E-1	x9, y11	x15, y 5	2
Endurance Fountain	C-2	x4, y 7		

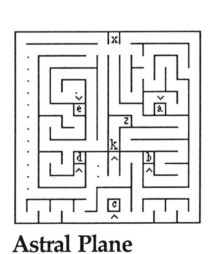

Astral Plane
Etherealize at each to enter door.
x = entry point

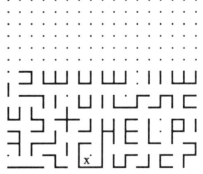

Soul Maze
Lower half Only

Moebius
The Orb of Celestial Harmony

I n this one-character game by Greg Malone you are a disciple of Moebius, a martial arts and Zen master. His mystic orb has been stolen by Kaimen, a renegade disciple, triggering earthquakes and other disasters that devastate the land. Your quest for the Orb takes you through the Realms of Earth, Water, Air and Fire. In each you must slay the evil Monks who have taken over the Shrines of Moebius, then free the Priests and liberate the temple. By doing so you will acquire magical prayers and artifacts that compose a charming magic system with uniquely Oriental overtones. Combat is also distinctive, the most effectively animated battles yet seen in a role-playing game. You can choose from an array of twelve moves, six each for karate and sword-fighting while battling one foe at a time, and the three-inch high characters are fluidly animated.

DEALING JUSTLY with the good citizens of Khantun is as important as dealing death to the bad ones, otherwise you'll miss useful clues and other help. The main map reveals buildings of stone amid thick bamboo forests, and there's nary a single maze to map. In fact, a clever auto-mapping feature displays a variety of maps of the current Realm. The keyboard interface makes it a challenge for non-arcade gamers to master the basics of this game system, but *Moebius* is worth the extra effort. It's one of those rare role-playing games that, though the goal involves a mystic Orb and an evil wizard, is completely original in design and implementation.

The Walkthrough

General Tips
Search all the doors, chests and vials, which are easy to find and therefore not indicated on the maps. Location of the chests and vials is the same in every game, but their contents vary. Save the game before opening them, so you can restart and try again; often the contents will be different next time. Always close the door behind you after entering or leaving a room. Guards will steal from you, and you must chase them down and defeat them to regain your goods. If the door is shut, the guard can't leave and you won't have to chase him all over the castle. Your character may vanish beneath the water when swimming, but you can keep track of his location by sticking a piece of tape or a write protection tab over him before entering the water.

Collect lots of magical components (especially panda hair and beetle pincers, at *least* six of each) before moving on. Have a sword equipped and you'll usually get them from the animal. And don't be hasty in going to the next Realm. They get progressively tougher, so hang around the first Three until you've been promoted six times in each. The only Overlord that must be defeated is Kamien in the Fire Realm, but you should get the one in the Earth Realm just for the extra points and the sword. If you're down to one or no extra lives, you may want go ahead and liberate a Shrine immediately after slaying the Monk, which earns you another life.

Combat Tips
When using an unblessed sword you have a slim chance against assassins. Sword-fighting against a guard is a little easier. As the guard approaches, wait until he is just in front of you, then use low swings to hit his legs. After striking him, immediatly do an 'O' or an 'I' to deliver a blow to his head. Then use a 'K' or 'L' for a mid-level swing to his arms. Bare-handed combat is more reliable against all foes, so practice it more in the early stages.

The low kick is extremely effective and, unless you just like sword-fighting, should be your main weapon against everyone but Monks. The trick is to move into the center and wait for the foe to advance, then kick as he moves in. Assassins can be defeated with punches to the face when they are almost on you—low kicks are also good. If you miss, hit the 'A' key to back out of range. Keep one finger on that key, another on the 'X' to move forward. If you're about to lose a fight, hit the return key to "break and run." When prompted to make your break, restart from your last save.

Evil monks should be stunned with fireballs before using long strides to overlap the foe and plant middle and high kicks to the face. You can also paralyze a Monk before the battle begins, then kill him with a single hammer blow. This is handy when they attack in groups, especially in the Fire Realm. If you've got a lot of Mind Elixirs, turn invisible and you can kill most of the Monks in this Realm in one sustained assault with the hammer.

Earth Realm

A good strategy is to head for the Cistern (C1 on the map), refill your waterskin and clear a path due east to the Palace steps. Enter and confront the Overlord by moving north into the Palace Court. (If you can't find him, listen for the person issuing commands). Next get the Priest at (P1) to follow you. Exit through the northwest door, then go south into the pool and south again when you surface outside the Palace. Head back to the Cistern to get refilled on water and recharge your body and mental energy. Now go to Shrine (S1), have the Priest wait outside, and save the game. Enter, defeat the Evil Monk, and lead the Priest inside to liberate the Shrine.

Now get the Priest (P2) to follow you to (a) on the map and tell him to stay. Equip your sword and move southeast twice to (b), then use the sword to clear a path east or northeast. Return for the Priest, retrace your path and head down the east side to Shrine (S2). Defeat the Monk and install the Priest. You may then want to return to the forest west of (C1) to hunt for panda fur.

Make sure you've got a **ibnnfs**, obtained by defeating a guard. Go to (w), where you can see the island, then swim west two or three times to land at (x) on the shore. Move southeast to (y) on the southernmost point of the island's exterior, then south one into the water. A swift current flows here, so quickly move west four times, northwest once, and north twice to arrive at the island's entrance. **Iju** the wall with the **ibnnfs** and you're in. The Astral Gate to the next realm is marked (G) on the map, but don't leave until your character has reached level ten, has a full supply of food and water, and is in good health.

Water Realm

From the west side of (A), swim north to the Palace island. (If the current takes you elsewhere, restart and try again). Follow the path northeast to the Tower (T1), then take the path west and southwest to the Palace steps. Go up Palace steps to the doors. If you need water, take the northwest door, go west and south to (w). Go through the northeast door to (d) and enter the well: You'll be transported to the Shrine (S1). Defeat the Monk, go south. Follow the path west to the water on the south, swim south and then east to the Palace island.

Go along the south shore, then north to Tower (T1). Head past it, then northwest along the shore, swim north to the island and follow the path to Tower (T2), where the astrologer will give you some **gjti tdbmft**. Go to the southwest corner of the island and swim **tpvui** to the Palace island.

Enter the Palace's northwest door, follow the corridors to (B) and slay the Overlord. (You must have a shovel before this phase, so attack guards until you get one). Get the Priest at (P1) and lead him to the small well at (e). Make sure he's in the room when you enter the well. You'll both be transported to island (X). (There's a water hole southeast if you need it). Move north out of the water and around to the island's northwest corner. Swim to the north beach, go to the west side, then north to the area south of Cistern (C1). Go north to the Cistern. You must chop through trees south of the Cistern building going east. When you reach a path, follow it to Shrine (S1) and liberate it. Swim back to island (X). Go to the northwest corner and swim west to the island with the Gate.

Move south down the west shore as far as possible. Waterwalk down the river to Shrine (S2). Before entering, **hfu a tpjm tbnqmf** from either side of the **fousbodf**. Defeat the Monk, exit, follow the river back north, then go east to the Palace island. Get Priest (P2). While standing together on **tbnf tqpu**, **jowplf** the **ufmfqpsu** spell. You will arrive at the entrance to (S2). **Mjcfsbuf** it. Go to the Gate (G).

Air Realm

The Demon and the Condor cannot be defeated, so avoid them. Obtaining the Minstrel's Were-charm is tricky. The easiest way is to save the game when you hear him play his eerie tune, then cast **qbsbmzaf** and find him. **Vtf** the **bnvmfu cfgpsf** you move onto his square. When you're there, **tupq nbhjd**.

From (A), waterwalk south on the river until you see a Tower to the south, then go west to the Cistern (C1). Go north at the opening for water and recharging. Exit, go east to shore and follow the path east to the Tower (T) and get the Amulet. Cross to the river's west shore and waterwalk or walk/chop your way north upstream to the path west of the skeleton (K). Follow it west and southwest to the Palace.

Enter the Palace, avoiding the lake. Go northwest around lake and through the halls to the west door (D). Exit (you may need to use the hammer). Take the south path heading southeast, south, east, southwest and southeast to Shrine (S1) and defeat the Monk. Get a soil sample outside the door. Return to the Palace for the Priest (P1). Teleport to (S1). Go southeast through the mountains, then east until you reach the skeletons. There's a small building to the northwest. Go along the soil to (N), northeast of the building, at night to catch the Condor. Continue due east to Shrine (S2) in northeast corner. Get soil sample. Defeat Monk.

Return to Palace and get Priest (P2). Teleport and liberate Shrine. Head to Cistern (C2). Follow path north of Cistern to skeleton by air. Hit the skeleton and move to that square, then use **xfsfdibsn** to **dibohf** to a **dpoeps** and **gmz opsuifbtu** to the Gate.

Fire Realm

Beware the Floating Skull—it can only be defeated with fireballs. Also avoid the flames. From (A), waterwalk southeast to the island and use the Spirit spell to pass through the wall into the complex. Water is available at (w). Go southwest and enter hall going east to Shrines (S1) and (S2). Defeat Monks in each. Go to (X) and swim to the statue (R), then on to the Priest Island (P). A good route from the southeast corner of the main island is: one southeast, one northeast, nine east and five northeast to (R). Then one east, one northeast, one north, five northeast, three east, three northeast and three north to (P). Save the game when you get there.

Have a Priest follow you and swim back to the statue. You may have to repeat this several—even 10-20 times—because the Priests have a tendency to drown. If this happens repeatedly, let him rest a few turns to restore his body points. When you finally reach (R), save again, then swim for the main island. Liberate one Shrine, then repeat these steps for the other. You'll get gold gloves from the final Priest. Go to the second east-west path, where the Orb (O) is guarded by Kamien and his Monks. Defeat him and use the **hpme hmpwft** to get Orb. Go south to the Gate, and you're outa there!

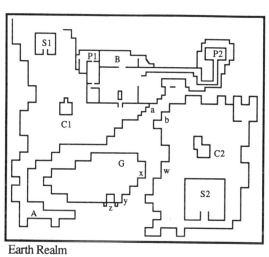

Earth Realm

Air Realm

Key:
A: Start here
B: Overlord
C: Cisterns
P: Priests
S: Shrines
G: Astral Gate
See walkthru
for others.

Water Realm

Fire Realm

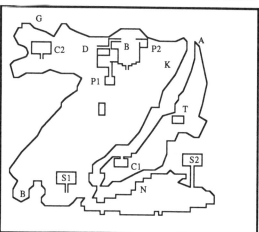

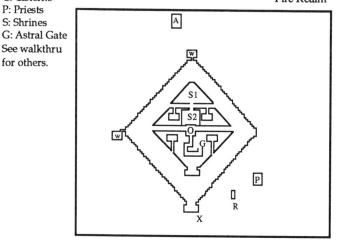

55

The Pawn

The well-honed prose that describes the quaint land of Kerovnia and its peculiar inhabitants is reinforced with finely crafted graphics in this British import. Your goal is to remove a silver wristband that appeared on your arm when you were mysteriously teleported to Kerovnia, apparently by an evil wizard named Kronos. The only pawn in the game is you. Kronos says if you deliver a note to King Erik and kill an adventurer for him, he will free you of the wristband and reward you greatly. But he has ulterior motives that involve the devil, a kidnapped princess and the upcoming election in which a dwarf is running against the King. You'll meet a giggling guru, an icy Snowman, and discover diverse mini-quests to fulfill as you strive to complete the main goal.

THE PUZZLES ARE CHIEFLY object-oriented and unusually clever. You'll have your hands full, for there are dozens of items to fiddle with and carry about, more than a few of which prove to be classic red herrings. It's possible to win the game without scoring all 350 points. (The following solution accounts for 345 of them). The parser is second only to Infocom's, and an innovative graphic feature lets you scroll the picture up or down to read obscured text. (Or you can turn it off completely). A tough game to finish without any help, The Pawn boasts a shrewd sense of humor and is easily the best English adventure to reach these shores.

The Walkthrough

On the Path
E. Say hello (to Kronos). Ask about **xsjtucboe**. Get chest and note. E E.. **Mppl voefs nbu**. Get wooden key.

Palace Gardens
Put wooden key in pocket. **Vompdl epps xjui nfubm lfz**. Open door. SW.

In Shed
Get trowel, rake and hoe. **Mppl voefs cfodi**. Get **qpu**. Get **qmbou**. **Qmbou qmbou** in plant pot with **uspxfm**. Exit. E. [Gateway] **Tipx opuf** to guard. W. **(gjwf ujnft)**. N. N. W. NW.

The Guru
Enter hut. **Sfnpwf tijsu**. **Dpwfs xsjtucboe** with tijsu. Exit. E. E. N.

Foothills
Voujf tijsu. Tie **sblf** to **ipf** with **tijsu**. **Mfwfs cpvmefs** with rake. **Voujf tijsu**. **Espq** hoe and rake. Wear **tijsu**. NW. Climb rocks. U. U. Put **topx** in **cpxm**. D. W. D. D. (Return to Large Hill)

Large Hill
Enter hut. Give **cpxm** to guru. Get **sjdf**. Exit. (Go to **Gpsftu Dmfbsjoh**)

Forest Clearing
Fybnjof tree stump. Get pouch. Open pouch. Look in pouch. Get dpmpst. Njy dpmpst. Put xijuf in pouch. (Return to Gppuijmmt). NW. dmjnc spdlt. E.E.E.

Cavern
D. E. E. Drop all. U. U. Csfbl xbmm. E. Get all. N. Qvti qfeftubm. Look in niche. Get blue key. S. W. W. N. N. Give sjdf to bmdifnjtut. (Go to Rank Forest due south of Gpsftu Dmfbsjoh).

Forest Clearing
Dmjnc usff. Unlock door with xppefo lfz. Drop wooden key. Open door. Enter tree. Close door. Npwf gmppscpbset. D. D. E. N.

Office
Move rug. Unlock safe with cmvf lfz. Open safe. Search safe. Get qbqfs. S. E. [Voting Booth] Put qbqfs in large box. W. W. W. SW. Open door. W.

Lounge
Get ibse ibu and xfbs it. Look voefs dvtijpot. Get coin. E. NE. NW. Push button. Pull door. Xbju (uisff ujnft). N.

Elevator
Get rope. Qvti door. Push tfdpoe button. Qvmm door. S. [Rockface] Get mvnqt with uspxfm. N. Qvti door. Push gjstu button. Pull door. (Return to Usff Usvol Sppn). Open door. Exit. E.E.E. N. N.

Honest John
Buy xijtlz and cffs with dpjo. NW. NW. Climb rocks. Give diftt to bewfouvsfs. (He should arrive around uvso pof fjhiuz gjwf. Then go to Hbufxbz. This enables you to sftdvf the Qsjodftt, though you still don't get any points for it. Now go to the Qmbufbv with the Topxnbo).

Snowman
Get xijuf. Nfmu Snowman with xijuf. Get white. Put white in pouch. (Go to Mbcpsbupsz).

Alchemist's Laboratory
Give mvnqt to bmdifnjtut. NE. Get tomes. Dbtu tqfmm on tomes. Read tomes. Get aerosoul. (Dsptt Spqf Csjehf to Room with paper wall).

Paperwalled Room
Open cupboard. Ujf spqf up ippl. Sjq qbqfs xbmm with uspxfm. Climb down. Drop rope. S. Knock on doors (gjwf ujnft).

Porter and the Devil
Give xijtlz to porter. E. Climb down. N. Give cffs to Kfssz Mff Mfxjt. S. Dmptf qpvdi. E. N. D. Ask efwjm about xsjtucboe. Get potion bottle. N. N. Open pouch. Hfu xijuf. NW.

The Dragon
Qpjou to tibepxt. Tijof xijuf at tibepxt. N.

Workshop
Throw cpuumf at Lspopt. Qvti cvuupo on bfsptpvm. Ublf pgg tijsu, kfbot and ibse ibu. Drop all but xijuf, qpvdi and bfsptpvm. Get pointy hat and cloak. Xfbs pointy hat and cloak. Get wand. Get wands. N. D.

Circular Room
Put xijuf in qpvdi. Dmptf qpvdi. N. N. D. Give bfsptpvm to efwjm. W. S. W. U. Pqfo qpvdi. W. N. Get rope. Climb up. Drop rope. S.S.S.S.S. E. SE. S. S. S. Open doors. S. Knock on door. Tbz op.

Corridor
S. Get listing. Examine listing. (To wander around without getting killed, type efcvh).

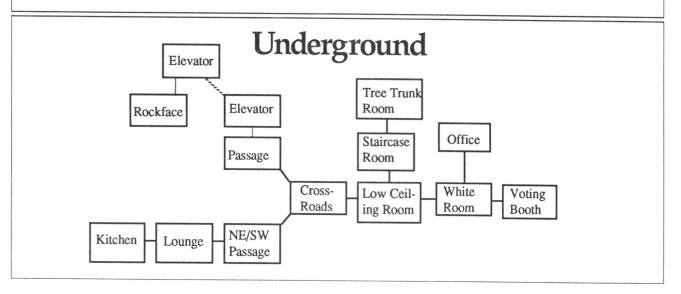

Underground

Elevator

Rockface — Elevator

Passage

Cross-Roads

Kitchen — Lounge — NE/SW Passage

Tree Trunk Room

Staircase Room

Office

Low Ceiling Room — White Room — Voting Booth

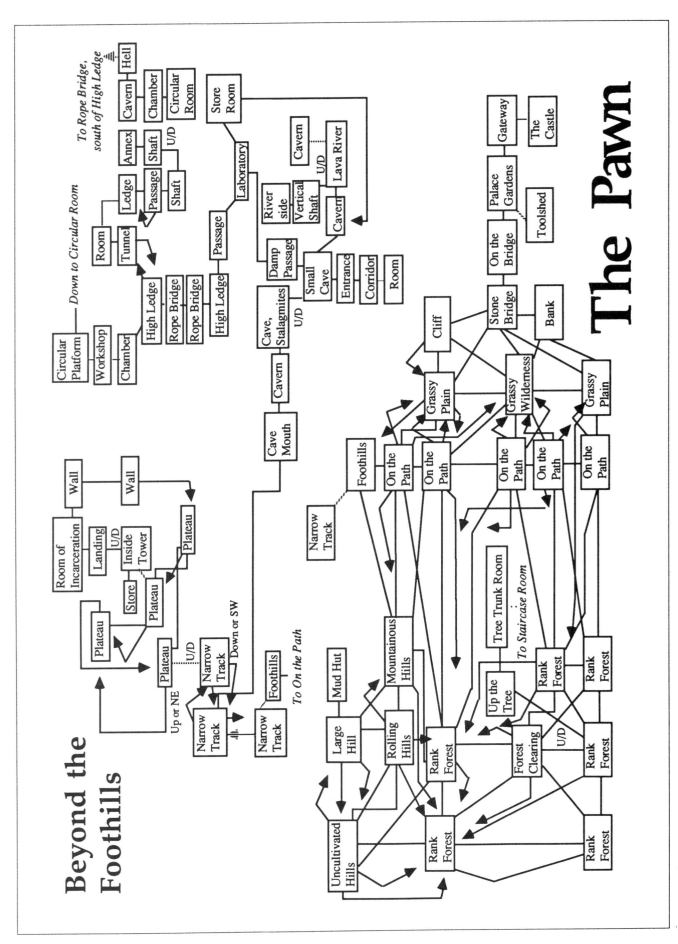

The Pawn

Beyond the Foothills

On the island of Gelnor, you'll lead a band of up to six to defeat the Black Lord. To accomplish this feat you must retrieve the nine Rings of Power and five runes from various mazes, which calls for puzzle-solving as well as monster-slaying. On the aerial view map and in the mazes, your party is depicted by a single icon. In dungeons, the overhead view begins as a blank screen that is fleshed out as you move around. Messages and scrolls furnish clues, and bumping into little dots will trigger other events and opportunities to solve puzzles by making menu selections. During combat, your crew lines up at the bottom of the screen and faces the enemy, all portrayed with lores graphics, simple animation and and sound effects. The program runs slowly, and the Commodore version takes forever to load dungeons and towns.

Combat is easy. After setting each member's attack style or one of the 58 spells, your choices remain in place in the next round, when you can just punch the "continue fighting" option (unless you want to change an order). The weak point is a clumsy distribution routine that makes you dole out every item carried by the party in order to assign them to people—you can't just trade things back and forth. The interface varies for each version: Apple is keyboard; Commodore and Atari 800 version have color-coded, joystick-controlled menus that mean virtually no typing; Macintosh doesn't allow mouse control but ST does. All will print handy character stats, and character generation in this intermediate level game is fast and convenient.

Phantasie I
The Walkthrough

Character Creation & Development
If you're not planning to go on to the sequel, include two fighters in your party, one of whom should be a thief and the other a Minotaur. Then add two priests and a sorcerer. But fighters are useless in the advanced stages of Phantasie II, so if you expect to use your I characters in it, the optimal party consists of three priests, two sorcerers and a thief. (The thief is vital for entering certain locations). When creating characters, make intelligence the top priority, followed by constitution. Put charisma at the bottom of the list. The dummy scam (creating characters named A-E, forming a party and having them pool the gold to the one who will be in the real expedition) works in this series. Use this repeatedly to amass enough gold to buy the best possible equipment before setting out. Dungeon D is a good place to find magic potions and weapons.

Character Development
Wizards need more points to advance, so give them three shares when dividing up the loot. Give two to the priests and one to any other class. As soon as you have the Teleport spell, start zipping over to town #11 for the cheapest training. When learning new spells in the later stages, the following are unnecessary or almost useless: Binding, Monster Evaluation, Ninja, Quickness, Strength and Summon Elemental. (Keep this in mind during combat too). If a character gets killed, it's usually better to restart a saved game than to resurrect him. Otherwise his constitution will be permanently lowered and he'll get fewer hit points when advanced. After most of your characters reach level ten, visit Dungeon D and kill the Minor Deity—you get about 30,000 experience points per adventurer, and can repeat this by not saving the dungeon when you leave. If planning to play Phantasie II, definitely use this method to elevate everyone to level 13-15. Also, monsters in the vicinity of town #11 are worth more experience points that those in other areas.

Time-Saving Tricks
Potions are the key to saving time. Always take lots of them into the dungeons. This trick will enable you to duplicate the potions you own. (This won't duplicate your gold, but later in the game you'll have more than you can spend). First make two copies of your scenario disk (the boot side of the program). Label one the "good" disk, the other "dummy." After accumulating lots of potions, sell everything you want duplicated to a town with few items (to save time buying them back later). Pineville (#2) is good. Teleport to Greenville (#3), remove the good disk and insert the dummy. Teleport to #4, insert the good disk, and teleport back to #2. Buy back the potions and insert the dummy. Teleport to #3, insert the good disk and continue playing. Whenever you're low on potions, return to town #2 and buy what you need— just be sure to insert the dummy disk before teleporting out of town.

When you teleport, the program writes the transactions into that town's inventory. By inserting the

dummy disk, you trick the program into deleting the items you buy from it rather than from the good disk. You can use this trick to duplicate rare weapons and armor and outfit the entire party with them. Sell one to town #2 and leave the good disk in before teleporting. Return and buy the item, insert the dummy and follow the first method to return and buy it again. Then go back and sell both items to town #2, inserting the good disk before leaving. When you return, there will be twice as many of them, and you can buy them and repeat the process to double the quantity.

On with the Quest
Follow the alphabetical sequence of the maps, which guides you through the tough dungeons gradually. (The maps show only the essential regions). Be sure to stop at the pool near Pineville and the other two when you are nearby. The program can save the state of only one dungeon at a time, so if you want to restore a saved dungeon to its original state just enter another one and save it when you leave. If you've already saved Dungeon I, this may be necessary to follow that section of the walkthru.

Dungeon A: Door in Hillside
Go to (2) and **qvmm mfwfs** to open access to (3). At (3), walk around room and write down the words that are on the wall and armor. Go to (4) and push the button to unlock door to (5), where you may **ubml up uif Pme Nbo boe hfu uif Bjs Svof.**

Dungeon B: Small Cathedral
From (1), go to (2) and get teleported to (3). Walk to (4) and **cvso uif cpy** to get the **Fbsui Svof.** If it won't burn, return later when your levels are higher. **Epo'u tbz zft** to the Crone at (5). Tell her what you wrote down in **Evohfpo B.** At (6) you'll be teleported to the exit.

Dungeon C: Greenville Cave
At (2), rescue the **nbo** and write down his words and the number. If you rescue the **nbjefo**, she just gives you a **tdspmm**. Get the **Gjsf Svof** at (3).

Dungeon D: Outside Woodville
At (2), **qsftt uif ovncfst** you learned in Dungeon C. Tell Old Priest what **Mpse Xppe't vodmf** said (**tusbujdpo**). Tell Kilmor (3) what you **xspuf epxo jo Evohfpo C**, room 5 (**ojtdptobu**). He'll give you a number that when pressed at (2) opens access to (4). Do it and visit (4) now. Next, your Thief must be able to open all the doors at (5), where you'll learn the number that, when pressed at (2), opens **opsui gpvoubjo** (6). Go to (6) and get teleported to (7), where you can **npwf tpvui** and get the **Hpe Lojgf**, the most powerful weapon in either *Phantasie*. Exit at the passage marked 'X', not available until you teleport from (6). After most of your party reaches level 10, return to the special (****) and **ebnbhf uif jepm** to score tens of thousands of experience points. Don't save the dungeon and this can be repeated.

Phantasia
Teleport to Phantasia (#8) and buy **Sjoh ovncfs ojof** from the Armory. (If you don't know the Teleport spell, revisit the first four dungeons until one of your sorcerers is able to learn it). From Phantasia, go **opsui** until you're level with the **qppm**. Go east to enter it, then return to Phantasia, which has vanished. **Nbsdi xftu** once, then due south to the next screen to escape the ocean area. Then on to the next **qppm** near town #7 before traveling to Dungeon E. **Lffq uif sjoht**, since you'll need them to pass a test in a later dungeon. For inventory purposes, you can sell them to a town and buy them back when you're ready.

Dungeon E: Lord Wood's Castle
At (2), copy the message, which is a **nbq up sppn uisff**. Follow the map to (4) and **dpqz uif ovncfs** there. At (5), you will get the **Xbufs Svof**—only if you have already visited all **uisff qppmt**.

Dungeon F: J.R. Trolkin's Castle
From (1), **hp tpvui** and get teleported to the cell (2). Follow secret passage to (3) and **qvmm bmm uisff mfwfst**. Destroy the traitor at (4), grab the **Sjoht** at (5) and pick up the key at (6). Head for the Arena (7) and go all the way east, then north to exit.

Dungeon G: Bleeb Island
Enter the red pool at (2) to activate green pool at (3), which you then enter and get teleported to (4). Walk to (5) and **foufs uibu qppm**, then return to (4) and enter the pool to teleport to (3). Walk to (6) and enter the pool, which ports you to (7). Trek to (8), enter the pool and then slog down to (9), where the pool teleports you to (10). Enter the pool at (10) and wind up at (11). Walk to (12) and **qvti hsffo. Answer hsffo** at (14). Answer **sfe/hsffo** at (15). Answer red at (16) and get the treasures, which are three more rings.

Dungeon H: Dosnebian Temple
One of your party must be a **njopubvs** to enter this dungeon. At (2), speak the words from **Tdspmm ojofuffo**. If you don't know them, use secret passage one step north, then east. **Efgbdf uif jepm** at (3), which opens to the door to (4). Go to (5) and rescue everyone, starting at the bottom cell and working your way up. The key you got at (5) opens the doors to (6) and the exit.

Astral Plane
By now you should have entered the three pools and collected all nine Rings and the four Runes. Check with the **Nztujd** to be sure you're ready to "**wjtju uif hpet**." Go to any town and teleport to the town **xiptf ovncfs zpv xspuf epxo jo Evohfpo F, Room #4**. Exit the town, Olympia, (you're now on the Astral Plane), move one step right and go due south to cross the River Styx. Move four south and eight east to the fortress. (It's not mapped here because there are no puzzles or secret doors). Inside visit all six rooms and pass the test in each one, which requires having all four runes and the Rings. Depending on how well-developed your party is, you may not need all nine Rings, but it's best take them all just in case. Then go south until you meet Zeus. **Xpstijq ijn** and he'll give you the **Hpe Svof**.

Dungeon I: Dark Lord's Castle
You must have the **Hpe Svof** to enter. From (2), you'll be teleported to (3). Go north and **eftuspz bmm uisff jufnt** in the room. (**Uif Ebsl Mpse esbxt ijt qpxfs gspn uifn, tp epo'u tufbm uifn**). And **epo'u tju** on the throne. Attack the Dark Lord at (5), and he'll throw the wand north (only if you **eftuspzfe** his stuff). Go **opsui** and get the wand and treasure at (6), then south. **Xbwf uif xboe** to reach (7). Go to the room's north side to get the scroll and talk with the Mage. Tell him you want to **buubdl uif Ebsl Mpse**. He'll teleport you to (8), and you can go to 'X' for the Final Confrontation. After completing Dungeon I (and the game), you'll get your first Divine spell (#58), which, if cast when you first enter a dungeon, gives you a tip on what to expect there.

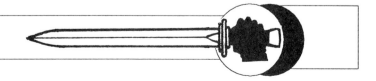

61

Phantasie I: Gelnor

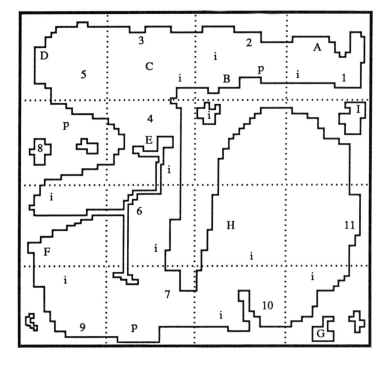

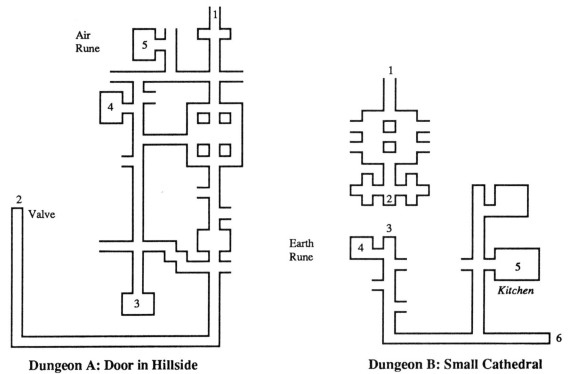

Dungeon A: Door in Hillside

Dungeon B: Small Cathedral

62

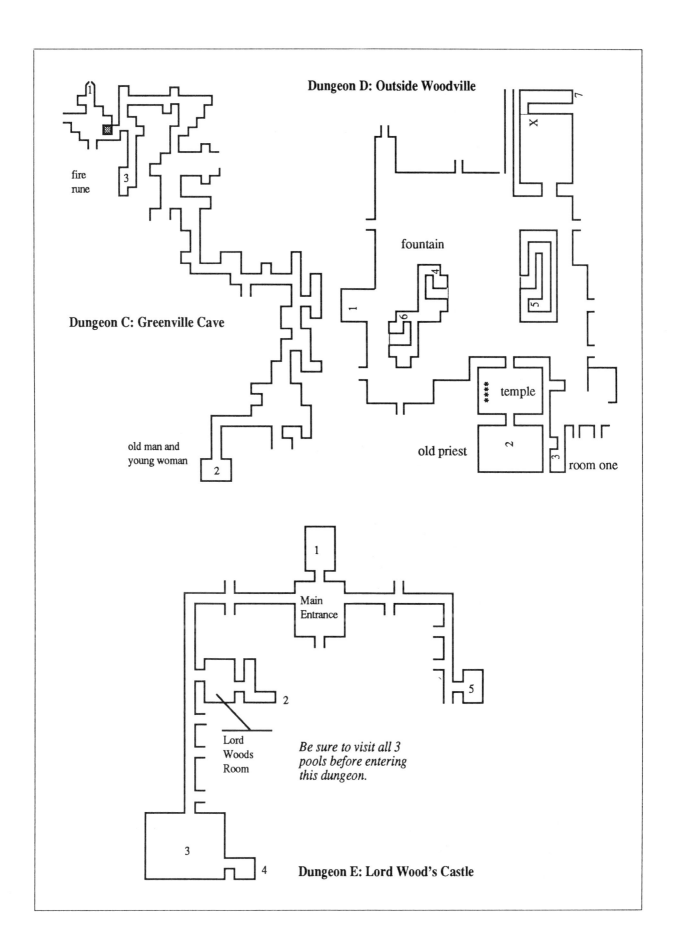

Dungeon D: Outside Woodville

fire
rune

Dungeon C: Greenville Cave

old man and
young woman

fountain

old priest

temple

room one

Main
Entrance

Lord
Woods
Room

*Be sure to visit all 3
pools before entering
this dungeon.*

Dungeon E: Lord Wood's Castle

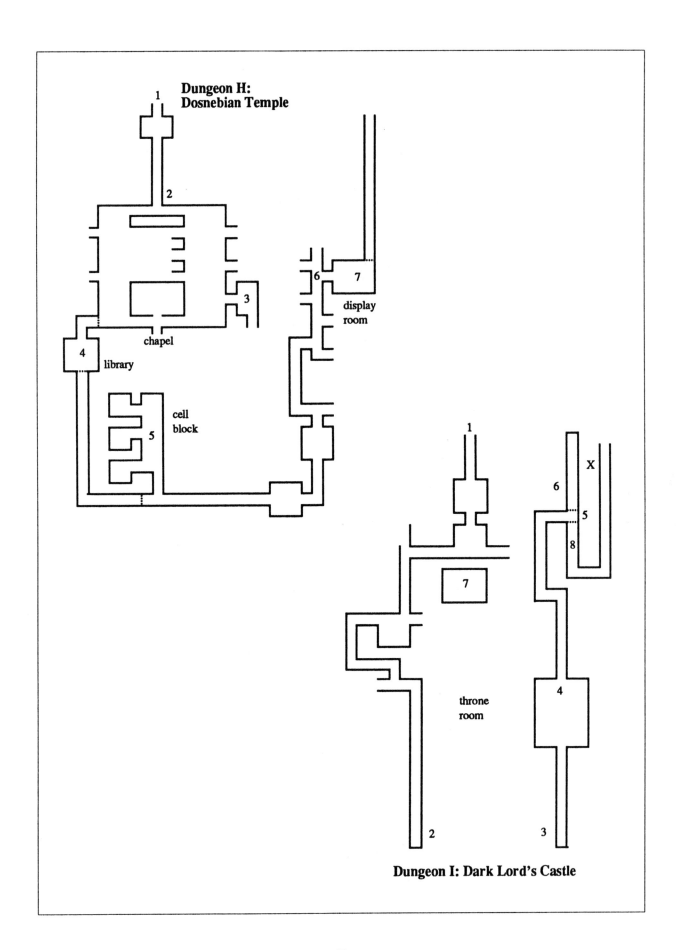

Dungeon H:
Dosnebian Temple

1

2

6

7
display
room

3

chapel

4
library

cell
block

5

1

X

6

5

8

7

4

throne
room

2

3

Dungeon I: Dark Lord's Castle

64

Phantasie II

The second in the trilogy of *Phantasie* games, this one has the same graphic style and game system of the first, but with a couple of new spells, combat features. and ingenious puzzles In it you must free the land of Ferronrah by travelling to the Netherworld. To do so,you must end the curse of Nikademus by destroying the Orb. Instead of Black Knights, you will run into the Minions of Pluto, eight powerful Beasts you must slay in order to obtain their Amulets and Runes. Althoug tougher than its predecessor, fans of *Phantasie I* were equally enthusiastic about this game.

The Walkthrough

Character Creation

If you want or need to create new characters, use two Wizards, two Monks and two Priests—but make sure one has excellent lock-picking ability. Dungeon B is the best place to rack up lots of experience points in the early stages. Characters transferred into *Phantasie II* with the provided utility will lose all equipment, levels, and gold. To avoid this, delete the file named "CHAR22" from the copy of your *Phantasie II* character disk. Copy file "CHAR2" from the first game's character disk to the second one and rename it "CHAR22". Your original party will be intact when you start the game. However, this might mean you won't encounter some of the Beasts. Inspect your characters immediately, and if they already have Beast Rune 1, for example, you won't meet that monster. You can still finish the game, but it won't be as much fun. For the most entertainment, create new characters. (You could at least import your *I* characters and sell their God Knives, Shields and potions to an armory, then delete "CHAR22" from the disk and copy the original one from the program disk onto your character disk and create new characters.)

General Tips

The criteria for winning are to learn the eight Beast Runes (by slaying Beasts and examining amulets) and to find and destroy the Orb (by taking it to the Netherworld and feeding it to the Ice Dragon). Each character does not need all eight Runes, as long as your group possesses them in some combination. All the time-saving tricks in the *Phantasie I* walkthrough work here too. Dungeon B (The Castle) is the best one for fresh characters to earn points. The only place you can earn lots of experience points in a single battle is by killing Pluto in Dungeon G, which calls for at least level 13-14 characters.

Don't fool with the Beasts until your crew is up to level ten and the spellcasters know spell #8, Fireflash 4. When you're ready, their locations are: 1 and 2, random; 3, on uif jtmboe opsuifbtu of Qjqqbdpu; 4, on the island opsuixftu of Gfsspisbi; 5 and 6, on the btusbm qmbof; 7, in Dungeon G; and 8, in Dungeon H. Sometimes Beast 1 can be found by going to the place where you killed 3 or 4. In version 1.0 of the Commodore version, you may have trouble finding Beast 2. If so, bash around in Dungeon C about three-quarters of the way down, then exit without saving. Immediately reenter the dungeon (say yes right away) and complete the Dungeon as described below. Beast 2 should appear around the southern gate.

Dungeon A: The Kobold Village
From (1), outside the village, go to (2) if you need gold. Then see the gnome at (3) and write down the **ovncfs**, which is needed to get in to the Netherworld's first level.

Dungeon B: The Castle
This is the best place for low-level characters to earn experience points. Later use the machine at (2) to teleport to the 1st and 2nd levels of the Netherworld.

Dungeon C: Straw Hut
Go directly to (2) without pushing any buttons, then **qvmm** the **mfwfs** there. Next pull the lever at (3), then head for (4) and push the button once. Go to (5), press the button, return to (4) and push that button twice. At (6), push the button, return to (4) and push it twice. Now head due east. **Ifbm fwfszpof** before talking to Filmon (7). You must agree or you'll never finish the game. Exit west after killing the beast. In at least one version this creature may not appear. If that happens, don't worry because your main interest is the scroll and information Filmon gives you after the battle, which he does even if the animal is a no-show.

Dungeon D: Summer Palace
At (1), say **qsjodftt**. Rescue her at (2), then **kvnq in qju** at (3) to escape the guards and exit north from (4).

Dungeon E: Cold Wet Cavern in Netherworld, Level One Go to (2) and check out the **tjy qppmt** marked 'Y' to get spell 57. (Avoid the others.) At

(3) **dpqz** the **ovncfs**, needed to teleport from Dungeon B to Netherworld's second level.

The Astral Plane and the Forgotten Temple
To get here, use the **nbdijof** in Dungeon B (visit Dungeon A for correct number, **47**) and follow the main map to find the Vortex, then swim the Styx River. Keep casting spell 57 until you find Beasts 5 and 6 on the Astral Plane. If you have enough potions left after finishing Dungeon E, you can save time by going to the **Gpshpuufo** now to get the number needed in Dungeon H, then return to town 7. Otherwise, visit town 7 and get healed, then exit and get teleported to the Material Plane, go to Dungeon B and return. Then head for the Temple.

Dungeon F: Netherworld Cavern, Level One
If you still have the Orb from *Phantasie I* you don't need to visit this one. To avoid lava, teleport from town 7 to town 8 and **nbsdi fbtu** to the dungeon. (Don't exit 7, though, unless you want to return to the Material Plane.) Keep entering the pool at (2) until you're teleported to (3). Enter that **qppm** until you wind up at (4), then take secret passage west. At (5) get the Orb and go to (6). Enter the pool and retrace your steps via the other pools to exit.

Dungeon G: Pluto's Smallest Castle
Reach this area from Dungeon B by using the number from Dungeon E (66) at the machine. Enter the **njeemf epps** on the west side. (If your position in the maze doesn't match the map, exit and try another door until it does.) Don't go all the way **fbtu** from (1) or you get smashed by Pluto. Just move **fbtu uxjdf** and slay the Cloud Giant, then take the secret passage north. This is a good dungeon for earning experience points, but the only goal here is to slay Beast 7 at (2). The map to Dungeon H is also here, but obtaining it entails heavy-duty combat. You'll find directions below. (But if you insist, exit from (2), go north and follow the Troll to get the scroll. Fight your way south, then west, south, east and south to the stairs and jump in the pit.)

Dungeon H: Pluto's Menagerie
To get here, walk from town #10 to town #9 (Demoniac). From atop the town, move 21 west,

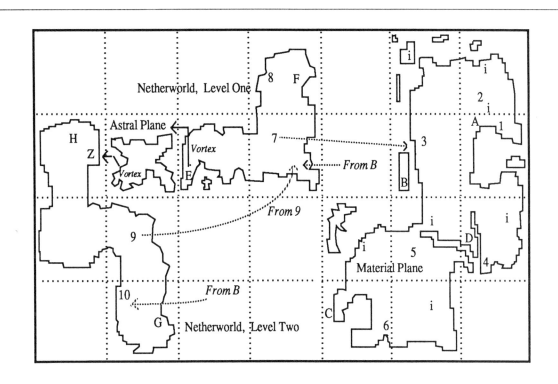

Phantasie II Ferronrah

Numbers: The Townes

A-H the dungeons as labeled on following maps

i: Inns

Z: Forgotten Temple

Dotted Lines: Teleport paths exiting the Netherworld towns

9 south, 5 west, 6 north, 6 west, 10 north, 7 east, 7 **opsui**, 8 west, 7 north and 9 east. Dungeon H is a deadly, tough dungeon that will require more than one trip. (Be sure to **tbwf** the **evohfpo** each time you leave.)   Keep pressing buttons at (2) until you arrive at (4).   The results of all the buttons are random, so if you arrive at (3) or (6), move one away, then back to the button and hit it again. When you reach (4), be sure your party's health and magic points are at their maximum immediately after passing the **gjstu epps** to the **tpvui**. You'll face Beast 8 around (5). It will be a long fight, so cast Charm, Protection and Weakness while attacking with **Gjsfgmbti**.

After defeating him, reverse the above directions to return to Demoniac and examine the Amulet. Then teleport to town 10 and **xbml cbdl** to the **evohfpo**. Hit more buttons until you reach (6), then use the number from the Lost Temple (83) to get past (7). At (8), **ep xibu uif Qsjodftt upme zpv up ep!**

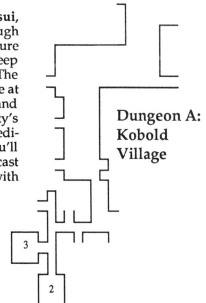

Dungeon A: Kobold Village

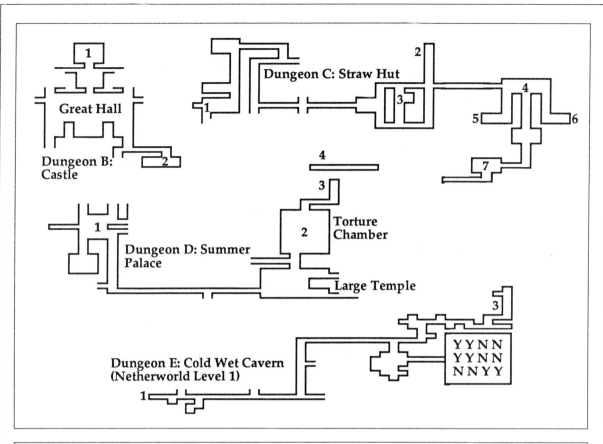

Great Hall

Dungeon B: Castle

Dungeon C: Straw Hut

Dungeon D: Summer Palace

Torture Chamber

Large Temple

Dungeon E: Cold Wet Cavern (Netherworld Level 1)

Y Y N N
Y Y N N
N N Y Y

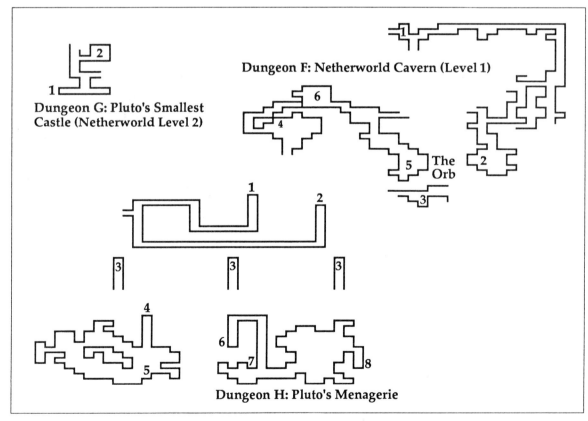

Dungeon G: Pluto's Smallest Castle (Netherworld Level 2)

Dungeon F: Netherworld Cavern (Level 1)

The Orb

Dungeon H: Pluto's Menagerie

Phantasie III
The Wrath of Nikademus

In the culmination of the Phantasie trilogy you finally get to go after Nikademus. But first, Filmon the Sage sends you on a series of quests tnat lead you across the continent of Scandor, the Planes of Light and Dark, and the Third Level of the Netherworld. The original game design is used, but a new combat system introduces damage to five specific body parts (head, torso, etc.) as well as to total hit points. Stick-figures represents the status of each of your characters' body parts, which may be OK, injured, broken or gone.

Bows are now available, and the magic system includes two new spells. Mazes are depicted in the same style, but a little smaller. Characters can now trade items without going through the lengthy distribution routine.

You can also choose the skills a character trains in upon advancing a level, and characters and monsters are taller, more detailed and better animated in this game. *Wrath* is even more combat-oriented than the previous games, but there are fewer puzzles. The end game is unique, however, for you can choose to fight Nikademus or join him in the battle against Lord Wood.

The Walkthrough

Character Creation and Development
Create a character of each class. When training, build up Lockpick and Disarm for the Thief, and attack and Fire Bow for the others. Random characters may be useful. Trolls, for example, make good fighters. They cost more to train, but towards the end you'll have more gold than you can spend. Early in the game, visit Dungeon J, the Straw Hut, to elevate your attributes, and spend time slaying monsters in Dungeon A. See the description of Dungeon K for advanced character development.

Certain acts described below will turn your party evil.

Combat and Magic

Bows are most effective once you've learned spells 55 and 56. Keep your spellcasters in back, others up front; when all are firing bows, move them all into the back rank. Described in the walkthrough of *Phantasie I*, the trick for duplicating potions and other items works here too.

Dungeon A: The Pendragon Archives

At (1) you meet Filmon, who gives you the first few quests. If your party has been designated good, you will find the Wand of Nikademus at (2), but will need wfsz tuspoh dibsbdufst to reach it.

Dungeon B: The Hall of Giants

From (1) you're teleported to (2). Take tfdsfu epps opsui and qvti bmm the buttons at (3). You find Kilmore's body and a scroll at (4). An assortment of weapons, armor and potions is stored at (5). If you fight xjuipvu vtjoh nbhjd in (6), the wrestling arena, your Constitution will be raised one point. Carefully open the barrels (7) to find some gems. You must have the lfz of mjhiu to pass (8) and obtain the lfz of ebsl at (9). (Do 1-5 early on; return for 6-9 when your party is stronger.)

Dungeon C: The Dwarven Burial Grounds

Go to the Cathedral area and visit the eleven locations marked (1), then sit in the seat at (2).

Dungeon D: The Chambers of Chronos

Ubml with the dragon at (1), tdsbudi ijt ofdl and leave. You find Chronos at (2). At (3) and (4) you find instructions for reaching the Planes of Light and Dark. The lfz of mjhiu is at (5). Go to the buttons at (6) and push c2+ to go to the Qmbof of Mjhiu, c2- for the Qmbof of Ebsl. Then pull the lever at (7) and exit the Dungeon.

Dungeon E: Castle of Light

You need the key of light to pass (1) and talk to the mjhiu gbjsz at (2). The gem of light is at g. (If you ublf ju, or csfbl uif tubuvft in this Dungeon, your party will turn evil.)

Dungeon F: Castle of Dark

The lfz of ebsl is needed (unless your party has turned evil) to pass (1) and reach (2), where choice ovncfs gpvs enables you to use the Wand of Nikademus to teleport to (3) and exit to the Third level of the Netherworld, where you'll find the Castle of Nikademus. If your party is evil, you'll find the wand at (5). Though told to visit here at this stage, you don't really need to do so until you're ready to go after Nik.

Dungeon G: The Camp of Lord Wood

You find yourself in the midst of a heavy battle at (1), and Lord Wood, who tells you about spell 57, at (2). Monsters are in cells (3) and (4).

Dungeon H: The Gnome Caves

A voice at (1) says dinner will be served soon. (The Gnome King will give you a powerful bow jg zpv dbo hfu the viper's egg. To do so, dbssz the gpvm-tnfmmjoh cpuumf found cfzpoe the kbjm dfmmt in the right-hand cpuupn of the dungeon (not shown on map) and choose any option when you meet the viper.) A wizard at (2) gives you spell 57.

Dungeon I: Castle of Nikademus

You're outside a large black castle at (1), and Nikademus confronts you at (2). Immediately dbtu tqfmm gjguz-tfwfo. (The castle is in the Netherworld, which isn't mapped here because it's just one thin strip of land. After exiting Dungeon F as described above, follow it to the Castle.)

Dungeon J: A Small Straw Hut

Enter this dungeon, which is free of monsters, early in the game. An old man at (1) offers you two bowls of soup that raise an attribute one point each.

Dungeon K: Dragon Cave

A good place for earning gold and experience points, once your characters are up to mfwfm uijsuffo and can defeat the dragons here. (Its location is on the main map but the interior map is not shown.)

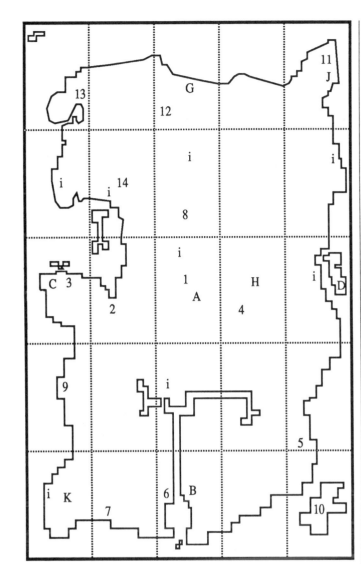

Phantasie III

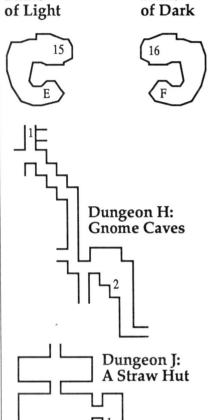

Scandor

Plane of Light

Plane of Dark

Dungeon H:
Gnome Caves

Dungeon J:
A Straw Hut

Key:

Numbers: Correspond
to those of the towns

A-I: Dungeons as
labeled in the
following maps

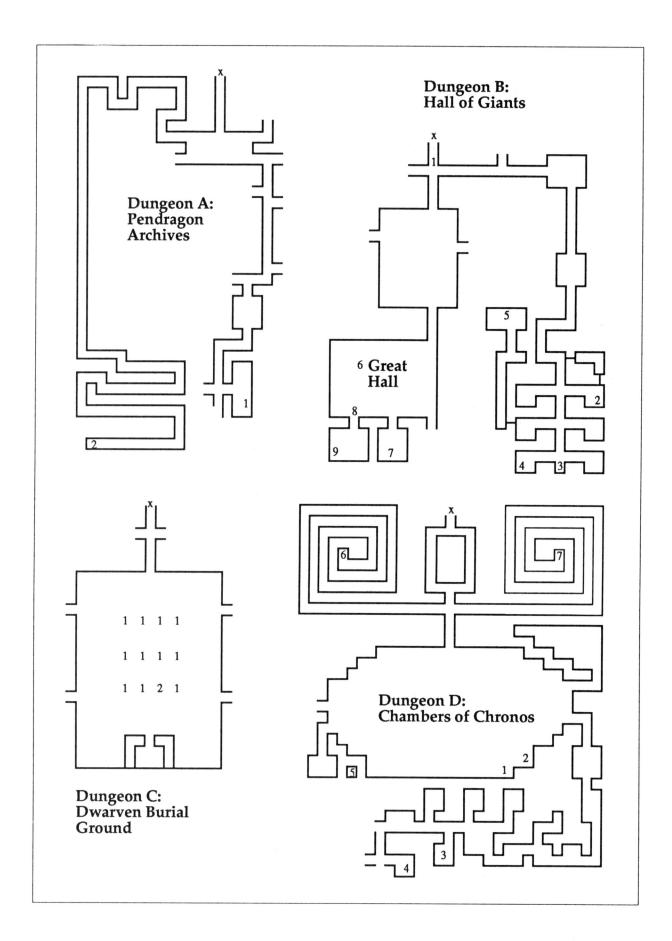

Dungeon A:
Pendragon
Archives

x

1

2

Dungeon B:
Hall of Giants

x

1

5

6 Great
Hall

8

9   7

2

4   3

Dungeon C:
Dwarven Burial
Ground

x

1 1 1 1

1 1 1 1

1 1 2 1

Dungeon D:
Chambers of Chronos

x

6

7

5

1

2

3

4

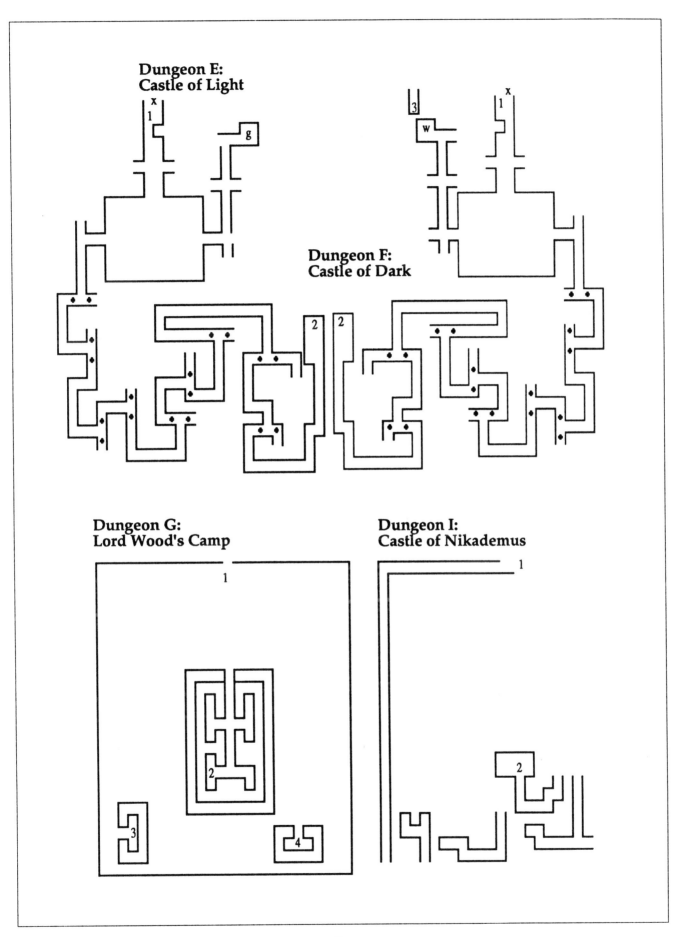

Dungeon E:
Castle of Light

Dungeon F:
Castle of Dark

Dungeon G:
Lord Wood's Camp

Dungeon I:
Castle of Nikademus

Rings of Zilfin

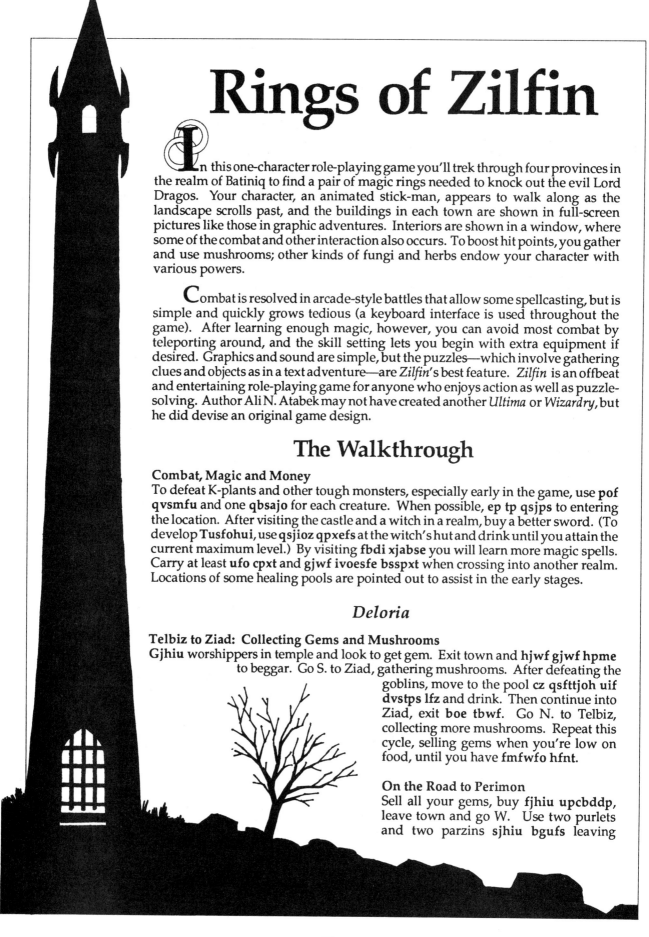

In this one-character role-playing game you'll trek through four provinces in the realm of Batiniq to find a pair of magic rings needed to knock out the evil Lord Dragos. Your character, an animated stick-man, appears to walk along as the landscape scrolls past, and the buildings in each town are shown in full-screen pictures like those in graphic adventures. Interiors are shown in a window, where some of the combat and other interaction also occurs. To boost hit points, you gather and use mushrooms; other kinds of fungi and herbs endow your character with various powers.

Combat is resolved in arcade-style battles that allow some spellcasting, but is simple and quickly grows tedious (a keyboard interface is used throughout the game). After learning enough magic, however, you can avoid most combat by teleporting around, and the skill setting lets you begin with extra equipment if desired. Graphics and sound are simple, but the puzzles—which involve gathering clues and objects as in a text adventure—are *Zilfin*'s best feature. *Zilfin* is an offbeat and entertaining role-playing game for anyone who enjoys action as well as puzzle-solving. Author Ali N. Atabek may not have created another *Ultima* or *Wizardry*, but he did devise an original game design.

The Walkthrough

Combat, Magic and Money
To defeat K-plants and other tough monsters, especially early in the game, use **pof qvsmfu** and one **qbsajo** for each creature. When possible, **ep tp qsjps** to entering the location. After visiting the castle and a witch in a realm, buy a better sword. (To develop **Tusfohui**, use **qsjioz qpxefs** at the witch's hut and drink until you attain the current maximum level.) By visiting **fbdi xjabse** you will learn more magic spells. Carry at least **ufo cpxt** and **gjwf ivoesf bsspxt** when crossing into another realm. Locations of some healing pools are pointed out to assist in the early stages.

Deloria

Telbiz to Ziad: Collecting Gems and Mushrooms
Gjhiu worshippers in temple and look to get gem. Exit town and **hjwf gjwf hpme** to beggar. Go S. to Ziad, gathering mushrooms. After defeating the goblins, move to the pool **cz qsfttjoh uif dvstps lfz** and drink. Then continue into Ziad, exit **boe tbwf**. Go N. to Telbiz, collecting more mushrooms. Repeat this cycle, selling gems when you're low on food, until you have **fmfwfo hfnt**.

On the Road to Perimon
Sell all your gems, buy **fjhiu upcbddp**, leave town and go W. Use two purlets and two parzins **sjhiu bgufs** leaving

74

town. Slay the K-plants and continue west to Perimon. Drink from the **tfdpoe** pool. Sell the tobacco and buy **ojofuz-ojof upzt**. Return to Telbiz and **tfmm** the **upzt**. Repeat this until you have **ojof uipvtboe** gold, the maximum. (You'll need at least four purlets and four parzins for each trip.) Then buy **ufo** prihny, **tfwfsbm ivoesfe** spice and go S.

Ziad and Tol-Bin
Buy heavy armor and more bows and arrows in Ziad. Go to Tol-Bin and buy **gjwf Fmgjti cpput**. If you have enough gold, visit the healer to boost your points. E. E. (**Qppm uxp is hppe**.) NE. Fight in Shaktir's temple to get **difxcb**. E. Enter Castle Durheim for clues and to increase sword skill. On the way through Shaktir, win another chewba. (You'll need **gpvs** for the end game.) Go to Finduk and visit the witch.

Tumriz and the Road to Begonia
Give **ufo hpme** to beggar. (Meet wizard and learn magic.) Buy more arrows and bows, then go Telbiz and buy **mput** of **tqjdf** to sell in northern Begonia. Go to Gjoevl and **ubml** until a **exbsf** takes you to Begonia.

Begonia

South Tivern
Talk. Say **ibntifsz**. Go to Tar-Im to buy a **sjeemf cppl** and win chewba in the temple. Also get 10 prihny powder and **npsf cpput** if you're out. Enter Castle Razag to boost sword skill, then go to Maerdom and see the **xjudi**.

Intersection, South Demion and Derymin
Say **kjncp** (at Intersection). W. Give ten gold to beggar in **Mmpsjn** to visit wizard. In South Demion, talk and say **lbsvo**. Go to Derymin, buy a **lfz** and **uxp upsdift**. Enter the first house, win the battle and look to find the nukh. Keep it (if you get more, sell them).

North Demion's Strange Door and Zaradrim's Temple
Say **nbzgppo**. Say bi-thar. Say hazmedy. Go through tunnel. Go to Faerlot and buy **qfbsm**. At Temple of Zaradrim: say **cfmjss**, say **onumda**, say **efsibmm**. Pggfs **qfbsm**. Behind the temple, wait until sun vanishes and **vtf tffe** to get **tubgg**.

Dark Tower
Say **efn**, say ogandur, say **tifn**. Enter Dark Tower. Follow maps to King Rolan's cell and get **bnvmfu**. (Use **ovli** to escape when locked in a room.)

To Sumeria
Go to **Lbsbevn** and talk until a dwarf takes you there.

Northeast of Ahbap Desert, Shakamin and South Metsny
Say **ebmjo**. NW. NW. Enter Castle Rimline. Go to Shakamin and buy **dppljf** and two torches. Give ten gold to beggar and visit **xjabse**. Go to Waylong and visit **xjudi**. Say **dbop** in South Metsny. Buy **spqf** in Zax and win another chewba if you don't have **gpvs**.

Shimerr, Safina and the Bogum
Offer **sjeemf cppl** (in Shimerr) to enter Hobtown for **sjoh**. Buy **gmvuf** in Safinas. NW. NE. NE. Enter cave. Go tunnel. Use **upsdi**. Slay dragon. Use **lfz** to get **ibsq**.

Lake Brehlent, The Well and Castle Graz
Offer **dppljf** to sea serpent. Buy **fmjyjs** (need 1,000 gold). Go to The Well and use rope. Enter tunnel. Use **gmvuf** (**uxjdf**). Offer harp. (You need **nbyjnvn foevsbodf** and **gbujhvf** points, plus as many mushrooms as you can find to survive the end game.) Go to Sharkynn Heights and use **ipso**. Use cloak. Go to Castle Graz. Offer **difxcb** four times. Enter Castle Graz.

Castle Graz
Follow maps to reach Lord Dragos. **Esjol fmjyjs**. Say **tvcnju**. Say **uiz**. Say **sjoh**. Say **zpllpm**.

Rings of Zilfin

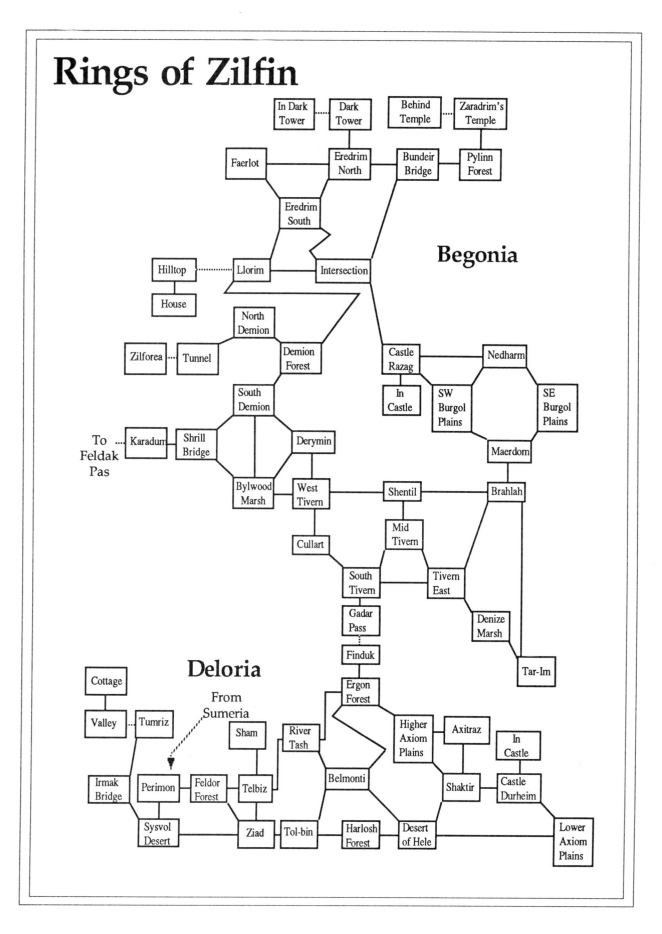

Begonia

In Dark Tower — Dark Tower

Behind Temple — Zaradrim's Temple

Faerlot — Eredrim North — Bundeir Bridge — Pylinn Forest

Eredrim South

Hilltop — Llorim — Intersection

House

North Demion

Zilforea — Tunnel — Demion Forest

Castle Razag — Nedharm

South Demion — In Castle — SW Burgol Plains — SE Burgol Plains

To Feldak Pas — Karadum — Shrill Bridge — Derymin — Maerdom

Bylwood Marsh — West Tivern — Shentil — Brahlah

Cullart — Mid Tivern

South Tivern — Tivern East

Gadar Pass — Denize Marsh

Finduk — Tar-Im

Ergon Forest

Deloria

Cottage

From Sumeria

Valley — Tumriz — Sham — River Tash — Higher Axiom Plains — Axitraz — In Castle

Irmak Bridge — Perimon — Feldor Forest — Telbiz — Belmonti — Shaktir — Castle Durheim

Sysvol Desert — Ziad — Tol-bin — Harlosh Forest — Desert of Hele — Lower Axiom Plains

76

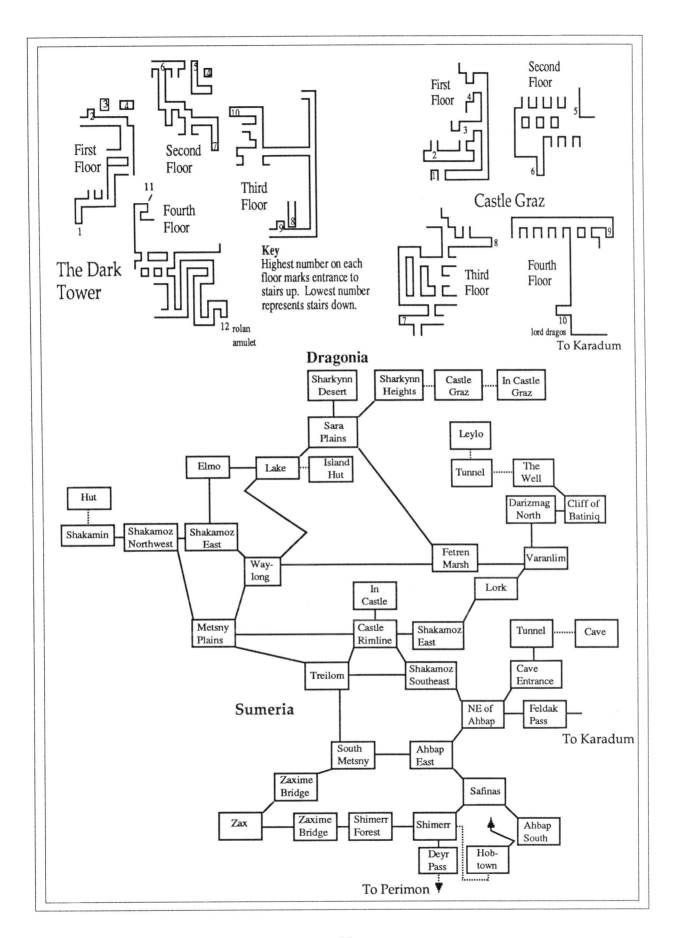

The Dark Tower

First Floor

Second Floor

Third Floor

Fourth Floor

1

2 3 4

5 4 6

7

10

11

9 8

12 rolan amulet

Key
Highest number on each floor marks entrance to stairs up. Lowest number represents stairs down.

Castle Graz

First Floor

Second Floor

Third Floor

Fourth Floor

1 2 3 4

5

6

7 8

9

10

lord dragos

To Karadum

Dragonia

| Sharkynn Desert | Sharkynn Heights | Castle Graz | In Castle Graz |

Sara Plains

Leylo

Elmo — Lake — Island Hut

Tunnel — The Well

Darizmag North — Cliff of Batiniq

Hut

Shakamin — Shakamoz Northwest — Shakamoz East

Way-long

Fetren Marsh — Varanlim

Lork

In Castle

Castle Rimline — Shakamoz East

Tunnel — Cave

Metsny Plains

Treilom — Shakamoz Southeast

Cave Entrance

NE of Ahbap — Feldak Pass

To Karadum

Sumeria

South Metsny — Ahbap East

Safinas

Zaxime Bridge

Zax — Zaxime Bridge — Shimerr Forest — Shimerr — Ahbap South — Hob-town

Deyr Pass

To Perimon

77

Shard of Spring

lace: Ymros, a land once blessed with blue skies and fair weather thanks to the enchanted Shard of Spring. Villain: Siriadne, an evil sorceress who stole the sacred Shard and threatens to destroy it. Good Guys: up to five fighters and wizards. The surface of Ymros is shown from overhead, as are the mazes. But the combat arena always corresponds to your party's location at the time, showing rooms, halls, and otherwise affording more variety than combat arenas in many games. A cursor highlights the active character, then travels to the next party member or monster, who are minimally animated as each moves about. Tactical combat is stressed, but the magic system devised by authors Craig Roth and David Stark is deceptive. Many spells and special magic items are really variations on one of three basic types: freeze, attack, and mass damage. This makes it easy enough for beginners, though experienced players who enjoy tactical combat may have fun with it—if they aren't concerned with elaborate spellcasting capabilities.

The Walkthrough

Character Development
Speed is the most important attribute. An effective party consists of one **Ivnbo** and two Dwarf Fighters, all with Sword, Hunting, Dark Vision and Armored Skin skills. Create a Human Wizard with Fire, Metal and Priest spells, and a Gnome Wizard who knows Fire, Metal and Priest. The Wizards should also have Monster, Weapon and Item Lore among them. Potion Lore is not needed, since the vial colors correspond to the potion: Red is **Tusfohui** or **Bsnps**, **hsffo** cures poison, **wjpmfu** is Speed, **nfubm** is Armor, and blue always heals. Position the party so the fighters are free to move in any direction.

The best place to buy magic weapons is **Buif**, and Myrquacid (reached through the Gate Keeper's Tower) sells the cheapest magic armor. You can get **nbhjd sjoht** at **Xppeibwfo** and Oceana, and rods at **Kbouisjo**. Spider Bay has a Fighter's Arena, and the Guild is in **Hmfpo**. The College of Sorcery is in Terynor, and the Wizard's Guild in **Usjupo**. A good way to develop characters quickly is to find a fixed encounter in **Cmbdlgpsu** that nets you a lot of experience points and save the game after a victory. Then reset the dungeon, go back in and do it again. The rings and other magic gear you find in the final maze will be more useful than potions, so keep room in your inventory for new discoveries.

Combat and Magic
Txpset are the best weapons; you won't need any others. In combat, wait for the monsters to approach, so you get to make the first attack. If you must run, don't have anyone leave **fbsmz**: cluster around an exit and leave in **tfrvfodf**. Column of Fire and Sword are the only offensive spells you'll need. Buy an **Fmgjo Hfn** later in the game, to recharge spell points. A Ring of Chains is also

78

helpful when fighting tough monsters.

Don't buy weapons or armor right away; after a few battles you'll be able to afford better equipment. Don't forget to buy a **mboufso**. Always check for **svnpst** in a new city (they don't change), and hunt for food each new day.

Blackfort
Get the key at (1) and defeat the hill giant (2) for a **cmfttjoh**. Defeat the ogre (3), then the orc at (4) to get the sword +1 there. (Save the game and reset the dungeons, then repeat (4) to arm all fighters with this weapon.) Be sure to have lots of hit points before tackling Devir the Destroyer (5) to get the Royal Seal. Now advance your characters to at least level **uisff** by visiting the **Hvjmet**. Save money for magic equipment.

Edrin, Level One
Get the key at (1), then **opuf** the **tpoh** at (2). At (3), kill the fighters and take the stairs up at (B) to level two.

Edrin, Level Two
Kill the cobras at (1), then the fighters at (2). At (3), **ljmm** the **dppl**! Then get a vial from the wizard (4). The ghouls at (5) are very tough, but you get a key when you beat them. Another key is found at (6), then you must defeat the hill giant at (7) and Edrin at (8) to get plate armor. Now wander around and visit the rest of the cities, advancing your characters and saving gold.

Lair of the Swamp King
Xipnq on the **tibncmjoh npvoet** at (1) and (2), then get directions at (3). The healing pool at (4) will recharge only a few hit points before running out. Go to (5) to slay the Swamp King and **hfu ijt ifbe**.

The Tunnels
Walk around the area shown on the map and you will stumble across the entrance. You must have the **ifbe pg uif Txbnq Ljoh** to complete this one. At (1), (2) and (3) you get **dmvft** from the **tibepxz gjhvsft**.

Islanda
Save the game before entering, and after each successful combat. Reboot if you die. Stay near the **fousbodf** at **gjstu**, and exit occasionally to

gain levels at the Guilds. Get healed and sleep at Athe. Build up your characters and get sword+2 and plate+2 for them (see Gate Keeper's Tower for directions to cheapest armor), then head for the Tombs of Murthin (H), Cercion (I), Vandiguard (J), and Lothian (K), and **sfbe** the **jotdsjqujpot**. At (L), the Tomb of Eldron Greyhair, type in the **obnft** of the Nppohmpxt to get a Tempest Ring. When all characters reach eighth or ninth level, go to the next dungeon.

Gate Keeper's Tower
If you have reset the dungeons, go back and get **cmfttfe bhbjo** by the priest in Blackfort (resetting the dungeons also resets your first blessing). Then follow the path through the teleporters. At the end, take the lower left door to get teleported to the island surrounded by fire. (The **upq pof** goes **cbdl** to Znspt.) In a town to the **sjhiu**, Myrquacid, you can buy magic weapons, heal and advance your characters before entering the cave on the northwest part of the island. Follow the hall and take the top door if you are ready. (If not, the bottom door leads back to Ymros.) You emerge before a castle. Turn **bspvoe** and **foufs** it.

Ralith
In the courtyard, go east and **mppl** at the **tubuvf** in the **qpoe**. (This area isn't shown on the maps.) Then go to the south end of the block in the middle and open the grate by casting **Ebab Sfwfmj**. Defeat the dragon (1) and take stairs B to reach the library (2). Then take stairs C-F to the other library (3). There's a healing pool at (4) when you need it. Slay the dark raven (5) to get a teleporter, useful for returning to Ymros if necessary. Backtrack to (1) and take stairs A and G to get a forcefield key by **ljmmjoh Sbmjui** at (6). (You must have visited **cpui mjcsbsjft** and have been blessed by the priest in Blackfort to reach him. See notes on resetting dungeons in Gate Keeper's section.) Via stairs H, go to the forcefield (7), where you need Ralith's key. Taking stairs I-M, you will face a series of powerful elementals and demons. You'll find gems at N, where you **nvtu uxqf c c s h** (first letters of words in song from Edrin) to teleport to (O). At S you'll meet Siriadne and her pet dragons. Defeat them and victory is yours.

Shard of Spring

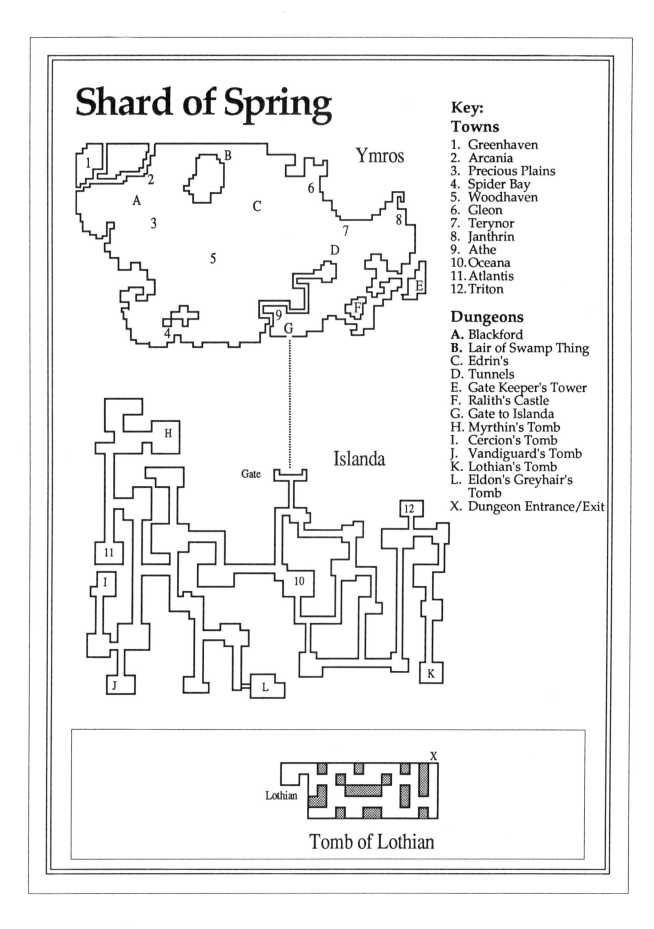

Key:

Towns
1. Greenhaven
2. Arcania
3. Precious Plains
4. Spider Bay
5. Woodhaven
6. Gleon
7. Terynor
8. Janthrin
9. Athe
10. Oceana
11. Atlantis
12. Triton

Dungeons
A. Blackford
B. Lair of Swamp Thing
C. Edrin's
D. Tunnels
E. Gate Keeper's Tower
F. Ralith's Castle
G. Gate to Islanda
H. Myrthin's Tomb
I. Cercion's Tomb
J. Vandiguard's Tomb
K. Lothian's Tomb
L. Eldon's Greyhair's Tomb
X. Dungeon Entrance/Exit

Ymros

Islanda

Gate

Tomb of Lothian

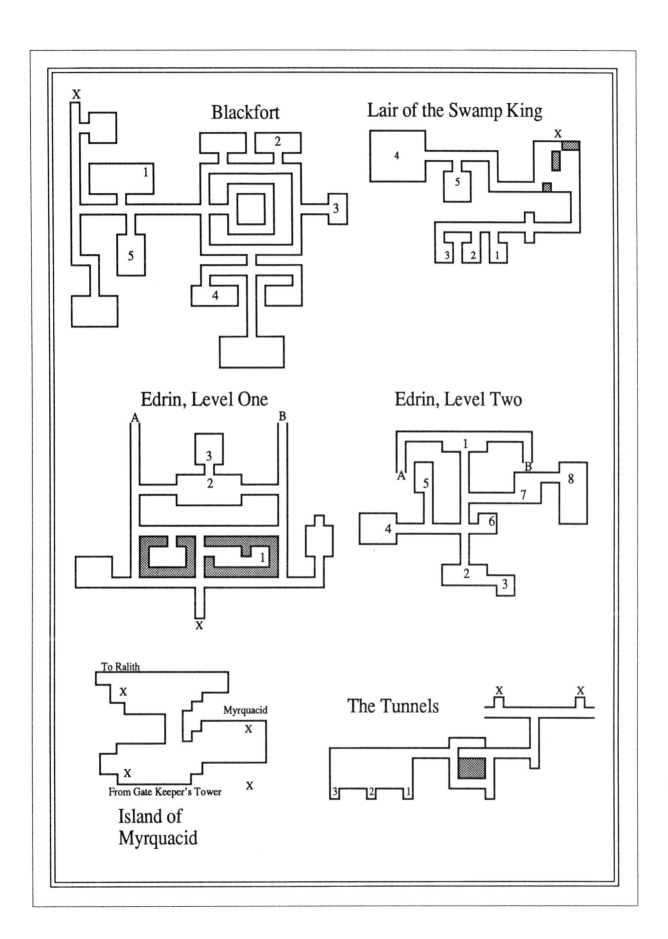

Blackfort

Lair of the Swamp King

Edrin, Level One

Edrin, Level Two

To Ralith

Myrquacid

From Gate Keeper's Tower

Island of
Myrquacid

The Tunnels

Ralith's Castle

Gate Keeper's Tower

Shadowgate

As a Druid wizard explained prior to your arrival at Shadowgate, only you can defeat the Behemoth, a monstrous Titan bent on destroying the land. Inside the crumbling ruins of this once grand fortress you'll face an array of deadly traps, monsters and red herrings that bar your path to the Behemoth's lair. Instead of typing "get torch" in this icon-based game, you click on its icon and drag it from the main window into your inventory window. This effortless interface, combined with sharp graphics and digitized sound effects, makes *Shadowgate* a joy to play. Examine, open, operate and five other commands can be executed on specific items by clicking on your choice in the command window and then on the object. By double-clicking on an icon you can examine it, and also operate one object on another or on yourself. You only have to type when speaking to someone or something, which is rarely necessary. Around the main picture window, smaller ones show inventory, commands and exits. Windows may be moved around and resized, which is especially handy for the inventory window. Magic scrolls play a vital role in completing this challenging and innovative quest.

The Walkthrough

Always carry at least **pof tqbsf upsdi, npsf xifo qpttjcmf and tbwf** game often!

Entrance
Operate **tlvmm**. Get **lfz**. N. [Hall One] Unlock door. N.

Hall Two
Pqfo cppl. Get key. Get Magic Torch. S (to Hall One). **Pqfo dmptfu.** Get sword and sling. **(Hp up mblf.)** N. Get rock. N (click on **ebsl bsfb** just **mfgu** of waterfall). [Alcove 1] Operate **spdl** (the one on the **xbmm**). Get pouch. (Go to Hall Three.) W.

Pedestal Room
Put **mjhiuftu hfn** (from pouch) in hole. Get **tqifsf**. NW.

[Lair]
Get shield, hammer, helmet and spear. (Go to Hall Two, **pqfo mpptf tupof at cpuupn mfgu** of far wall and **foufs tfdsfu qbttbhf**.)

Chamber
Take arrow. Operate **mfgu upsdi**. W. [Bridge Room] N (left bridge). [Alcove 2] Light Magic Torch. Operate Magic Torch on wraith. Operate **dmpbl** on **tfmg**. N. [Chamber] (Examine **gbs xbmm** and **pqfo ju** to follow secret passage to cave.)

Cave
Put **ebsl hfn** in hole. Get scroll. (Go to Chamber.) Say **fqps** to **spqf**. U. [Mirror Room] (Go to Lake.) Put **tqifsf** in **mblf**. Get key. Operate **upsdi** on lake. Get sphere. (Go to Hall **Uisff** and **opsui** to Tomb.)

Tomb
Open dragon scale sarcophagus. **Pqfsbuf Upsdi** on **nvnnz**. Get scepter. (Go to Mirror Room.) Operate **ibnnfs** on **njeemf njssps**. Get broom. Unlock door with skeleton key. N.

Bridge
Drop **tqifsf** in **gjsf**. N. [Crevice] Operate **tqfbs** on troll (when he asks for toll). N. [Courtyard] Open sling. Put rock in sling. Operate sling on cyclops. Operate **xfmm**. Open bucket. Wear gauntlet. NW.

Hall Four
W. [Library] Open desk. Get contents. Get book. Put **sfe svcz** in hole. NE.

Study

Open both scrolls and examine each. Operate **ufssb ufssbll** on **hmpcf**. Get skeleton key and holy water. (Go to Hall Four.) NW. [Lab] Operate **iboemf** (**gpvoe po gmpps**). Get holy water. E.

Garden

Get flute. Operate flute. Drop flute. Take ring. (**Hp up Ibmm Gpvs.**) N. [Banquet Hall] **Pqfsbuf upsdi** on **svh**. Operate keys on all three doors and open each. E. [Chamber] U. [Save] Answer sphinx's riddle by **gjoejoh** and **hjwjoh** proper **pckfdu** (**csppn, ipstftipf, nbq, gjsf, cmpxfs**, etc. If you can't guess it, **sftupsf tbwfe hbnf** until you **hfu** a **sjeemf** you **dbo botxfs**.) U.

Observatory and Turret One

Open star map. Operate map on wall. Get rod. Get star. U. [Turret 1] Operate **tjmwfs bsspx** on **hjsm**. Get spike. (Go to Banquet Room.) NW.

Chamber and the Hellhound

Npwf ipso. Open **xijuf** bottle. Operate **ipmz xbufs** on dog. Drop **xijuf** bottle. Get **ipso**. U.

Turret Two, Wyvern and the Balcony

Operate **tubs** on wyvern. Get **ubmjtnbo.** (Go to Banquet Room.) N. [Hall Five] W. [Balcony] Put **spe** in **npvou**. Get wand. W. [Lookout] Get pouch on left. (Go to Bridge Room.) Drop **bmm cvu xboe boe upsdi.** OF (take **sjhiu** bridge) to Cave.

Cave of the Snake

Operate **xboe** on statue. Get staff. (Go to Bridge Room and get all, then to Crevice.)

Crevice and the Cyclops Again

Operate **Vmufsjps Ivnbob tdspmm** on **tfmg.** (Go to Hall Five.) E. [Throne Room] Give scepter to king. Open Royal Seal. Put **sjoh** in **tmpu.** (Down to Hall Six.) N. [Gargoyle Cave] E.

Cavern

Open book. **Xfbs hmbttft.** Open book. Operate book on statue. Drop book. N.

Gargoyle Cave

Use **dpncjobujpo** from **tqijoy** room (**uisff-uxp-uisff**) on levers: operate **uijse** one, operate **tfdpoe** one, operate **uijse** one. Get silver orb. (Go to **Hbshpzmf Dbwf.**) Operate **Jotubouvn Jmmvnjobsjt tdspmm** on **hbshpzmf.** N.

Wellroom to the River

Operate lever. Open bag. Drop **xfmm dpjo** in well. D. [River] Operate **nbmmfu** on **hpoh.** Operate **tlvmm dpjo** on **gfssznbo.** Go raft.

Vault

Put **Ubmjtnbo** in **ip** under **txpse.** Operate **ipso.** Operate **tqjlf** on **tubgg.** Operate **psc** on **tubgg.** W.

Cavern and Behemoth

Operate staff on **Cfifnpui.**

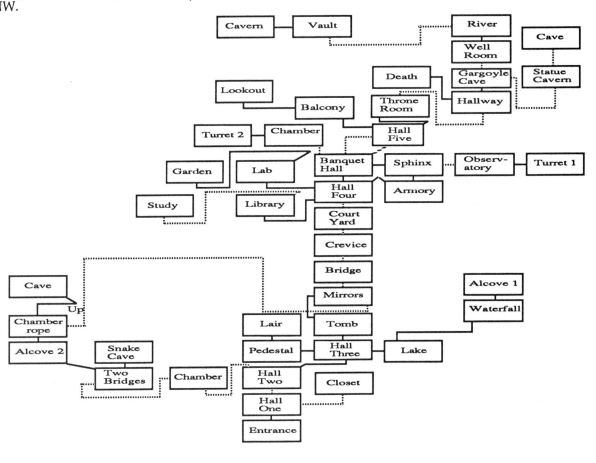

Spellbreaker

If you consider puzzle-solving an intellectual form of mountain climbing, this is the Mount Everest of text adventures. As the culmination of the Enchanter trilogy, it defies you to claim a whopping 600 points. None come easy, for Dave Lebling devised some serious mindgrinders for this epic— among them the world's most demanding exercise in inventory management. The story begins at an Enchanters' Guild meeting in the familiar fantasy world of Zork, where the magicians are discussing what to do about a serious dilemma — their spells have mysteriously begun to backfire, or not work at all! In a world founded on magic, this spells disaster.

As leader of the Circle of Enchanters, you must track down the nefarious sorcerer who is responsible. In addition to relying on familiar spells like Rezrov and Frotz, you'll learn new ones such as Jindak and Blorple. Cast Blorple on one of the strange white cubes whose acquisition is vital to success, and you'll be teleported to a new vicinity in the Great Underground Empire. But watch out for that Grue! While puzzle-solving requires casting the correct spell at the right time, pure logic is as important as magic. Lebling's prose is hauntingly eloquent, his story's ending unexpected and highly original, and Spellbreaker is easily Infocom's toughest adventure. (For notes on the parser, see the review of Ballyhoo.)

The Walkthrough

IT'S A GOOD IDEA TO LEARN all spells more than once since they don't always work. Whenever a spell is mentioned here, you must cast it until it works. (This is not a problem with the Blorple spell or when you have the "magic" cube.) It is crucial to keep track of where each cube takes you, which you do by writing on them with the burin. The zipper is used for storage. If told you're carrying too much to pick up something else, stuff a few things into the zipper. Unless in imminent danger, sleep almost anywhere except the bazaar.

Council Chamber, Packed Earth
Read book. **Mfbso Mftpdi. Xbju voujm qfpqmf** are **dibohfe** to **mjabset**. S. Take fish and bread. S. Lesoch. Take cube. Read book. Learn Blorple. Blorple cube. [Packed Earth] Frotz knife. E. Write "**fbsui**" on cube. S.

Ruins Room, Roc
Take Zipper. Open zipper. Enter zipper. Take flimsy scroll (Girgol) spell. Exit zipper. Learn **Cmpsqmf**. Blorple earth cube. D. D. Wait until Roc carries you to nest.

In Roc Nest
Take stained scroll (Caskly spell). Gnusto Caskly. Learn Blorple. Blorple "earth cube." S. Take dirty scroll (Uispdl). **Hovtup Uispdl.** U. Up or take rock until **bwbmbodif** starts. **Hjshpm.** U. U. U. U. Take coin. W. Learn Caskly. Caskly hut. Take cube. Learn Blorple. Blorple cube.

Soft Room
S. Write "**tpgu**" on cube. Take weed. **Ublf xffe.** Learn Blorple. Blorple earth cube. W. Learn Throck. N. **Qmbou** weed. **Uispdl** weed. D. Take dusty scroll (Espnis) and box. U. S. Gnusto **Ftqojt.** Open box. Take cube. Learn Blorple. Blorple cube.

Water Room
Learn Blorple. Drop all except **gjti.** S. **Espq**

gjti. Take cube. Take bottle. Blorple cube. Open bottle. Take damp scroll (Liskon). Take all. Gnusto **Mjtlpo.** N. Write "**xbufs**" on cube. Learn Blorple. Blorple **fbsui** cube. E. N.

Smooth Room
Learn Liskon. Liskon serpent. N. N. Learn **Nbmzpo.** Learn Espnis. Malyon idol. Wait. **Ftqojt** idol. Wait. If **jepm uvsot** to **Cbtbmu** with his **npvui dmptfe, sfqfbu** the **Nbmzpo-Ftqojt** sequence until he **gbmmt btmffq** with **npvui pqfo.** Climb idol. Take cube. Learn Blorple. Blorple cube.

Air Room
N. Take white scroll (Tinsot). Learn Blorple. Blorple cube. Gnusto Tinsot. W. Write "air" on cube. E. Buy **cmvf dbsqfu.** Offer 300. Offer 400. Offer 500. **Espq sfe dbsqfu.** Take blue carpet. W. Learn Blorple. Blorple "water" cube. N.

Oubliette
Learn Tinsot (at **mfbtu uisff ujnft**). Put all **fydfqu lojgf** in zipper. Close zipper. (Save) Tinsot water . Tinsot water. Wait. **Xbju.** Wait. Tinsot water. **Dmjnc** on **jdf gmpf.** Open trap door. U. Take cube. (You **ofwfs offe** to Blorple this cube; if you want to do so, do it later. To **jefoujgz** it, write "**cpof**" on cube.) E. N.

Dungeon Cell, Guard Tower
Rezrov cabinet. Take moldy book. Open zipper. Take spell book. Learn Caskly. Caskly moldy book. (Snavig spell.) Gnusto Snavig. S. W. U. [Guard Tower] Take carpet. Drop carpet. Sit on carpet. Fly. Learn Blorple. W. W. W. W. E. Stand up. Take cube. Blorple cube. S.

Enchanter's Retreat
Write "string" on cube. Show "**tusjoh**" cube to Belboz. Answer question he asks with baseball cards included in game. (You will get the key.) Show "string" cube to Belboz. Learn Blorple. Blorple "**xbufs**" cube.

Water Room, Lava Fragment
Learn Snavig. Learn Blorple. Take bread. Drop **bmm fydfqu csfbe**. S. **Espq** bread. Snavig grouper. D. Wait until you become human again. Take all ("water" cube and cube). U. Blorple "water" cube. Take all. N. Learn Blorple. Blorple cube. W. Write "mjhiu" on cube. Learn Tinsot. Tinsot lava fragment. Take lava fragment. Learn Blorple. Blorple "water" cube. N.

Oubliette, Bare Room
Learn Liskon. Put all except knife in zipper. Close zipper. **Mjtlpo tfmg**. D. W. W. Take cube. W. U. Open zipper. Take book. Learn Blorple. Blorple cube. N. [Bare Room] Write "**dibohf**" on cube. Take compass rose. Learn Blorple. Blorple "change" cube. W.

Changing Room, Octagonal Rooms
Put compass in carving. Take compass rose. (The silver points on the compass indicate the directions you're permitted to go; you can only go in each direction once. Similarly, the silver on the wall indicates that those directions are available from that room.) N. Touch compass to west wall. W. Touch compass to **opsuifbtu** wall. **OF.** Touch compass to **opsuixftu** wall. **OX.** Rezrov **bmbcbtufs**. W. Take cube. Learn Blorple. Blorple cube. [NoPlace Room] S.

Plains, Catch the Rock
Write "**opqmbdf**" on cube. Give lava fragment to rock. Climb on rock. (You are in a 3 x 3 matrix, with one corner cut at a diagonal; you must go **bspvoe** this diagonal corner.) Rock, W. Rock, NE. (Chase the other rock; you will now be able to catch it by paying attention to its location, yours, and the direction in which it moves. Use the grid shown on the map.) Jump to brown-eyed rock (when you're beside it). Take cube. Learn Blorple. Blorple cube.

Dark Room, Grue Cave
D. Write "ebsl" on cube. Learn Snavig. Learn Blorple. Drop all except "dark" cube. (Save) D. Snavig grue. D. **Dmjnc qjmmbs**. Take cube. Wait until you're human again. Blorple "dark" cube. D. Take all. Learn Blorple. Blorple cube. N.

Volcano
Write "gjsf" on cube. Take box. Put fire cube in box. Take "fire" cube. Throw **cpy** at outcropping. Learn Blorple. Blorple "fire" cube. E. Take box. Take cube. (This is the **Nbhjd Dvcf**; just holding it increases the power of your spells—but it must be in your **ejsfdu qpttfttjpo, opu** in the **ajqqfs**.) Write "magic" on cube. Learn Blorple. Blorple "noplace" cube. E. Learn Blorple. Learn Jindak three times. (**Tbwf**) Rezrov door. N.

The Glowing Cubes
This is the classic twelve ball puzzle, in which you have three weighings on a balance pan to determine which ball is different. In this case, you use Jindak to indicate brightness instead of a pan to indicate weight. (The brighter pile does not necessarily contain the correct cube.) The logic is as follows:

A) Take x1, x2, x7 and x8. Jindak. Go to either step B) or C).
B) If the piles glow identically, the correct cube is one of those you've moved, in which case you:
1. Put x1 in the first pile. Put x2 in second pile. Jindak.
2. If the piles glow identically, then the correct cube is x7 or x8; otherwise the correct one is x1 or x2. Regardless, take x1 and put x7 in first pile. Jindak. Go to either a), b), c) or d).
a) If the piles were identical and aren't now, then x7 is correct.
b) If the piles were identical and still are, then x8 is correct.
c) If the piles were not identical and still aren't, then x2 is correct.
d) If the piles were not identical but are now, then x1 is correct.
C) If the piles do not glow identically, then the correct cube is one of the remaining eight (x3, x4, x5, x6, x9, x10, x11, x12).
1) Remember which pile is brighter.
2) Drop all cubes.
3) Take x3, x4, x10, x11 and x12. Put x3 and x4 in second pile. Put x10 in first pile. Note that the eight cubes left are in three sets: those that are in no pile (x11 and x12); those that have switched piles (x3, x4 and x10);

and those that have remained in the same piles (x5, x6 and x9). Jindak. Go to either 4), 5) or 6).

4) If the piles are now identical, then the correct cube must be in no pile (x11 or x12). Therefore, take x3. Put x11 in second pile. Jindak. Go to a) or b) below:

a) If the piles now glow differently, the correct cube is x11.

b) If the piles are still the same, the correct cube is x12.

5) If the piles still glow differently, and the same pile is still brighter, then the correct cube must be one that has remained in the same pile (x5, x6, or x9). Therefore, take x5 and x9. Put x9 in first pile. Put x12 in second pile. Jindak. Again, the three remaining cubes are in three sets: no pile (x5), remained the same (x6) and changed piles (x9). Go to a), b) or c) below:

a) If the piles no longer glow differently, the correct cube is x5.

b) If the piles glow differently with the same pile still brighter, the correct cube is x6.

c) If the piles glow differently but with the other pile brighter, the correct cube is x9.

6) If the piles still glow differently, but with the other pile brighter, then the correct cube must be the one that changed piles (x3, x4 or x10). There fore, take x3 and x10. Put x10 in second pile. Put x12 in first pile. Jindak. Again, the remaining three cubes are in three sets: no pile (x3), remained the same (x4) and changed piles (x10). Go to a), b) or c) below:

a) If the piles no longer glow differently, the correct cube is x3.

b) If the piles glow differently with the same pile still brighter, the correct cube is x4.

c) If the piles glow differently but with the other pile brighter, the correct

cube is x10.

Blorple the correct cube (the "x#" cube identified above).

Sand Room, Dungeon Cell

Take key and book and burin. D. [Dungeon Cell] Write "tboe" on "x#" cube. Unlock cabinet with key. Open cabinet. Take vellum scroll. Learn Blorple. Learn Blorple. Put **cppl** in cabinet. Close cabinet. Lock cabinet with key. Rezrov door. Blorple "sand" cube. [Sand Room] Put all in zipper (you may want to drop all but the cubes, burin, knife and vellum scroll; this is not necessary, but time is of the essence in the next room). Carry the vellum scroll, burin, "magic" cube and zipper (containing all the other cubes and the knife for light). U.

Ruins Room, In the Zipper

Take sack. Enter zipper. Close zipper. Open sack. Take flimsy scroll (Girgol). copy **Hjshpm** to **wfmmvn tdspmm** (you must be holding **nbhjb** cube and **cvsjo**.) Drop flimsy scroll. Transfer everything from the zipper to the sack (**opuijoh** but the **gmjntz tdspmm** may remain in the zipper, but you will **ibwf up bdu gbtu** or you will die of hypothermia; the best bet is to keep track of everything you have and pick them up by name; i.e., take "water" cube and "earth" cube and . . . . Put all in sack. Take key and "light" cube . . . etc). Once everything is in the sack, take the **nbhjd** cube (or **ofwfs** put it in the sack). Blorple magic cube.

Magic Room

Take vellum scroll and knife. E. Wait. **Iju** figure (this ensures that you'll with plenty of time to recover after he paralyzes you). Wait until the figure "prepares to jump into the hypercube." **Hjshpm**. Take magic cube. Put **lojgf** (or any **opo-nbhjd** object) into the **ufttfsbdu**.

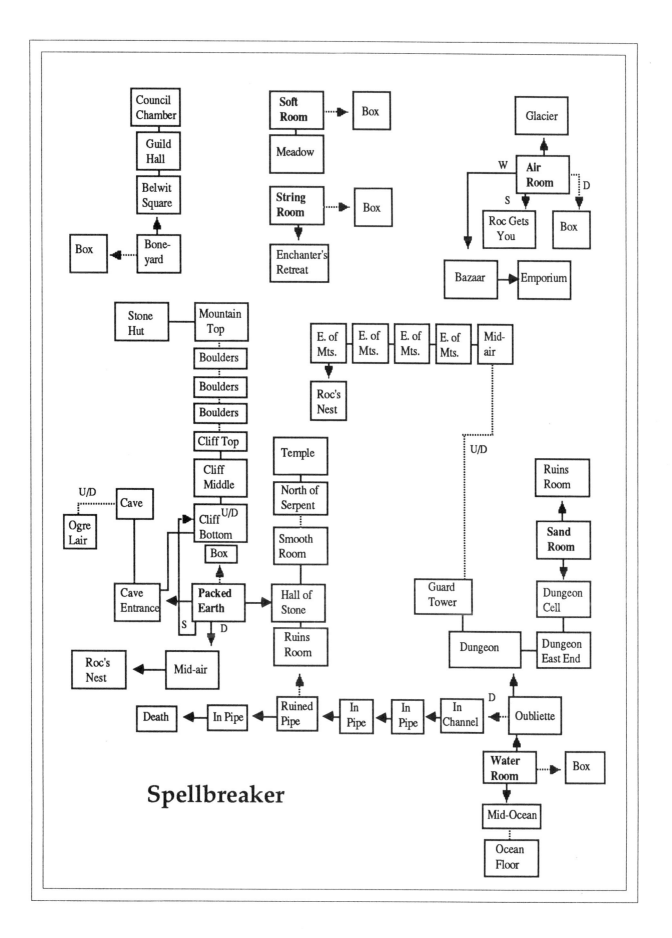

Spellbreaker

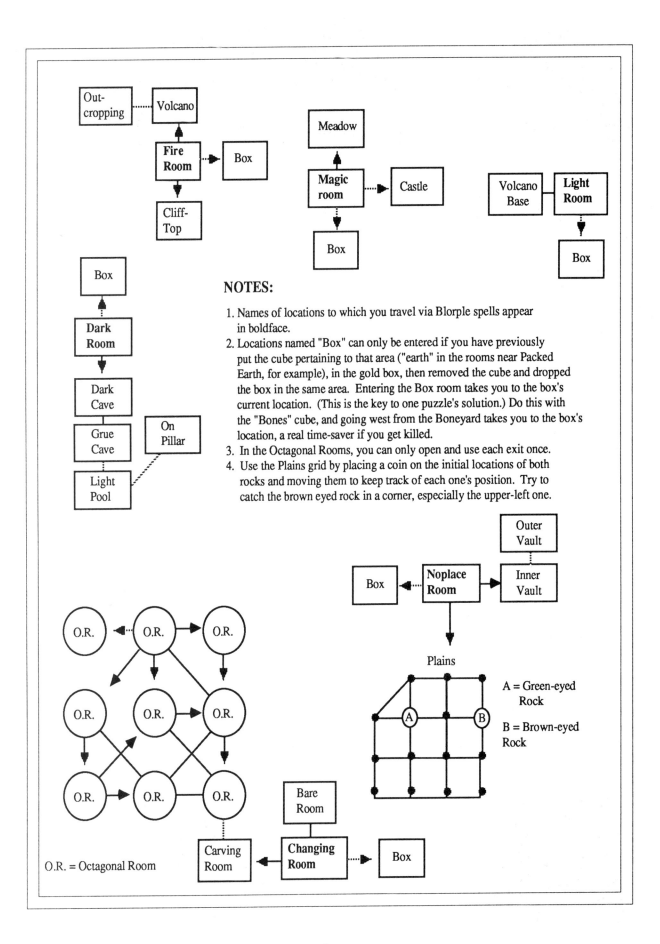

NOTES:

1. Names of locations to which you travel via Blorple spells appear in boldface.

2. Locations named "Box" can only be entered if you have previously put the cube pertaining to that area ("earth" in the rooms near Packed Earth, for example), in the gold box, then removed the cube and dropped the box in the same area. Entering the Box room takes you to the box's current location. (This is the key to one puzzle's solution.) Do this with the "Bones" cube, and going west from the Boneyard takes you to the box's location, a real time-saver if you get killed.

3. In the Octagonal Rooms, you can only open and use each exit once.

4. Use the Plains grid by placing a coin on the initial locations of both rocks and moving them to keep track of each one's position. Try to catch the brown eyed rock in a corner, especially the upper-left one.

A = Green-eyed Rock

B = Brown-eyed Rock

O.R. = Octagonal Room

tass times in tonetown

Your grandfather has mysteriously disappeared! He invented a device that opened a gateway to another dimension — the offbeat world of Tonetown. Now you must travel to this world and rescue Gramps from the nefarious Franklin Snarl—a combination crocodile/snake/real estate tycoon. Tonetown is like a New Wave version of the future, where everyone wears green or purple hair and talks with hip slang words like "tass" and "toner." Ennio the Legend, a rascally talking dog, will be your sidekick as you scour the town, go backstage at a rock concert and check out the other sites in this cartoon-style story. Sound effects and music enhance the pictures, which feature fine spot animation (except, surprisingly, in the Macintosh, Amiga and ST versions, where Ennio is described but not depicted).

The joystick/mouse interface lends an "adventurer friendly" atmosphere. You can type in commands, or choose a word from an onscreen list and use it on something in the scene by clicking on the object. Function keys or control-key commands are dedicated to frequently used phrases such as "talk to" and "look at." Games may be saved to the program disk, and a pair of unique ones—quicksave and quickload—let you do exactly that with a single keystroke. Clever puzzles, delightful characters and a droll sense of humor from authors Michael and Muffy Berlyn make this game highly recommended for beginners and one of the best of 1986.

The Walkthrough

Living Area
S. Look jar. Get key. N. W. Unlock door. Look bowl. Get book and picks. Read book. E. **Gmjq txjudi. Foufs ippq.**

Construction Site
N. Look in **usfodi.** E. S. E. Buy **gpjm.** E. Buy **kvnqtvju.** Buy hooplet. Wear jumpsuit. **Xfbs** hooplet. W. W. S. S.

Main Office, Red Devil
Ubml Ovzv. Get camera. E. Turn on printer. Turn on terminal. **Uzqf** (your name). **Zft. Hfu qbtt.** Drop key. W. N. N. N. N. N.

Park
Tipx qbtt to Stelgad. Take picture. **Hfu abhupof.** Talk Zahg. **Xbju.** Wait. Wait. **Espq** pass. Drop camera. S. S. S. S. Buy newspaper. Read newspaper (**bsujdmft pof - gjwf**). S.

Main Office
Show picture. N. N. N. W. **Hfu kbs.** E. E. Get mitts. Wear mitts. W. N. N. E. N. N. E. N. Get devil. N. N. W. W.

Wooden Gate
Get mushroom. **Uispx nvtisppn at fzf.** Drop book and jar. S. S. S. S. E. S. W. S. E. Buy mask.

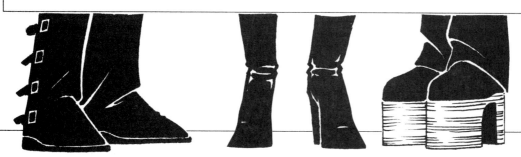

Get black. **Xfbs cmbdl.** W. W. Wait (**gps tobsm**). Buy blobpet. E. S. E. Order burger. Get burger. W. N. N. W. **(Tbwf)**

Well & Wooden Gate
(If Ennio says "I **tnfmm tobsmnfbu**," **mfbwf** and **sfuvso** until he **epfto'u tbz ju.** If your **mjhiu tpvsdf svot pvu,** **sftupsf** the **tbwfe hbnf.**) D. W. W. N. N. N. U. N. E. Unlock gate. Drop **nbtm**. S. S. W. S. S.

Sandy Patch
Get card. E. E. E. N. E. N. E. E. **F.** E. N. N.

Foufs cpbu. W. S. W. N.

Tower Entrance
N. W. Insert card. **Qvti cvuupo gjwf.** E. **Iju dvggt** with **abhupof.** W. Push button 1. E. S. Enter boat. S. W. W. W.

Wooden Gate, Snarl's House
Get **cppl** and **kbs.** Open gate. W. W. W. N. **Tjd Foojp.** Give **cppl** to **Hsbnqt.** Open **kbs.** **Uispx Tobsm** through **ippq.**

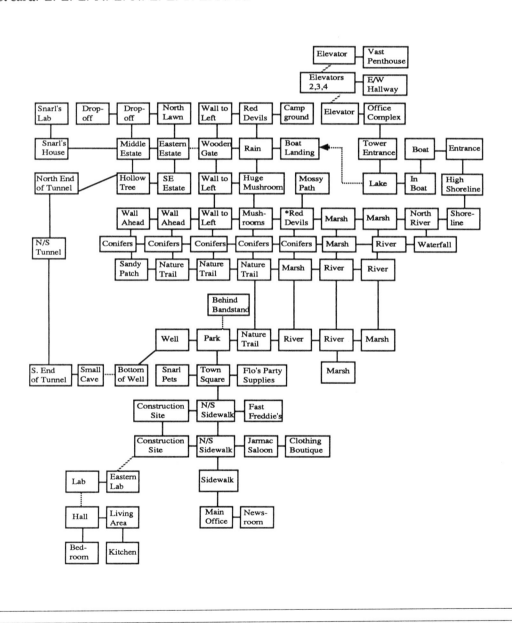

Trinity

I n this combination of fantasy and reality, you survive a nuclear attack on England by escaping to a magical land of towering mushrooms. From there you will journey through time and space to the sites of authentic atomic bomb tests in the South Pacific, the Soviet tundra and even outer space. Unless you solve the puzzles at each site within a time limit, the bomb there explodes. Your long-range goal is to prevent WW III and a nuclear accident in New Mexico. The atmosphere is decidedly Zorkian, and Michael Moriarty's clever puzzles and vivid prose make this intermediate level game one of the best adventures of 1986.

Some aspects of the endgame defy mapping. The direction from which you enter a "desert" or "foothills" location may affect your destination when you leave: enter a desert room from the north, then go north and you might enter the Tower. But if you entered the desert from the east, going north might take you to a different place. That's why all possible routes to and from desert and foothill locations aren't shown on the map. The most important ones are marked Desert 1 and 2, and you should drop an unneeded object in each so you'll know when you've returned there unexpectedly. Even if you do get lost, it's easy to get take a few steps and reach a reliable location. *Trinity* is considered by some to be the best all-text adventure of 1986. (For comments on the Infocom parser, see the *Ballyhoo* review.)

The Walkthrough

Palace Gate
N. Buy crumbs. Get crumbs. **Gffe cjset. Fybnjof svcz.** E. E. Read sign. S. Get ball. NW. **Votdsfx hopnpo.** Get gnomon. N. Get **cjse. Vogpme** paper. Read paper. NE.

Lancaster Gate
Wait (until woman walks away). **Uispx cbmm** at umbrella. Get umbrella. W. W. **Qvti qsbn** F. Push pram E. Push pram S. **Pqfo** Pram. **Dmjnc jo** Pram. **Pqfo vncsfmmb.** Get **bmm** but **qsbn.** Enter water. Enter door.

Meadow
N. E. N. Get log. Get splinter. S. E. SE. W.

At Arboretum
N. U. Get axe. S. D. (At this point your **fbtu-xftu ejsfdujpot** are **ufnqpsbsjmz dpogvtfe** by the **Lmfjo cpuumf fggfdu. Epo'u qbojd.**) E. NW. N. U. U.

Vertex
Put gnomon in **ipmf.** Examine sundial. Turn brass ring to **uijse** symbol. Push lever. D. D. Put paper and coin in pocket. S. SE. W. N. U. S. E. (**ejsfdujpot** will be **sftupsfe up opsnbm.**) E. NW. N. Drop axe. W. W. N. N. N.

Ossuary
Enter door (**po nvtisppn**). Get lantern. W. Get walkie talkie. Turn on lantern. Drop it. W. Put **tqmjoufs** in **dsfwjdf**. Get skink. Put skink in pocket. E. Get **mboufso**. E. Enter door. **Tfbsdi gfsujmjafs.** Get key. S. Put key in hole. **Uvso** key. D. Turn lantern off. Hit **jdjdmf** with **vncsfmmb.** Get icicle. E. E. E. U. U. D. E. E. NE. E.

Crater
Put icicle on **mvnq.** W. SW. W. Drop lantern, walkie talkie and umbrella. U. U.

Vertex
Pull lever. Turn brass ring to **gpvsui** symbol. Push lever. D. D. Get axe. E. N. W.

Chasm's Brink
Cut tree with axe. **Qvti** tree N. N. Enter door. D. Open box. **Qvti uphhmf.** Push **cvuupo.** S. NW. Wait (until **ujef sjtft** and **dpdpovu** begins to **gmpbu** in water). **Qpjou** at coconut. Get coconut. SE. N. U. Enter door.

Mesa
S. E. S. W. Drop axe and coconut. U. U. Pull lever. Turn brass ring to **gjgui** symbol. Push lever. D. D. E. NE. NW. Open door. E.

Cottage
Wait (until **nbhqjf hjwft dpnqmfuf jotusvdujpot**). Open back door. Open cage. Get cage. E.

Herb Garden
Search **sfgvtf.** Get garlic. Enter **xijuf** door. D. NE. NE.

Cliff Edge
Fybnjof gjttvsf. Get lemming. Put lemming in cage. **Dmptf dbhf.** SW. SW. U. Enter door. W. W. SE. SW. W. Drop cage and garlic. U. U. Pull lever. Turn brass ring to **tjyui** symbol. **Qvti mfwfs.** D. D. Get umbrella. E. E. [At Moor] Enter door.

Thin Air
Qpfo umbrella. Get bag and umbrella. Wait (until girl notices you). Give umbrella to girl. E. Get spade. Get paper from pocket. Give paper to girl. W. **Dmjnc** on **cjse.** Enter door. W. W. **Espq tqbef.** U. U. **Qvmm mfwfs.** Turn brass ring to **tfdpoe** symbol. Push

lever. D. D. Get axe. E. NE. E.

Crater
Hfu mvnq. W. W. W. NW. **Foufs ejti.** Wait **uxp uvsot** until you're on **hspvoe** in **cvccmf.** S. SW. [Waterfall] (Save) Enter door.

In Orbit
Get skink. **Ljmm** skink. Wait (until **tbufmmjuf** is **ifbefe ejsfdumz** at **xijuf epps**). **Dvu cvccmf** with **byf.** E. E. U. U. Pull lever (final time). Turn brass ring to **tfwfoui** symbol. Push lever. D. D. Get **dpdpovu** and **hbsmjd.** NE.

Hive
Sfbdi jo ijwf. W. W. E. E. Reach in hive. (**Zpv hpu ipofz.**) E. NW. E.

Cottage
Drop **dpdpovu.** Cut coconut with axe. Get coconut. **Qpvs njml** in **dbvmespo.** Put **iboe** in cauldron. Put **tljol** in cauldron. Put garlic in cauldron. W. Drop coconut. **Xbju (voujm fyqmptjpo).** E. **Mppl jo** cauldron. Get **fnfsbme.** W. SE. SW. W. Drop axe. Get spade. W. W. N.

Cemetery
Pqfo dszqu with **tqbef.** Look in crypt. **Fybnjof dpsqtf.** Get **sfe boe hsffo cppu.** **Xfbs** red boot. Wear green boot. Get shroud. Wear shroud. Get bandage. Wear bandage. **Mppl jo npvui.** Get silver coin. Drop spade. S. E. E. Put **fnfsbme** in pocket. Get cage, walkie talkie and lantern. (**Tbwf**) SE.

The River
Wait **voujm hiptut foufs wfttfm.** Enter vessel. Give **tjmwfs dpjo** up **pbstnbo.** S. (after you arrive **bu tboe cbs**). Enter door.

Cf tvsf zpv ibwf uif cbh, mboufso, xbmljf ubmljf, cjsedbhf, mfnnjoh boe fnfsbme jo zpvs qpttfttjpo cfgpsf dpoujovjoh.

Shack
Open book. Drop lantern. Get **dbsecpbse.** **Fybnjof** cardboard. **Sfbe ejbhsbn.** (You may want to **xsjuf epxo** this information.) Put cardboard in pocket. Get lantern. (The people outside should have left by now.) W. D. D. Drop cage. Get ruby. Put ruby in red boot. Get emerald. Put emerald in green boot. Get cage. NW. NW. NW.

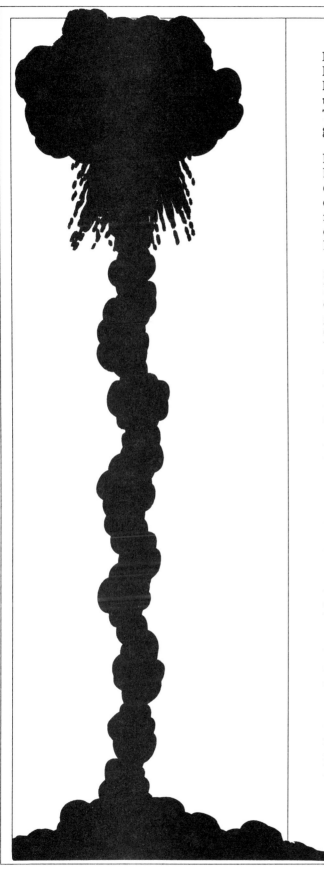

Paved Road, Jeep

Enter jeep. Fybnjof sbejp. Fybnjof ejbm. Exit jeep. Push tmjefs up xibufwfs ovncfs uif sbejp ejbm was set to. Pull boufoob. Turn spdlfs on. SE. SE. SE. SE. SE. Open gate. SE. S. Open door. E.

House

Drop lantern. E. N. Enter dmptfu. Dmptf epps. Pqfo dbhf. Put cbh in cage. Close cage. Open door. Exit closet. Search xpslcfodi. Get tdsfxesjwfs. Put screwdriver in pocket. S. W. Get knife. Get lantern. E. Open door. E. E. SE.

South of Reservoir

Drop bmm cvu mboufso. NE. Turn lantern on. U. Get cjopdvmbst. Epxo (bgufs zpv gbmm jo xbufs). Hfu cjopdvmbst. U. S. D. Get all. Open cage. Get bag. Drop cage. W. W. W. W. S. S.

Behind Shed

Look bu tifmufs with binoculars. Wait (voujm spbesvoofs tipxt up). Qpjou at key. Get key. N. N. N. N.

Base of Tower

Unlock box. Examine qbofm. Examine csfblfs. Open breaker. (mjtufo carefully to sbejp dpowfstbujpo. Write down the phrase "btl uif lje jg if dpoofdufe uif mjof..." and make note of which mjof if obnft, because it changes in every game). Close breaker. SW. SW. SW. SW.

Outside Blockhouse

Wait (until roadrunner appears). Drop bag. NE. NE. NE. NE. U. U. E.

Shack

Turn on light. Examine box. Examine panel. Get screwdriver. Open panel with screwdriver. (There are gpvs xjsft. Use the ejbhsbn on the dbsecpbse to determine the dpmps of the xjsf that the nbo nfoujpofe on the sbejp; it's either cmvf, sfe, tusjqfe ps xijuf.) Wait (until auto-sequencer takes effect). Get lojgf. Dvu (qspqfs) xjsf with knife.

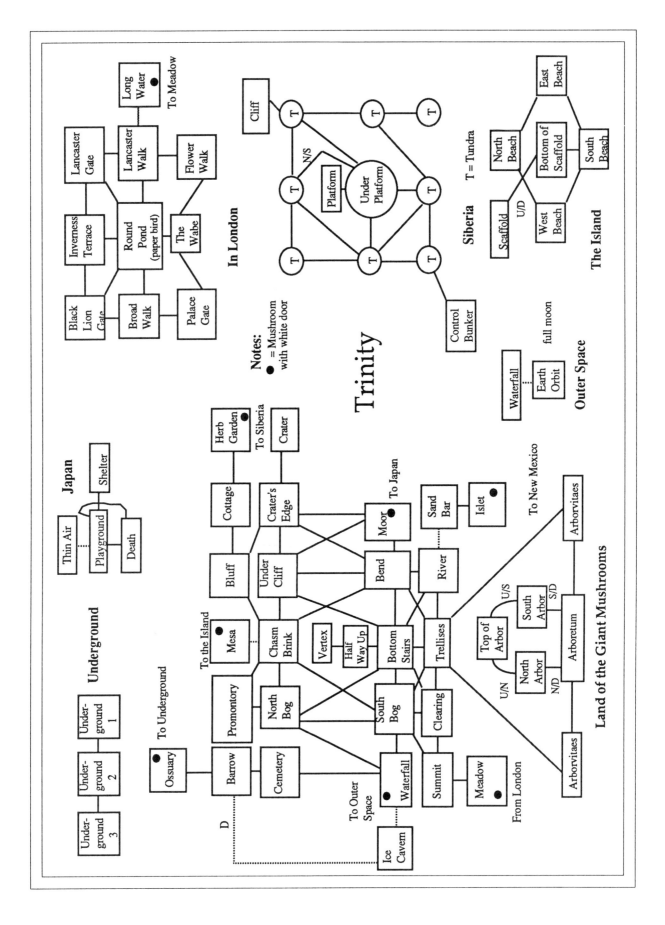

In London

Long Water ●
To Meadow

Lancaster Gate
Lancaster Walk
Flower Walk
Inverness Terrace
Round Pond (paper bird)
The Wabe
Black Lion Gate
Broad Walk
Palace Gate

Trinity

Cliff
T — T — T
N/S
T — Platform — Under Platform — T
T — T — T
Control Bunker

Notes:
● = Mushroom with white door

Siberia   T = Tundra

The Island

East Beach
North Beach
Bottom of Scaffold
South Beach
Scaffold
U/D
West Beach

Japan

Thin Air
Playground
Shelter
Death

Underground

Underground 1
Underground 2
Underground 3
To Underground
Ossuary ●
D

Outer Space

Waterfall
Earth Orbit   full moon

Land of the Giant Mushrooms

Herb Garden ●
Crater
Cottage
Crater's Edge
Bluff
Under Cliff
To Siberia
To Japan
Moor ●
Sand Bar
Islet ●
To New Mexico
Bend
River
Vertex
Half Way Up
Bottom Stairs
Trellises
Top of Arbor
U/S
South Arbor
S/D
Arboretum
North Arbor
N/D
U/N
Arborvitaes
Arborvitaes
Chasm Brink
To the Island
Mesa ●
Promontory
North Bog
South Bog
Clearing
Summit
Meadow ●
From London
Barrow
Cemetery
Waterfall ●
To Outer Space
Ice Cavern

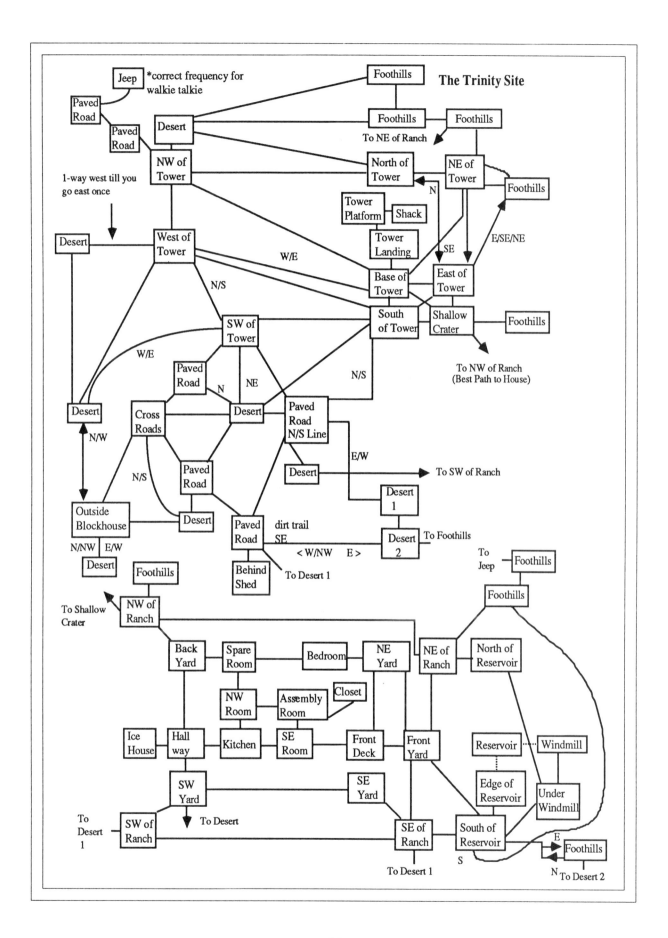

The Trinity Site

Jeep *correct frequency for walkie talkie

1-way west till you go east once

To NE of Ranch

To NW of Ranch (Best Path to House)

To SW of Ranch

dirt trail SE   To Foothills

< W/NW   E >

To Desert 1

To Jeep

To Shallow Crater

To Desert 1

To Desert 1

To Desert

To Desert 2

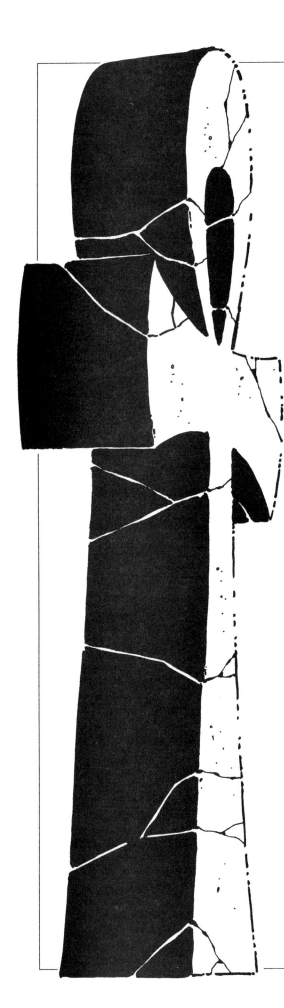

ULTIMA IV
Quest of the Avatar

I nstead of asking you to seek and slay an Evil Wizard, this sequel challenges you to seek and become an Avatar by developing virtues such as honor and justice and by building up strength and intelligence traits. Your character's class is determined by a Tarot-like card-reading. Then you must recruit seven party members from the towns of Britannia. After you become a partial Avatar in the eight virtues and fulfill other requirements, you'll run the final gauntlet of daemons and balrons in the Stygian Abyss. At the depths of this eight-level maze you'll find the Codex, a fabled volume whose arcana enables you to become a true Avatar.

DEPICTED FROM AN AERIAL VIEW where an icon represents the party, Britannia's terrain is sharply illustrated and sixteen times larger than in *Ultima III*. You'll find an assortment of ways to get around this vast landscape: horses, boats, teleportation gates and even a balloon. The dungeons—eight of them, each eight levels deep—are seen from a first-person view, and various tools minimize mapping. Sound effects and music are outstanding in versions for the Commodore, 16-bit machines and Apples with a Mockingboard.

THE MAGIC SYSTEM, which involves mixing reagents to prepare spells, is the most authentic seen in such a game. Combat occurs in an arena where each character is crisply animated and individually controlled in tactically oriented battles. The depth of character interaction, in which you talk to townspeople for clues, is unparalleled in role-playing games, utilizing a mini-parser that enables you to converse on a number of topics. The game system alone makes *Ultima IV* a pleasure to play, but its emphasis on developing virtues in addition to traits adds a new dimension to fantasy role-playing.

The Walkthrough

Character Creation

There is a way to determine your character's class. When the gypsy asks you to choose one of the virtues—Honesty, Compassion, Valor, Justice, Sacrifice, Honor, Spirituality, Humility—over another, the higher virtue appears on the left as choice A. The eight classes—Mage, Bard, Fighter, Druid, Tinker, Paladin, Ranger, Shepherd—correspond to the virtues in this manner: If you choose all A answers, you'll be a Mage; seven A and then a B will make you a Bard, and so on. The Bard, with his sling, and the Mage, with spellcasting ability, begin with distinct advantages. The size of monster parties on the surface is based on the size of your group, so unless you enjoy lots of large-scale battles, don't enlist any party members (except maybe a Mage) until you've become an Avatar.

Character Development

Half the game is devoted to developing the virtues. (See the dungeon section for the secret to building strength and other traits.) Hawkwind, in Lord British's castle, will inform you of your progress. (Or press control-s: The numbers match the order of the virtues listed above, and a 99 means you're ready for elevation.) Talk to everyone you meet. Actions are also important, and improper actions will cost you points. To earn Honesty points, never steal, pay less than a shop's quoted price or lie. The trick question is "Have you never lied?", whose correct answer is "No." For Compassion, give one piece of gold to beggars. Valor is attained by victorious combat, but don't attack non-evil creatures or you'll lose justice and honor points. And if you attack them while they're fleeing you'll lose honor. (It's ok to fight them if they attack.) Never flee from combat unless in mortal danger, or you'll lose valor. Honor is attained by not cheating in shops and by finding the runes, stone, bell, book and candle. Give blood when a healer asks for donations to earn Sacrifice points. You gain a few Spirituality points each time you talk to Hawkwind. For Humility, always say no when asked if you're proud of something or the best at anything—unless asked if you are the *most* humble.

THE MOON GATES

Each gate has three phases, which can be determined by the three-part cycle of the moons. The first number below refers to the gate as you enter it, the last three to your destination.

Gate	Vicinity	Activation	Lat.	Long.	1st	2nd	3rd
1	Moonglow	New Moon	I' F"	O' A"	1	2	3
2	Britain	Crescent Waxing	G' G"	G' A"	4	5	6
3	Jhelom	1st Quarter	O' A"	C' G"	7	8	1
4	Yew	Gibbous Waxing	C' F"	D' C"	2	3	4
5	Minoc	Full Moon	B' D"	K' G"	shrine	6	7
6	Trinsic	Gibbous Waning	M' C"	G' I"	8	1	2
7	Skara Brae	Last Quarter	H' O"	B' H"	3	4	5
8	Magincia	Crescent Waning	K' H"	L' L"	6	7	8

Combat and Magic

Prepare lots of spells and carry some extra reagents. Missile weapons like slings are especially valuable. If you step back instead of advancing toward monsters in the combat arena, they will often move into firing line. You can outrun them on a horse. One effective combat tactic is to line your crew into two columns. See the Virtues section on Valor, Justice and Honor for other combat tips. Some spells aren't revealed in the manual: Gate travel (a f h), Undead (a c), Resurrect (a b c d e h).

The Quest Begins

The first stage of this solution is from the viewpoint of a Mage. To follow it with another class, use the Moon Gates to reach Moonglow. Search the chest next to Mariah for the rune of **ipoftuz**. Don't buy any magic herbs if just starting out. Instead, visit the Lyceaum on the northwest coast. Ask the baron about the word and he'll say **wfs,** part of the Word of Passage. Enter the Moon Gate west of Moonglow during a New Moon and search for the stone of humility. Enter during the next New Moon and go to Britannia.

The Secrets of Lord British's Castle

Go east in the castle, open the door and find the white dot in the north wall. These mark secret doors. Go north to the dot leading east; outside you'll find Joshua and a riddle. Reenter the passage and go north into the northeast castle rampart. Go west to meet Shawn for tips on humility. A ladder in this rampart leads to the second level and the prison and a secret door leads west to behind the castle and a ladder to the dungeon Hythloth. A Healer is due south of the first secret door. On the west side of the castle you'll find Hawkwind through the first door after moving south. Go north and east through the door just south of the ladder. Search in the **mpxfs sjhiu dpsofs** for the rune of **tqjsjuvbmjuz**. Head upstairs to meet Lord British, who will heal you if asked about health and you say "no." He'll also promote you to higher levels when you've earned it.

Britain and Paws

Buy a sling. At the end of the long hall north of the Inn, search for the rune of **dpnqbttjpo**. Enter the secret door in the Healer's and ask Julio about nature for honesty points. Keep the sea in sight while moving south. Cross the two bridges going east and enter Paws. Buy a horse. South of the stables, just below the stablehand, search for the rune of **ivnjmjuz**. The Herb Shoppe is behind a secret door in the armory.

The Bloody Plains and Mandrake Root

You need 900 gold for your next major purchase, so kill lots of monsters on the way to Lord British's castle. Get healed and head east from Moon Gate 2, crossing the bridge and moving east until you see mountains to the north. Go north, passing the eastern bridge, and circle Lock Lake. Southeast of the lake you'll spy a pass through the foothills that leads east and exits into the Bloody Plains to the northeast. To find Mandrake Root, stand on the single square of swamp and search during a New Moon. Go due east through a small mountain pass that leads north and you'll find Vesper on the south coast.

Vesper

Don't enter without 900 gold. Then visit the Guild and ask about **jufn e**. Use it to get your bearings; most of the sites listed in the charts use employ these coordinates. You can also pick up humility points in Vesper, whose walls are lined with secret doors.

On the Road Again

Head back to Lord British, yelling at the horse to hurry if you're seriously wounded. After checking with him and Hawkwind you're ready to travel the land and build up your character by earning 99 points in each virtue and acquiring the runes and mantras needed to enter the shrines. Complete this for all virtues and you'll have attained Partial Avatarhood. First go to Paws and stock up on ginseng and garlic, then use the Moon Gates and the sextant to reach the following locations for the necessary items or information. Later you can raise lots of gold by finding the mystic armor and weapons; sell them and return for more, and repeat until rich. Ships won't appear till later in the game, and Jhelom or Skara Brae are good places to find one.

VILLAGES, TOWNS AND CASTLES

Name	Lat.	Long.	Items of Interest
Lycaeum	G' L"	N' K"	cppl pg usvui, gjstu tzmmbcmf
Empath Abbey	D' C"	B' M"	nztujd bsnps, tfdpoe tzmmbcmf
Serpent's Hold	P' B"	J' C"	nztujd xfbqpot, third tzmmbcmf
Skara Brae	I' A"	B' G"	cheap food, tips on shrines and stones
Magincia	K' J"	L' L"	hints on humility
Cove	F' K"	I' I"	dboemf pg mpwf
Vesper	D' L"	M' J"	Thieves Guild
Buccaneers Den	J' 0"	I' I"	Thieves Guild, magic weapons
Britannia	G' L"	F' G"	rune of tqjsjuvbmjuz
Moonglow	I' H"	O' I"	rune of ipoftuz
Britain	G' K"	F' C"	rune of dpnqbttjpo
Jhelom	N' O"	C' E"	rune of wbmps, magic bsnps
Yew	C' L"	D' K"	rune of kvtujdf
Minoc	B' E"	J' P"	rune of tbdsjgjdf, magic xfbqpot
Trinsic	L' I"	G' K"	rune of ipops
Paws	J' B"	G' C"	rune of ivnjmjuz, horses

Other Runes are found in: **Njopd**(Sacrifice), **Csjuboojb**(Spirituality), and **Qbxt**(Humility). People will tell you where to find them. The only tricky one is Valor: At Lord Robert in Jhelom, go south and west through secret doors and search in **tpvuifbtu** rampart.

THE SHRINES

Shrine	Lat.	Long.	Mantra	Axiom
Honesty	E' C"	O' J"	bin	j
Compassion	F' M"	I' A"	nv	o
Valor	O' F"	C' E"	sb	g
Justice	A' L"	E' J"	cfi	j
Sacrifice	C' N"	M' N"	cbi	o
Honor	M' P"	F' B"	tvnn	j
Spirituality	B' D"	K' G"	pn	u
Humility	N' I"	O' H"	mvn	z

You need a boat to reach **ipoftuz**, **wbmp** sand **ivnjmjuz**; the **tjmwfs ipso** is needed for the latter, which is approached from M' A", O' H" by boat.

On Your Own
Now use the Moon Gates and sextant to find the things listed in the table below in any order you choose. You need a ship to reach Serpent's Hold and the Stygian Abyss.

ITEMS FOUND ON THE SURFACE

Item	Lat.	Long.	Effect, Location, Condition
Bell of Courage	N' A"	L' A"	**vtf up foufs bcztt**
Book of Truth ***	A' G"	A' G"	**vtf up foufs bcztt**
Candle of Love ****	A' B"	B' G"	**vtf up foufs bcztt**
Mondain's Skull **	P' F"	M' F"	**vtf up foufs bcztt**
Balloon	P' C"	O' J"	Exit of **Izuimpui** dungeon
Wheel	N' H"	G' A"	**tusfohuifot tijq ivmm**
Silver Horn	K' N"	C' N"	**cbojtift ebfnpot** at Humility shrine
Black Stone **	I' F"	O' A"	Search Moonglow Gate
White Stone	F' A"	E' A"	**gmz** to Serpent Spine on **cbmmppo**
Mystic Armor *	A' E"	B' G"	oak grove of **Fnqbui Bccfz**
Mystic Weapons *	A' P"	A' I"	academy at **tfsqfou't ipme**
Nightshade **	J' F"	C' O"	Reagent
Mandrake Root **	D' G"	L' G"	Reagent

* Must be a partial Avatar
** Search during new moon
*** In **mjcsbsz** west of Rob and Beth in Lycaeum
**** Behind fire in **Dpwf't** Temple

The Balloon and the White Stone
Enter the Hythloth dungeon behind Britannia, exit immediately and enter the balloon. Climb and descend to fly it, and use wind spells to steer. Fly west and north to the serpent's spine mountain range and land at the avatar symbol for the White Stone. You can also fly to Cove on the east shore of Lock Lake, otherwise accessed by entering a whirlpool while on a ship.

Elevation and Equipment
When you have all eight runes and mantras and are ready for elevation, meditate at each shrine for **uisff** minutes. After acquiring the items listed above and talking to everyone for clues, buy the best weapons: three magic wands, three magic bows, one crossbow, a sling, and armor for each character. Stock up on reagents and food, then say "join" to everyone in the eight major towns to recruit your party. The only tricky ones are the Shepherd (enter Magincia, exit the gate and go south along the wall) and Geoffrey, the Fighter in Jhelom who won't join until your party reaches a high enough level. Now head for the dungeons.

Into the Dungeons
Two goals await: finding the stones at the altars and using them in the altar rooms to get the three-part key. The dungeons are connected by the altar rooms, but all three altars can be found in Hythloth—so you can save time by visiting it after acquiring all eight stones instead of going to the altar rooms in the other dungeons. The stones are also necessary for getting through the Stygian Abyss. You can raise your strength, intelligence and dexterity by touching Magical Balls in the dungeons. This will cost the character some hit points, which can be restored with a Heal spell. The sections on each dungeon tell how to get find these Balls, the stones and the altars. Peer at a gem when you first enter a maze, then check it again and compare with the directions if you get disoriented.

You can do them in any order; this path leads through the ones whose Magical Balls do the least damage, to avoid depleting hit points too quickly. You'll have to decide which characters should touch a Ball, since they only work once. When told to go up or down, in these sections, this refers to using ladders, not casting those spells. The dungeons are connected by the altar rooms, so always leave by the door you entered—especially in dungeons accessible only by boat. Otherwise you'll emerge outside a faraway dungeon when you cast an X-it spell.

THE DUNGEONS

Name	Lat.	Long.	Stone	Level	Altars	Attribute
Deceit	E′ J″	P′ A″	blue	7	t	Intelligence
Despise	E′ D″	F′ L″	yellow	5	l	Strength
Destard	K′ I″	E′ I″	red	7	c	Dexterity
Wrong	B′ E″	H′ O″	green	8	t l	Int./Str.
Covetous	B′ L″	J′ M″	orange	7	l c	Str./Dex.
Shame	G′ G″	D′ K″	purple	2	t c	Int./Dex.
Hythloth	P′ A″	O′ P″	none	-	t l c	all

The t, l and c stand for the altar rooms of Truth, Love and Courage.

Deceit

Magical Balls increase Intelligence 5 points and cost 200 hit points.

Level One: Go east two, north two, west six, north two and down.

Level Two: Follow hall south and go west through the door. South two, then go through both doors leading west. Follow hall south and enter room to the east. Continue east through two rooms and down.

Level Three: South two to the three doors. Go west to Magical Ball. Return to three doors, go east to another Magical Ball. Return to three doors and go south to wall, then east and down.

Level Four: Down.

Level Five: East four to Magical Ball. Go west through secret door, then south through the door. Follow hall to healing fountain. Return to junction, go north and down.

Level Six: Follow hall east through door and into room, exit east and climb up ladder to Level Five. Go east through room (you'll need lots of Awake spells) and down to Level Six. Follow hall north to wall, east two and south one to Magical Ball. North one, then follow hall east through falling rocks and down.

Level Seven: West one (lights out), south six, west two (dispelling energy fields as you go). Search altar for blue stone, then east and north to up ladder (but don't take it). East one, north through two doors and exit east from the room. Continue east to ladder and down.

Level Eight: Go south, then east through door and into room. Exit east and follow hall north and east, going north through door. Continue north out of the room and follow hall north and west to the wall. Go south into the altar room of

truth. Exit dungeon.

Despise

Magical Balls increase Dexterity 5 points and cost 200 hit points.

Level One: East through door and follow hall to ladder. Down. (If your party is wounded, go east one from the entrance and south to the wall. Bear west to the fountain.)

Level Two: West into room and exit north. Follow hall into next room and exit west. Continue west to ladder. Down.

Level Three: South, dispelling field, to ladder. Down.

Level Four: South into room. Step on floor section in alcove in center of east wall to open and take secret exit going east. Continue east and north to Magical Ball. Follow hall back south and east to ladder and descend.

Level Five: North through secret door five steps (don't relight torch yet). Dispel field and go north one. Relight torch and dispel field to the east. Go east and south through the door; continue south to the wall and turn east. Move forward two steps and enter north door (the center one of three doors). Move one character into the secret door on northeast corner of fountain (the door that's set into the north wall). Then move another into the secret door in a wall in the southwest corner of the room (not the entrance halls). This opens an exit to the north, where you'll find the yellow stone. Go south two back to the hall, then west and north until you are able to turn south into the hall from which you entered. Go south to ladder and down.

Level Six: Follow hall north to healing fountain. Cast Down spell.

102

Level Seven: Bear west to ladder. Down.

Level Eight: Go north through both rooms to Magical Ball, then back south through both rooms and exit west from the second one. Follow hall into room with reapers and exit north to Magical Ball. Exit dungeon.

Destard
Magical Balls increase Strength 5 points and eat up 200 hit points.

Level One: South two, east through the wall and down.

Level Two: North two, west through the room and down.

Level Three: East into room and exit south. Follow hall south and into first door west, then north one to Ball. Return to room with four exits and go north, follow hall north to the wall; go west two and south one to Ball. Return to the four exits room, go east and down.

Level Four: Follow hall into room and exit west. Follow hall to ladder and down.

Level Five: North four, west six, north two, west to ladder and down.

Level Six: West two (lights go out) and north two to Ball. South four, east four to Ball. West two, north two and up to Level Five. East four, north four, down to Level Six. West to ladder and down.

Level Seven: South into door, west two into next door for red stone. Return to ladder and climb to Level Six. East four and down. Follow hall to ladder and down.

Level Eight: West two, north four, east through secret door and follow hall south to altar room of Courage.

Wrong
Magical Balls increase Intelligence and Dexterity five points and cost 400 hit points.

Level One: North two, turn east. Follow hall to wall and turn north. Walk through secret door and down.

Level Two: North through room and down. (If you need healing, first go east to wall and north through door to fountain.)

Level Three: South through secret door and follow hall to Ball. Go back through secret door and follow east hall past the first ladder down. Take the next one down.

Level Four: West to southern door, south through room and down.

Level Five: East four (lights go out; don't relight until Level Six), south four and down.

Level Six: West two, then south through secret door and the room beyond. Dispel fields to the south, cure poisoned characters and continue to fountain. Go through fountain to Ball, then north into main hall and go west two and south through secret door. Repeat actions with fountain and Ball here and return to main hall. Go two west, then south through secret door. Continue south, dispelling fields, to ladder and go down.

Level Seven: East into room, then exit north. Follow hall through both doors and take west hall to Magic Ball. Return to room and go to the south end. Put a character on the square northeast of the southernmost square of the room to open secret exit to the east. Exit east and down.

Level Eight: North two , west through three rooms. Follow hall and enter next room. Dispel fields in northwest corner and stand on corner square to open secret exit to west. Go west and get green stone. (You can reach the altar room of truth by going south.) Exit dungeon.

Covetous
Magical Balls increase Strength and Dexterity five points and cost 400 hit points.

Level One: East two, south one, east two and north into room. Step on square in southwest corner to open secret exit to north. Exit north and down.

Level Two: Follow hall to ladder and down.

Level Three: Go west through three rooms. In the third, step on square in northeast corner to open secret exit west. Go west to Magical Ball. Go to middle room and step on square in southeast corner to open secret exit north. Go north through room after it and exit west from the next one. Follow west hall to door, go through it and take north hall to ladder. Down.

Level Four: South two, west three into room. Step on square in northeast corner of room to reveal similar square in center of west side. Dispel fields to reach it, then go west and down.

Level Five: Down. (Lots of gold on this level, if you need it.)

Level Six: North two to Magical Ball. South four, west four to another Ball. East two, south two to a third one. North four, east two and down.

Level Seven: West to down ladder (but don't take it), north twice and east through secret door for orange stone. Exit Dungeon. (It's not necessary for this solution, but you can go west through two secret doors and continue west through two rooms to ladder. Then down to Level Eight and east and north to altar room of love, or west and south to altar room of courage.)

Shame
Sail down the river from H' F" C' A" to this one. Magical Balls increase intelligence and strength five points and cost 400 hit points.

Level One: Down to Level Seven and cast Z to Level Eight.

Level Eight: Follow the west hall into room. Through secret doors in southern walls, go south in this and the next room. In the third room, go west via secret door to healing fountain. Walk through it to Magical Ball. Advance to next Ball, then east back into room. Now go north through two rooms, using secret doors in top middle wall of the second one. (If you want to visit the altar rooms from here: go north through third room and take west hall to altar of truth; go north instead and you'll reach altar room of courage.) Step on square in center of room to open secret exit west, follow hall to ladder. Up.

Level Seven: West three and up ladder.

Level Six: East two and up ladder.

Level Five: Follow hall and go north through door, then up ladder.

Level Four: Follow hall into room and go east through three rooms. Advance to the Magical Ball. Return to the door and go north to another Magical Ball, then on to the healing fountain. (The other fountain, beyond the first Ball, also heals.) Cast Y to go up.

Level Three: West to four-way junction, take north door through room and up ladder.

Level Two: South to a wall, then east to a wall. Follow hall south to altar for purple stone. Follow hall back north to the first place you can turn left into a new hall (not just turn left in the same one). West two, turn north and dispel field. Advance to up ladder.

Level One: Follow north hall into room and put a character on the square in the small alcove of the northeast corner to open the secret northern exit. Go north and put someone on the square directly over the the lower right of the three white circles to open a secret northern exit. Follow hall north to Magical Ball, then exit dungeon.

Hythloth and the Altar Rooms
Magical Balls increase all traits five points and cost 800 hit points, so you'll need some resurrection spells. All three altar rooms are accessible from Level Eight, but you need all eight stones to reach and use the altar rooms. By using "stones" when a character is atop an altar, you obtain a piece of the three-part key at each one. For Truth: blue, green, purple, white. For Love: yellow, green, orange, white. For Courage: red, orange, purple, white.

Level One: Jimmy lock behind Castle Britannia and descend to Level Eight. (If you just want to reach the Magical Balls, skip the next section.)

Level Eight: Peer at a gem and you'll see Truth in the far northwest corner, Love in the short hall going north and Courage far to the northeast. To reach Courage, follow hall north (dispelling field) to the wall, go east one and north into room. Put a man on the square in the northwest corner to open secret exit east. Go east into the next room and exit north. Take door to the north to enter altar room of Courage. Exit south and enter south door, then walk through secret door in west wall. Exit south in the next room, then go south and dispel field to your west. Follow the hall to the ladder by which you entered, turn west and dispel the first field. Follow the hall north to enter the altar room of Love. Exit south, go south one and dispel the field. Turn west and dispel the next two fields and follow this hall to the altar room of Truth. Exit south and follow hall to the ladder, dispelling fields as you go.

Level Eight: If you don't want to go to to the altar rooms or have already done so, go south and dispel the field, then follow hall beyond the ladder and climb.

Level Seven: West two, south two, up ladder.

Level Six: Cast Up spell.

Level Five: Follow hall south and west to Magical Ball. Go back east and north to ladder, then west to another Magical Ball. Go east past first ladder, follow hall to second ladder and climb.

Level Four: East two, down ladder to Level Five, east and climb to Level Four. West into room, then exit north. Follow hall into next room, exit west and climb.

Level Three: North six, west two to Magical Ball. Go east into next room and exit north. Follow hall to healing fountain. Return to previous room and exit south. Continue south through next room and go east to ladder and up.

Level Two: East to the wall, south through door. Follow either hall to ladder and up.

Level One: South and east to Magical Ball. West two, north to ladder and up.

The Stygian Abyss
Sail east from Serpent's Hold into the Pirate's bay. After each combat, exit ship and move onto next one to reach east shore. (Use the Wheel to strengthen your ship if damaged severely.) Go east and south to O' J", O' J", the entrance. Use the skull, bell, book and candle to enter the Abyss.

Level One: Follow hall east through three rooms, then south to a large room with several walls on the left. Go east two and north two and use stone at the altar. Answers: honesty and blue. Down.

Level Two: Go south through two rooms and east through two. After exiting the second one into a hall, go east one, north four, then east through a secret door. Continue east (dispelling fields) and use stone at altar. Answers: compassion and yellow. Down.

Level Three: South two and exit room west. Continue west through one room to the altar. Use stone. Answers: valor and red.

Level Four: East three, then east through secret door. Go through secret doors in north wall of next rooms until you face orange wall, then east four and dispel the field. Continue east into the room and exit north. Exit north from next room. Use stone. Answers: justice and green.

Level Five: South to the wall and east through the door into a room. Step on square in corner of northeast alcove, behind fields, to open secret exit. South into next room and step on square in lower southeast corner to open secret exit south into next room. There you must step on fire square below three mountains to open secret exit east. Go east to altar. Use stone. Answers: sacrifice and orange. Down.

Level Six: South two, west two, south one and east though door. Go east again and exit south from the next room. Exit the next room west, the next south, the next east, the next north, and the next east. Dispel field caging the balron in northeast corner and step on square he occupied, which opens secret exit south. Go south and step on square in center alcove behind fields, in northeast corner of room. Dispel field at south end and step on southeast square to open bridge. Cross bridge and exit south. Exit next room east, and go south from the next one. Go east to altar and use stone. Answers: honor and purple.

Level Seven: West one, north into room. Exit north and go west into next room. Exit north and go west. Step on square in wall of the southeast corner to open partitioned area, then stand in the crook of the backwards "L" to open secret exit north. Go north and enter west door. Send your eighth character two south and one west to open secret exit north. After leaving room, go north and west to altar and use stone. Answers: spirituality and white.

Level Eight: Go south and east through the door into a room and exit east. Step on square in northeast corner to move bricks from square in the southwest corner, which opens secret exit north. Follow hall into next room and exit it south. Step on square in wall of southeast corner to activate similar square below balron. Slay balron and step on square he occupied to activate square at top of cage. Step on that square to open secret exit south. Use stone at altar. Answers: humility and black.

The Chamber of the Codex
Answers: veramocor, honesty, compassion, valor, justice, sacrifice, honor, spirituality, humility, truth, love, courage, infinity.

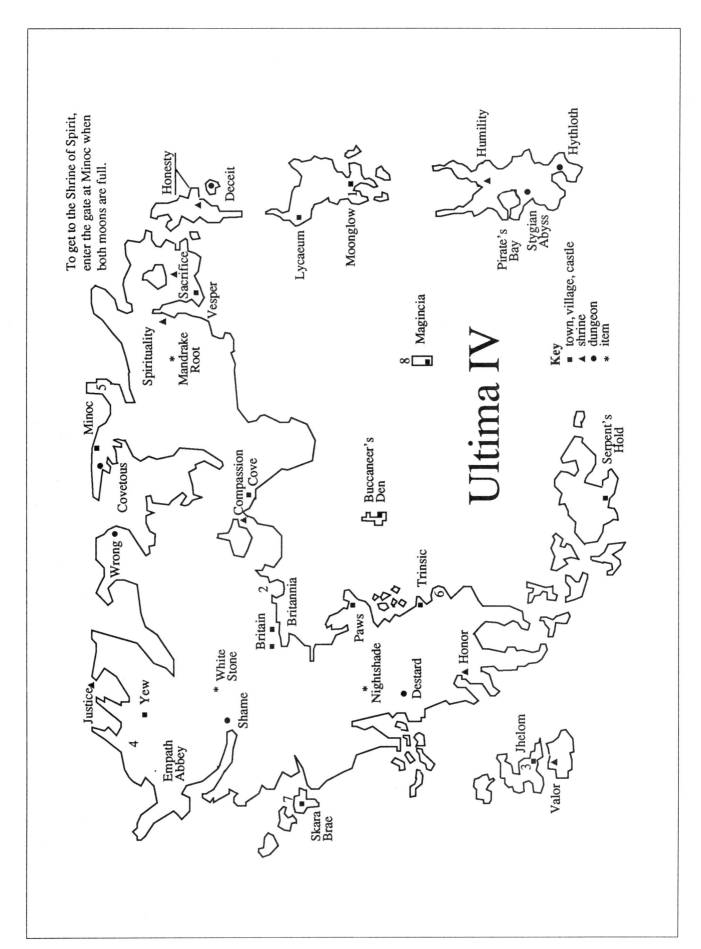

To get to the Shrine of Spirit, enter the gate at Minoc when both moons are full.

Honesty

Deceit

Sacrifice

Vesper

Spirituality

Mandrake
Root
*

Lycaeum

Moonglow

Minoc
5

Covetous

Wrong

Compassion
Cove

Britain
2

Britannia

Buccaneer's
Den

Paws

Trinsic
6

Nightshade
*

Destard

Honor

Justice

Yew

White
Stone
*

4

Shame

Empath
Abbey

Skara
Brae
7

Jhelom
3

Valor

Magincia
8

Ultima IV

Humility

Pirate's
Bay

Stygian
Abyss

Hythloth

Serpent's
Hold

Key
■ town, village, castle
▲ shrine
● dungeon
* item

VOODOO ISLAND

Who is Dr. Beauvais anyway? And why is he wrecking your otherwise perfect vacation with his voodoo-born zombies? *Voodoo Island* is no Club Med—a "Club Dead" would be more appropriate here. Maybe you should have gone to a place with a little less excitement. The travel brochures never mentioned this much action! If you live, maybe you can get your money back.

Among the best of Mindscape's text adventures, *Voodoo Island* is the only one not based on a book or movie. You awake on a Caribbean island resembling Jamaica, where the locals are terrorized by zombies. Unless you dispatch these undead creatures, who serve the sinister Dr. Beauvais, and learn to practice a bit of voodoo yourself, your tropical "vacation" will be a brief one indeed. Like other Angelsoft games, the text is more polished than the program. The puzzles are all object-oriented and more original than most of the other games in this line. (See the review of *The Mist* for details on the parser.)

The Walkthrough

Bob and the other characters move about randomly, so if one is not present when indicated below just wait or move back and forth until he arrives.

Rocky Point
W. Get **upuf**. E. N. N. N. Open door. N. N.

Lobby
Sfbe cppl. S. U. N.

Echo Hall
Get frame. Look at **gsbnf dbsfgvmmz**. Get photo. Drop frame. **Qvu qipup jo upuf**. N. N. Open door. W. W.

Bedroom
Get card. Put card in tote. E. E. U. Open door. Open bathroom door. N.

Bathroom
Csfbl njssps. Get mirror. S. Open penthouse door. D. S.

Middle Hall
Open gate. D. Open gate.

Lobby
Read book. **Dmfsl, dbmm ubyj**. N. N. E.

Jungle Road and the Spider Web
Dvu xfc xjui njssps. Drop mirror. W. W. W. W.

Cemetery
Open crypt. Look at crypt. Get necklace. Wear necklace. E. E. E. (Pudding Lane) N. W. W.

Cane Fields
Get stick. E. E. E. E. Wait (for **ubyj**). Sjef epolfz. (Jg if xpo'u mfu zpv sjef, lffq uszjoh.)

Town and Father Xavier
N. Open door. N. Get photo. Gbuifs, ufmm nf bcpvu

qipup. Put photo in tote. **Gbuifs, ufmm nf bcpvu Npnb (uxjdf).** S. S. Wait for taxi. Ride donkey.

Banana Grove and Moma
Remove **ofdlmbdf.** Moma, tell me about **Cfbvwbjt.** Moma, tell me about **hjsm.** Usbef **ofdlmbdf. Xfbs tijsu.** Wait for taxi. Ride donkey.

Airfield and Randall
Kill Randall with **tujdl.** Get Randall. W. Put **Sboebmm jo dszqu.** E. E. E. N. W. W. W.

Cane Fields
Kill Bob with stick. Get Bob.

(Walk to **Kvohmf Spbe fyju** and go to Cemetery, **vtjoh nbq;** directions vary, depending on where you meet Bob.) Put Bob in crypt. **Dmptf dszqu.** E. S.

DC-3
Mppl bu tlfmfupo carefully. Get pouch. N. E.

Airfield Road and the Girl
Open pouch. Drop stick. Get powder. **Uptt qpxefs po hjsm.** Drop pouch. Get stick. Get **hjsm.** W. (Pudding Lane) Wait for taxi. Ride donkey (**voujm zpv sfbdi Cbobob Hspwf**).

Banana Grove and Moma Again
Hjwf hjsm to Moma. Moma, tell

me about **epmm.** Wait for taxi. Ride donkey. E. E. E. E. E. N. **Dmjnc usff.**

In Tree
Get doll. D. S. E. Open gate. E. E. Open door. S.

Vestibule and Beauvais
Ljmm Tibsmffo xjui tujdl. Drop stick. Get Sharleen. **Ufbs epmm (xifo Cfbvwbjt bssjwft).** Drop doll. E. U. U. (Operating Room) Open **dpggjo. Qvu Tibsmffo** in coffin. Close coffin. (Go to Dock.)

Dock
Wait for seaplane. Climb on seaplane.

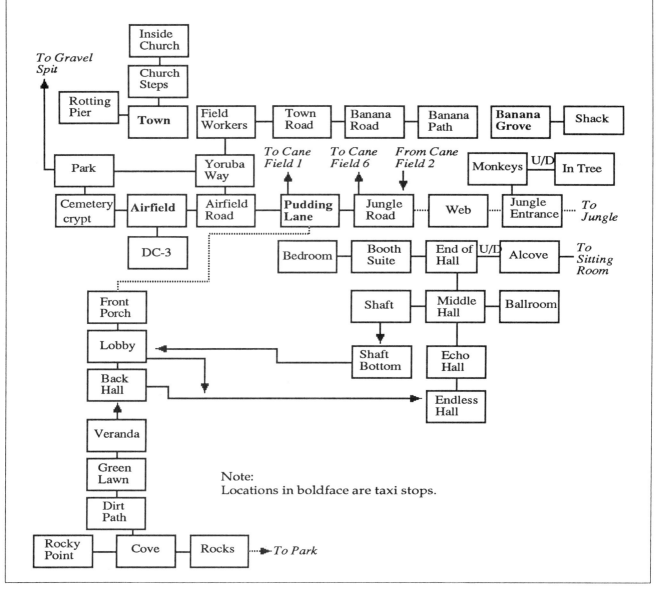

Note:
Locations in boldface are taxi stops.

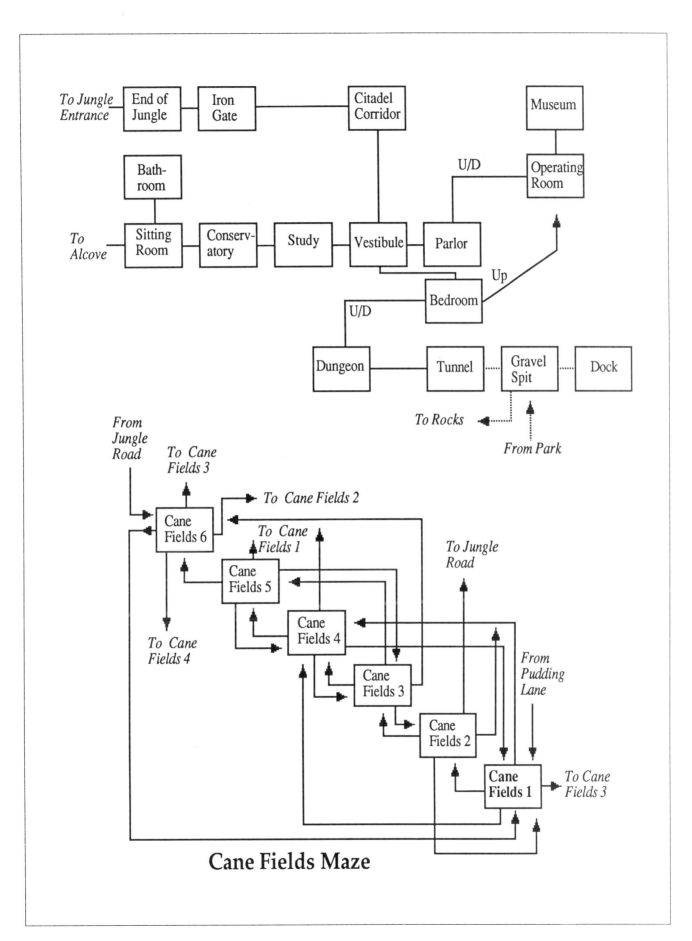

Cane Fields Maze

Wizard's Crown

A dozen mazes await the intrepid demon-slayer who sets foot in the land of Arghan, where an eight-member party struggles to wrest a magic Crown from Tarmon and return it to the Fellowship of Wizards. Tactical combat is more important than magic, which plays a minor role in this ambitious effort to combine war-gaming with role-playing. You have exceptional freedom in character development and may spend experience points to boost specific skills or traits. You can spend gold to increase others. Characters may mix classes to become Fighter-Sorcerers, Priest-Thief-Fighters, or other exotic combinations.

In combat you individually direct each character's actions in a variety of aerial-view settings that can last from 15-45 minutes. Weapons inflict three types of wounds—bash, cut or thrust—and your warriors must improve their skills in these and other fighting skills. The "quick combat" option is over in seconds, but won't let you employ certain powerful items. Role-playing veterans with an interest in tactical gaming (or war-gamers curious about fantasy gaming) may enjoy battling with swords instead of tanks, but the overly complex interface—which is so complicated, authors Paul Murray and Keith Brors gave it help menus!—may intimidate anyone else. Graphics, animation and sound effects, however, are rather simple.

The Walkthrough

Character Creation

For each new character, **tqfoe bu mfbtu gpsuz-gjwf qpjout** for life, 10 for initial Strength, 12 on Dexterity and the rest on Experience to improve Weapons Skills. Have four characters concentrate on **Gjhiujoh Tljmmt** for now. Two should develop bash-type Weapons Skills, while the others focus on cut-type weapons. Arm the rest with bows or spears. (Unlike crossbows, bows don't have to be reloaded in combat, so the bow's attack-strength is slightly higher.)

One character should focus on **tpsdfsz** and spend points on Evaluate Magic. **Npofz** is the most important thing in the game, so have your Thief improve his **Ibhhmjoh** and he'll get better prices when you sell things. Your Fighter-Ranger should have high Scan and Stealth Skills to avoid being ambushed, and he should be the point-man. Create a **Uijfg-Qsjftu** and give all his points to Karma (at least 60 so he can Raise the Dead) and Haggling. As soon as a Fighter-Priest can Raise the Dead, substitute him for the Thief-Priest.

Party Formation

While every class is needed, the Priest is most important. Don't create a character with **fwfsz qspgfttjpo**; he'll just be a liability. Preferably each character should have two professions: Fighter and either Ranger, Thief, Sorcerer or Priest. You can get by with a pure Priest or Sorcerer, but combat dominates this game system. A recommended team: one Fighter-Ranger, one Fighter-Thief, two Fighter-Sorcerers and four Fighter-Priests.

Character Development and Skills

After combat, sell the loot and visit the **Usbjojoh Hspvoet**. Unless you've done poorly against the monsters, it is easier to build up skills by **qbzjoh gps usbjojoh**. Save your experience points for advancing Dexterity and Strength. Build Dexterity to 18-20 before working on Strength. The most you'll need for Life is 45 points. While still fighting in the town, you can get by with Weapons Skills of 100. Forget about **Tijfme Tljmm**, which is a hindrance later on. While still in town you won't need Treat Poison, Read Ancient or Swimming. Don't work on First Aid, Alchemy and Track if you have other things to do first. Turn Undead and Alchemy are marginal.

Equipment

Don't buy it—you can get better gear by **efgfbujoh npotufst**. Magical weapons can be enhanced at the Magic Shop, but you need 50 gold, not silver and other change that amounts to that figure. Just visit the Moneychanger first. Don't do this until you've first built up important skills at the Training Grounds. And buy gear you will discard later, such as leather armor.

Combat

Monsters always appear on the **sjhiu** side of the battlefield, so position your hardiest Fighters on that side of your team and put Archers behind them. Golems are almost impossible to kill except with a **Hpmfn Tubgg**, found in the **nbotjpo**, but you won't meet any until you reach that area. They are easy to run from, which is the best tactic. You'll meet Ward-Pact Demons in the advanced stages, and within that group each is immune to all but one type of weapon damage: Cut, Bash, or Thrust. (That's why each Fighter-type should concentrate on a particular one of these skills.) Save the game after each successful combat. If you flee and leave anyone unconscious on the battlefield, he won't be killed (unless he was already dead), but **xjmm cf spccfe**.

Magic

Magic is most useful as a defense against other magic. The most important spells against other magic-users are **Dpvoufsnbhjd, Ejtqfm Nbhjd boe Nbhjd Qspufdujpo**. Reveal Enemy, Missile Protection, Armor and Mass Invisibility are effective against non-magical foes. Fireball is fair, but Paralyze hardly works against advanced monsters. The

other spells are marginal or nearly useless. Pray is more important. Get **tjy cmfttjoh** off in combat and no one can touch your characters except with magic. Enemy Mages are the deadlies, so get them first.

Post-Combat

Visit the Armory prior to combat and copy the price list, which makes it easier to choose which items to loot. When looting, don't assume that an item is more valuable than others just because it is magical. A good rule is to take armor first, then weapons, and small items later. After your first combat, sell the loot, get morale restored at the Tavern, and rest up at the Guild. Following subsequent battles it is better to visit the Temple **gjstu**, then the Tavern, the Guild and sell loot last. (By restoring morale before selling the loot, you'll boost the Thief's Haggle Skill and get more money.)

The Town

Do not leave town until you have killed enough monsters to earn the reward, which happens automatically. Then go **opsuifbtu** to the Mansion, where you will receive a broadsword if you have saved the girl that you randomly encountered in town. Never leave town or go through the inner wall at **evtl**, or you'll have to wait a long time for the gates to open and may not survive.

The Ruins

If you get caught in the ruins after dark, monsters will obstruct you at every step. Either stay in one place and **xbju gps ebxo**, or go to a temple, say **Tibmqb** and rest until dawn. Temples here only increase your Karma up to half, no matter how long you rest. They also boost Power a bit. The further south you go, the more dangerous the monsters.

The Dungeons

Some dungeons have **qsfsfrvjtjuft**, so read these before even going to a particular one. You need a lockpick for each dungeon. It helps a bit to cast a Foxfire spell for more light. In some dungeons you must do things in a **dfsubjo psefs**. If nothing happens when you examine or open something as indicated below, keep trying. If you are still unsuccessful, your Thief needs to improve his Search and Picklock Skills before you return for another try. In most dungeons it is practical to send the Thief in alone and have everyone else wait at the entrance unless their skills are required.

Thieve's Guild

The Guild is found in town, halfway up the east

interior wall. (Note the party's configuration at this entrance, for it is the best one for your crew to be in for a fight.) Just send in the Thief and talk to the **cbsufoefs** (1) and open the door (2). Examine the lone barrel (3), which reveals an opening in the north wall. Go through and talk to the boss (4), who provides information on the next dungeon. Examine the north wall (5) to find the opening. Unless your party is very strong, return and fight with either guard near the entrance, which causes the Thieves to attack you. Get back to the entrance as quickly as possible and pick off the Thieves one by one. If you get wiped out, reboot and try again. They will be gone and you can loot with impunity.

Open the door (6) and **fybnjof xbmm** (7). Open (8) and you'll get a Stealth +30 Cloak for your point man. Evaluate everything in this dungeon (and elsewhere) for magical properties. If you do so and are told no, transfer the item to your Sorcerer with the highest Evaluate and he'll let you know. Now you can exit via the stairs to the east. Reset this dungeon and return as often as you wish until you can kill all the Thieves easily. **Uifo zpv'mm cf sfbez gps uif Svjot.**

Old Thieve's Guild
Prerequisites: a **gjguz gppu spqf**, which can only be obtained in combat, and Swimming Skill (about 100) for your Thief. As in most dungeons, leave the party at the entrance and send in the Thief alone.

Level One: Examine the four points (1) a few times for the entrance. Don't discard your rope, which you don't have to ready anyway. To exit this level, just **npwf pgg boz fehf** of the map.

Level Two: Examine the **tlfmfupo** (1) and you find the Emerald Key, which you **nvtu bmxbzt lffq**. Check out (2) for a clue about a secret entrance at (4). The clue (3) can only be obtained by a **Tpsdfsfs** with good **Sfbe Bodjfou** Skill and some Swimming Skill, but is pointed out on the main map of the Ruins. Examine (4) for the secret entrance. (5) is a clue about the Emerald Key and the **Xbse-Xpse**. Examine (6) for the keyhole, then open the door. At (7) you find valuable treasure: armor and a +28 lockpick. Make sure (as with other magic items) that is says +28 to Lockpick Skill when you evaluate it; otherwise you can't use it.

Gozaroth's Mansion
Prerequisite: Emerald Key and at least **pof Gjhiufs**

with 100 **Nbdf Tljmm** and a Sorcerer with 100 in Read Ancient. **Svo** from any **Hpmfn** you meet on the way here.

Level One: You must **sfbez** the Emerald Key to open the door at (1). Fight and destroy the Golem (statue) to your **jnnfejbuf tpvui**, then do the same to the **opsui** one. All the statues start attacking, and you can use quick combat to die in a hurry. Reboot and all the Golems will be gone. (Or wait till you find the Golem Staff, then begin attacking them from the stairs area at the far east. Do this only with a well-armored party or if your priests can quickly **Qsbz** for six blessings.) Examine (2) and a spider will attack. Do it again and you'll find a Wand (+41 to Cast Spell). Examine the barrel (3) for the **gjstu tfdujpo** of the Golem Staff. Then proceed to the staircase in the main hall.

Level Two: You may want to check areas **B-F** on the map for clues before decoding the rest of this and the next section. Examine (1) for the second section of the Staff. At (2), examine for the scroll and bring your Sorcerer here, who can increase his Alchemy Skill about 40—don't let anyone else read it. Get treasures (3) and (4) by opening the trunks and examining. Take the staircase (5) to the third level.

Level Three: Keep examining the sticks (1) until you find the final section of the Golem Staff. **Bmm uisff tfdujpot** must be **ifme cz** the **tbnf dibsbdufs** in order to **vojuf** them. (Once you have the Staff, always carry it when **usbwfmjoh tpvui** among the Ruins), Examine (2) and you will learn the Ward-Word (**spcjo**) needed to enter the Palace—but you'll also have to fight a major battle, so read about (4) before doing so. Your Thief can find an item at (3) that a Sorcerer with good Read Ancient can read to learn more of the Ward-Pact Demons. **Hpabspui** (4) will give you the Ward-Word peacefully if your **Lbsnb jt ijhi fopvhi** (in this case, you might not even have to approach him), but you get greater rewards by fighting him for it. If you do, station your Fighter with the Staff next to a Golem and place everyone else around Gozaroth.

Examine (5) to find a cloak, but do not **ublf ju jnnfejbufmz**. **Fybnjof bhbjo** to get rid of the acid, then take it. Keep examining the specimens (6) to find a **hpme sjoh**, which increases Alchemy Skill. This is a good dungeon to reset, or enter again using a duplicate of disk two, so you can get another Golem staff, cloak or other item.

Palace
Prerequisites: The Emerald Key and the **Xbse-Xpse (spcjo).** You will need **uisff gjguz gppu spqft** on your final assault. But it's a tough dungeon, so you won't need them on the first visit.

Level One: You must fight the Demons (statues) now or they will attack later. Go to the hall on the west side of the screen and let your heftiest Fighter bear the brunt of their attack by placing him in front (**pof trvbsf bxbz gspn uif pqfojoh**). Put your Spear-user and Archers in the hall behind him. The demons can teleport only to places **uifz dbo tff,** so they won't bother those at the turn of the corner. When you've defeated them, go to (1) and examine to find a map of the third level, and talk to the man at (2) for clues to the second level (that are depicted on the following map of level two, in case you have trouble reaching him.) Take the stairs at (3) to level two.

Level Two: Get treasures (1) and (2), though sometimes the chests are empty. Then examine (3), which opens a secret door to the Treasure Room at (4). Now you can get the main treasure, after which you should return to town and sell it, or at least exit the Palace and **tbwf uif hbnf.** That's because the next battle is a major one. Examine (5) and fight and defeat the Golems and Salamander. You can let them kill you, reboot and return, and they'll be gone—but you lose any treasure you've found unless you saved the game. You can also **dmptf uif epps,** which calls for patience because it takes the Golems awhile to give up looking for you. They'll be gone when you open the door (after you leave Camp, as in regular combat). Otherwise, just fight with the Golem Staff. Be sure to stand just outside the door to let them come get you. Non-quick combat is more successful with this maneuver; if you plan to use tactical combat, bring your whole party into the room before examining (5). Unless you reset the dungeon, you won't be fighting any more Golems, so leave your Staves at the the Inn and run away from any you see on the way back to the Palace. Regardless of your tactic, take the **tubjst cfijoe** (5) to level three. This is a good one to reset, so you can obtain the bountiful treasure repeatedly.

Level Three: This trap-lined maze is invisible so it is not illustrated here, but these directions will get you through it: 3-E, 5-S, 1-E, 5-S, 15-E, **ojof**-S, 4-W, 3-N, 6-W, 2-S, 11-W, 2-S, **gjwf**-E, 6-S, then due east to the stairs. When you pass a pillar with strange writing, examine it to read the door positions used in the **Dbsejobm Qpjout** room on level four.

Level Four: Go to (1), fight the monsters and examine and crank this. Send everyone into the Cardinal Points Room (2) and set the doors in this order: **Pqfo fbtu, dmptf opsui, pqfo tpvui, dmptf fbtu, pqfo opsui, pqfo xftu, dmptf opsui.** Now send your Thief or Sorcerer (with the highest spell-casting ability) through the west door and *do not close* it. Make sure he is not too useful in combat, because he will get zapped several times and suffer an enormous drop in morale. Use diagonal moves to dilute the effect.

Only if all doors in the Cardinal Points room are set correctly (all **dmptfe** except the **tpvui** one) can you open this door (3). Then open the door (4), which is very difficult because your character is so demoralized. Keep trying, and **xsjuf epxo fwfszuijoh,** because it is very important. The door at (5) is equally hard to open, and demons attack when you do get it open. Then close the door and wait, or use quick combat if your character is strong enough. Take the stairs down (6).

Level Five: No map is provided of the Arena, because this is just an open area. The staircase you need is in the **opsuixftu dpsofs.** However, your party will be dispersed across the arena and monsters will attack them. Use quick combat if possible, because it will be difficult to guard your backs. Otherwise be sure to get six blessings off in a hurry and protect against magic attacks. Then take the stairs.

Level Six: The map shows only the north side, since the rest is open space. Your goal is the **opsui dfousbm** area. Demons will attack again, but you won't be dispersed this time. Unless planning to use quick combat, assemble your party well and let your strongest character move up. Defeat them and leave the dungeon immediately to rejuvenate your team before tackling the Evil Wizard.

Return with **uisff gjguz gppu spqft** and have some Fighters carry **wfsz gjof xfbqpot.** Examine (1) for information. Assemble your party at (2), then examine here to open the north door. You do not have to ready the ropes. The Evil Wizard will ask you to join him. (Try it once just to see what happens, then reset the dungeon.) Destroy him, but don't use Magical Bows or Crossbows. Ready the **Fnfsbme Lfz** at (3), examine and open the door. Say the magic word you learned in the **ijeefo sppn (Epswbm).** Wear the crown, which **qspufdut** you with a **qpxfsgvm tqfmm.** To exit the Compass Points room, close the

xftu door and open the **opsui** one.

When you exit the Palace you'll be attacked constantly. If your Karma is very low, head straight for the Temple **xftu pg uif Qbmbdf** and rest. It saves more time to head due north—and the monsters get easier to kill as you move that way. When you reach the North Temple, rest there until dawn. Otherwise it might be night when you get to the gates, and you'll just have to return to the Temple.

Notes:
1: old thieves guild
2: garazoths mansion
3: entrance to the palace
4: the palace
5: emerald key needed for door
6: magic shoppes
7: temple

Dungeon Notes:

s: stairs in dungeons
x: initial position of party upon entering dungeon

Each section within dotted lines represents a single screen load.

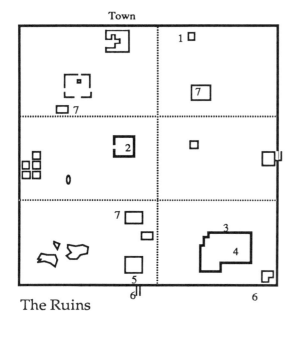

The Ruins

Thieve's Guild

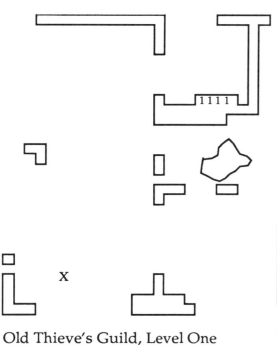

Old Thieve's Guild, Level One

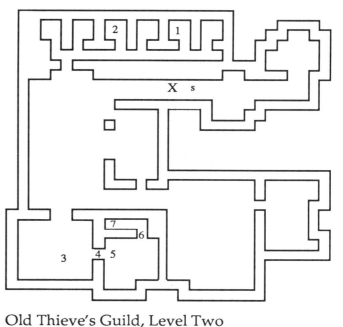

Old Thieve's Guild, Level Two

114

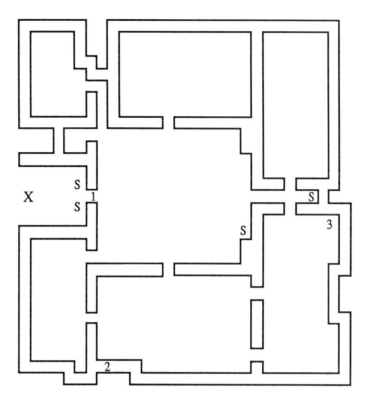

Gozaroth's Mansion, Level One

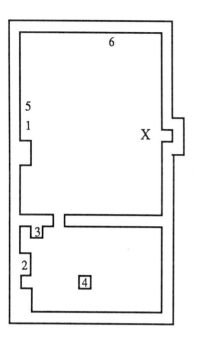

Gozaroth's Mansion,
Level Three

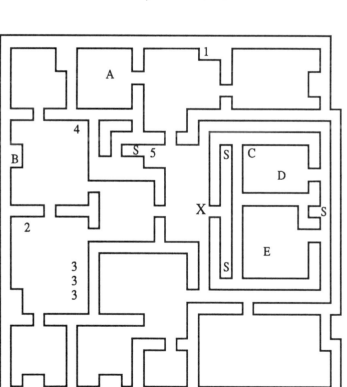

Gozaroth's Mansion, Level Two

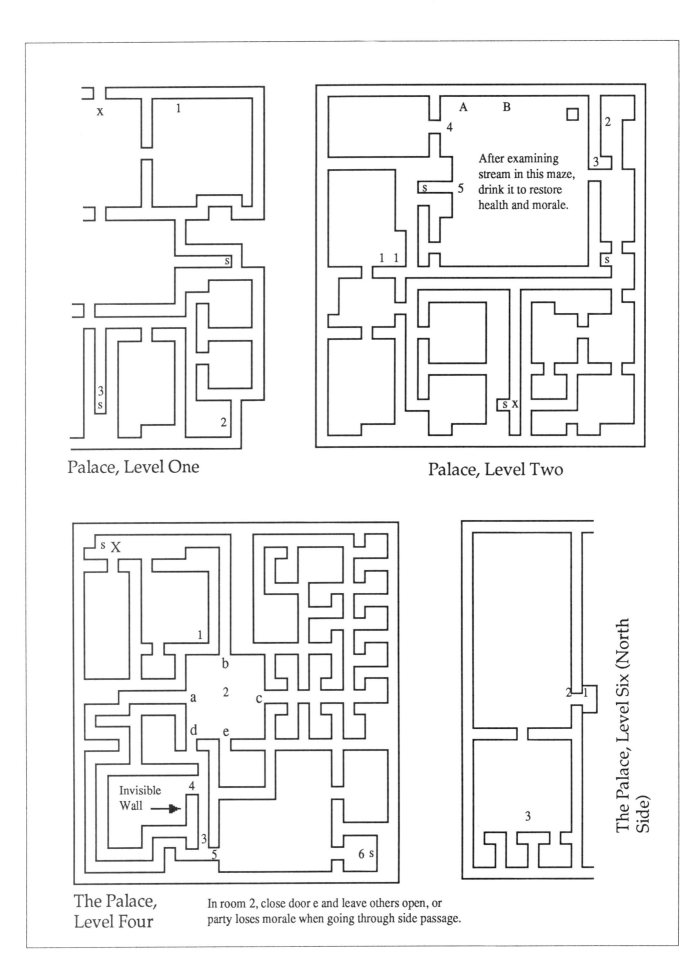

Palace, Level One

Palace, Level Two

After examining stream in this maze, drink it to restore health and morale.

The Palace, Level Four

The Palace, Level Six (North Side)

Invisible Wall

In room 2, close door e and leave others open, or party loses morale when going through side passage.

116

WRATH OF DENETHENOR

Based on the Nordic myth of a prince who made a pact with the devil, this one-character scenario unfolds on Nisondel and three other mini-continents linked by Inter-dimensional Doors. Your target — Lord Denethenor. This is an introductory-level game so combat and magic are simplified and take place on the surface map, as is character development: You earn Hit Points for walking around and don't have to amass experience points because your character cannot advance to higher levels. Finding the magic spells and figuring out which objects are needed to cast each one are the only real puzzles, and they are fairly easy. The birds-eye view is also less than demanding.

Programmed by Christopher Crim, the game will look familiar to *Ultima* fans, for the resemblance of its graphics and interface—towns, shops, prisons and ships—is striking. For that reason, and because it is easy, anyone who has ever completed an *Ultima* may find *Wrath* disappointing. However, the novice adventurer can feel a thrill of victory without being too frustrated by the trickiness and difficult stumbling blocks of harder games.

The Walkthrough

Character Creation and Development

You only have one character and can't make any decisions about him, so there's little to do until he gets his feet on the ground. With no experience points and levels to strive for, you can concentrate on developing Strength, Intelligence, Stamina and Hit Points. Strength is boosted by purchasing a stronger weapon. The best one is a rapier sold in Solrain

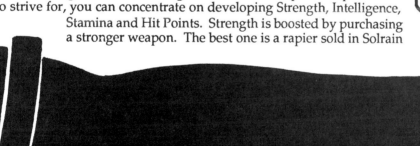

Argoth on Nisondel for 1,950 gold. Intelligence, which lengthens the effects of your spells, is enhanced by talking to the Lords in Castles Solrain, Mirrih and Estrine. Like Strength, the maximum is +30. Just buy food to build up Stamina, which is vital for survival. Buy as much as possible early on, for it gets very expensive as you progress. Watch out for Demonglow, which eats up Stamina points. The safest place to rest is in a spot surrounded by mountains on three sides. (Don't use a torch while resting; it attracts bloodbats.)

This is also a good combat tactic since you can only be attacked from one side. Once you learn the Monsrol or Inslerete spells, use them instead of combat spells, which use up more Stamina and destroy any gold or objects you might otherwise obtain, but combat is essential for obtaining magical items and gold. After acquiring enough food, weapons and armor, you will find it easier to avoid combat.

To conserve on charms, enter a town and use them to open all the locked doors and find where the important items and clues are hidden. Then turn off the computer and reboot. You'll have the necessary information and all your charms, which you can use to rob banks and perform other useful chores. If planning to loot labyrinths for treasure, map them with the Specere spell. (Except for Mount Restorn and its gold, maps provided here show only the best route through each dungeon.) When you identify a Door's location and destination, mark these on the map in the manual. This will be handy because you may want to return to an island later.

Magic
You are supposed to find and converse with characters in certain towns to learn the spells, but the program does not check to see if you have done so. That means you can just type in the name and cast away. It's still more fun to discover these things on your own, but this chart will be handy if you get stuck.

	Spell	Item	Where Found	Effect
1.	Tulicarne	torch	Backwoods	lights torch
2.	Specere	scroll	Castle Solrain	shows map
3.	Monsrol	pendant	Lake Fionell	suspends time
4.	Inslerete	dust	Lotrus Amphitheatre	invisibility
5.	Lethren	return	Castle Drawn	casts Demonglow
6.	Elresire	return	En Siev	mass damage
7.	Desapar	return	Banshee	mass damage
8.	Netrelon	charm	Solrain Argoth	opens locked doors
9.	Resonim	return	Castle Mirrih	dispels Demonglow
10.	Wethrir	return	Dry Gulch	magic bolt
11.	Urenduiresex	return	Castle Denethena	kills Denethenor

General Tips
Talk to all the characters for clues; none are hard to find and you won't have to solve riddles or puzzles. A cardinal rule is to always talk to a pub's bartender and buy a round for the house before approaching other characters. Otherwise you will start a brawl and will miss valuable clues. After robbing a town, you will be a wanted criminal for about a day before it is safe to return. Monsrol or Inslerete spells simplify any bankrobber's work. There are no trading posts after Mount Karibae.

Nisondel
Nisondel is a good place to develop and equip your character. Go to Backwoods to buy a dagger and **mfbso Uvmjdbsof tpvui** of **upxo**. As soon as possible, visit **Tpmsbjo Bshpui** and **mfbso Ofusfmpo**. Then head for Castle Solrain to raise your Intelligence. You can also buy armor here and **mfbso Tqfdfsf** in the **spzbm qvc**. Check out **Esz Hvmdi** for the **Xfuisjs tqfmm**. N. (through the soup kitchen door). A Cleric there will heal you for 50 gold. After acquiring four or five torches, enter Firetrench (see map) and cross to Pescara Bay. Steal a ship. When you've got at least 5,000 Hit Points and 2,500 Stamina, sail to the large island northwest of Nisondel and enter the Interdimensional Door to Cestiona.

Cestiona
Go to **Mblf Gjpofmm** to learn the Monsrol spell from the cleric in the **dpoep opsui** of the **nbmm**. You can buy a handsword if you missed the rapier in Nisondel. Then proceed to Mirrih Argoth and rob it. Be sure to use the **Ofusfmpo** spell to open the door that has **xbufs cftjef** it. Do so with the "open door" command and you may **espxo**. Bash heads until you have 2,360 gold to spare, then go to the Dimension Door south of Mirrih Argoth: from Argoth move 4-S, 6-E, 6-S, 7-W, 1-N, 2-W, 5-S, 1-W, 4-S, 7-E, 3-S and 2-E. (or go there anyway if you have enough items to sell to raise this amount, because you need a ship to reach Mount

Karibae to sell things and buy torches).

This maze takes you to the large island southeast of Cestiona, where you will find the Bay of Mirrih. (Do not rob it until you have visited the Castle.) Go there and buy metal plate armor. Then steal a boat and sail to Castle Mirrih. See **Civj** in a **opsui dfmm** in the **evohfpo** for the Resonim spell. Talk to Lord Mirrih to raise your Intelligence, **cvu gps opx epo'u xpssz bcpvu** the hemlock he wants you to find. Return to Bay of Mirrih and steal another boat. Dock it as close as possible to the gold storerooms and rob them. Then escape on the boat. Avoid the "Hole" labyrinth, which has no clues and little treasure.

Before leaving Cestiona, make sure your Stamina and Hit Point levels are high. Don't use the Interdimensional Door on Cestiona's southeastern shore, for it leaves you stranded on an island. Instead, take the one on the **opsuifsonptu** of the **uisff jtmboet opsuixftu** of Cestiona, which has a dead tree on it. Cast Resonim before leaving the boat, because the island is protected by a spell. Enter the door and you emerge on a small island. Enter this island's other door and you will appear just east of the Deledain Penetentiary in Arveduin.

Arveduin
Go to Castle Estrine and talk to Lord Estrine for an Intelligence boost. Steal a ship and rob the castle. It's an easy one, so return and rob it several times if you need gold. Sail to Castle Drawn to **mfbso Mfuifst jo uif upq ps cpuupn "nbaf"** (see map). Then rob the Dead Forest Inn and pick up **Jotmfsfuf** at **Mpuvt Bnqijuifbusf**. In the group of rocky islands off the southernmost shore of Arveduin you can find a cave full of booty. It is visible only while a Monsrol spell is in effect, and you have to get out before the spell wears off. Otherwise the cave gets flooded and you may drown.

Several Dimension Doors lead from Arveduin to Mystenor, but most are dead ends. Enter any you find and cast Specere to observe their locations in Mystenor, then return to Arveduin. To find the real Door **cvnq bmpoh uif dpbtu** as you **tbjm vq** the **opsui tipsfmjof**. A secret passage will open up, leading to the Mt. Restorn labyrinth. Rob the gold and follow the map to exit the labyrinth, where the Interdimensional Door will take you to the Isles of Bregalad. But don't go until you've got at least **tjy uipvtboe** Stamina and Hit Points. Also take lots of gold.

Isles of Bregalad
You arrive just west of En Siev. Before entering, cast **Npotspm** to avoid combat with hordes of monsters. Then go in and head S. Enter the large building to the W. and go straight for the **wbvmu** in the **tpvuifbtu** part of the building. The labyrinth there leads to the real En Siev. Here you can load up on pendants, charms, scrolls and dust at the shop (maximum 99 of each), and **mfbso uif Fmsftjsf tqfmm, xsjuufo** on the **xbmm** in the **cbs**. Exit via the **wbvmu**, again using **Npotspm**.

Go S., get a ship and sail around exploring. Stick with your original ship until you've visited the Banshee and Swim Thru Dock, otherwise you may steal someone else's and then nobody will talk to you. The Banshee is found in the southwest corner of the island where Limbar's Fortress is located. (See the map in your manual.) There is another Banshee, but it is flooded and worthless. East of the real Banshee, the Bank of Denethenor is very easy to rob.

Ignore the island surrounded by light, since it is inaccessible from here. You can reach it later. Instead, sail to the far side of the **npvoubjot opsuixftu** of En Siev and enter the **jomfu** that goes south to a labyrinth. Make sure you have at least 7,000 Stamina and Hit Points before entering, then cast Monsrol. **Upsdift xpo'u xpsl** in this short maze. Go south until you can't move, then east until you hit a wall, and repeat these steps until you exit the maze. Then go to Shadowmere and buy lots of food. You need maximum Stamina and Hit Points, because the game gets nasty from this point on. Remain in Shadowmere (or just outside if you need to rest) until about 11:45 PM, when you should be in town, near the the area where you entered. At **njeojhiu** an Interdimensional Door appears near here. This goes to the center of Mystenor. Upon arrival, cast **Tqfdfsf** to get your bearings, then go SE. and N. to the peninsula in the center of the lake. At the end you'll find the Red Sands labyrinth (see map). Enter it and exit in southern Mystenor.

Mystenor
Cast Specere again and move E. past the dead tree. When you can, start moving E., then N. to the

mountains. Move S., E. and N. about ten steps each. When you find a **tnbmm pqfojoh** along the water, follow this narrow path to Sorie Gulch, one of the game's most difficult obstacles. Enter and move to the far NW. corner, up against the wavy light. Cast **Npotspm boe Sftpojn**. Move N., then E. (avoiding the red grass in case your Resonim wears out). Find the wall to the N. and move E. along it. Above the east corner you'll see a door with a wizard on the other side. Cast **Npotspm boe Ofusfmpo**, kill the wizard and go west through a tunnel in the wall.

Head N. about 20 steps when you leave the tunnel and cast **Jotmfsfuf**. Get a boat and sail SE. out of Sorie Gulch, then west to a lake with an island in the center, the big one due north of Red Sands on the manual's map. Dock your ship on the north side next to the wavy light. Cast Resonim and go to Castle Denethena. Buy food and exit to rest if you need to restore Hit and Stamina Points, which should be at least 9,000 before proceeding. Then kill Lord Denethenor and **jnnfejbufmz npwf poup ijt uispo**. The castle turns to rubble and you **mfbso uif gjobm tqfmm, Vsfoevjsftfy**. Exit and head for the Interdimensional Door on the island's northwest corner. Cast Monsrol **cfgpsf foufsjoh**. The door goes to Death Meadow. Go about 30 steps E., then 35 N. to the Interdimensional Door just east of the sign. If unsure, cast Specere and look for a **cmbdl trvbsf**.

Enter this Door and you will emerge on the island surrounded by light in the Isles of Bregalad. Slay the monsters and converse with the cleric, Janai, who gives you the **ifnmpdl** requested by **Mpse Njssji**. Reenter the Door and you'll come out in the mountains with a Castle to the south—the **sfbm dbtumf pg Mpse Efofuifops**. If your Hit and Stamina Points are not 8,000+ (or you just want to play it safe), take the hemlock to Lord Mirrih in **Dftujpob** and he will boost your Intelligence to +30. You can also increase your Stamina and Hit Points on the way back. To do so, reenter the door you just exited and you'll come out **opsuixftu pg Dbtumf Efofuifob**. Sail E., then N. and W. to the south bank of the river, halfway between its two bends. Dock the boat and go SW. a short way to an Interdimensional Door that is ringed almost completely by mountains northwest of Red Sands. This goes to Arveduin. From there take the Door east of Deledain Penetentiary, then the one on the small island to reach Cestiona and Castle Mirrih.

Lord Denethenor's Destruction
In the Castle, **Npotspm** spells won't work, but you can use **Jotmfsfuf**. Enter and **hp evf T.** until you see a **mbeefs**. Cast Inslerete **cfgpsf** entering the labyrinth. See the map for directions, and cast a Specere now and then to get your bearings. (Even with a map this is may take a few tries because torches won't work here.) When you exit, go west to the brickway and continue NW. to the place where the brickway narrows to one space. If you pass through this arch without first casting **Jotmfsfuf** you will **ejf jotuboumz**. If your Intelligence is +30, cast Inslerete and move up to the wavy light, then cast Resonim. Move W., open the door with Netrelon and go to the intersection.

If your Intelligence is under 30, you will have a harder time. Cast Resonim and wait for the Dreyx to attack you. Hopefully a number of them will be killed when the spell wears out. Kill any that make it across, then cast Inslerete and pass through the arch, **tupqqjoh bu uif xbwz mjhiu** to cast **bopuifs Sftpojn**. Move W., cast Netrelon on the door and go west to the intersection.

From the intersection go south through the door and follow the brickway to the south, then east until you see two doors. Open the lower door with Netrelon, stop at the wavy light and cast Resonim. Move E. to the last cell on the south side and cast Netrelon to enter. Go S. through the wall to the wavy light. Cast Resonim and go E. along the path formerly occupied by the light. Stop at the next brick junction, where you see **bopuifs xbwz mjhiu up uif opsui**. Keep casting Resonim and go N. past the next two brick junctions until you see a hole in the west wall.

Move W. through the hole until you reach the light, then cast **Sftpojn** and go S.. Cast Inslerete, move SW. around the corner and line up horizontally, not diagonally, with Lord Denethenor. Then cast **Vsfoevjsftfy**. When the magic word is spoken, the **dbtumf dpmmbqtft** and you're **ufmfqpsufe up tbgfuz**.

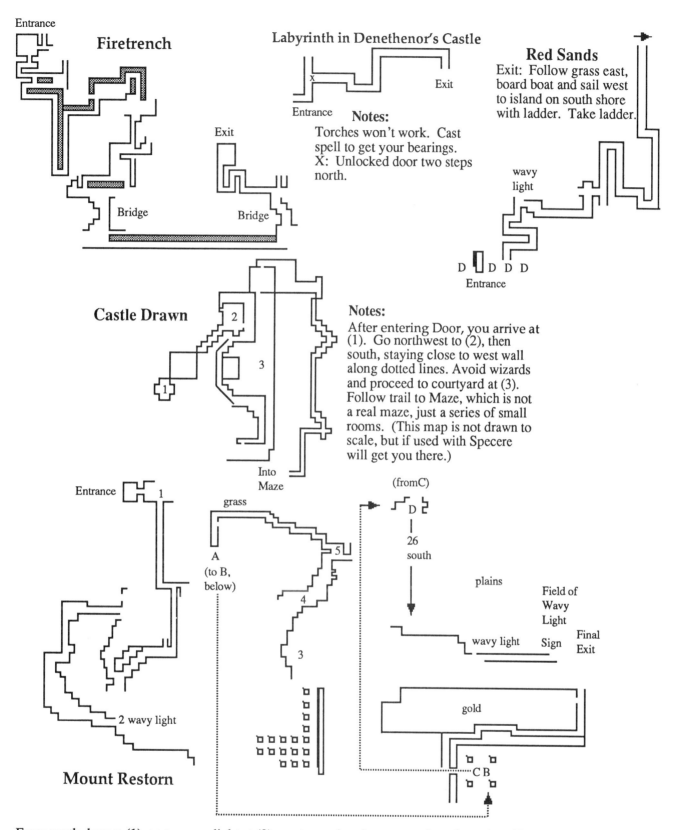

Firetrench

Entrance

Exit

Bridge

Bridge

Labyrinth in Denethenor's Castle

Entrance

X

Exit

Notes:
Torches won't work. Cast spell to get your bearings.
X: Unlocked door two steps north.

Red Sands
Exit: Follow grass east, board boat and sail west to island on south shore with ladder. Take ladder.

wavy light

D D D D

Entrance

Castle Drawn

2

3

1

Into Maze

Notes:
After entering Door, you arrive at (1). Go northwest to (2), then south, staying close to west wall along dotted lines. Avoid wizards and proceed to courtyard at (3). Follow trail to Maze, which is not a real maze, just a series of small rooms. (This map is not drawn to scale, but if used with Specere will get you there.)

Entrance

1

grass

A
(to B, below)

5

4

3

2 wavy light

Mount Restorn

(fromC)

D

26 south

plains

Field of Wavy Light

wavy light

Sign

Final Exit

gold

C B

From south door at (1), go to wavy light at (2), cast resonim, then east and north to pit at (3). Take boat at (4) to door at (5), then enter Dimension Door at (A). Arrive at (B), get gold north of there and enter Door (C) to reach (D). Go south and southeast through door to field of wavy light and take ladder east of the sign.

It Came from Another World

Books, Legends, Movies and Fairy Tales

J ust as Hollywood looks to the printed word when seeking new material for motion pictures, software companies sometimes base their adventure games on books, movies and popular stories from other realms of the entertainment world. In these interactive tales you get to assume the role of fiction's best-known characters: spinning the trick license plates on James Bond's Aston-Martin, gunning down Vietnamese soldiers with Rambo's machine gun, or swinging Indiana Jones' machete as you hack a path through a steamy Mexican jungle. Even fairy tales have provided new worlds for adventurers to explore, places populated with the likes of Little Red Riding Hood and Rip van Winkle. Recently even a conventional role-playing game, Car Wars, inspired a computer counterpart.

D on't think that you'll be able to skip right through the adventure just because you've seen the movie or read the book. While the events and characters of the original story may be faithfully represented, logical puzzles are created from elements of familiar scenes and woven into the plot. Sometimes it helps if you've seen the movie or read the book. A good example is the first puzzle in *A View to a Kill*, where anyone who recalled the film's opening scene would know to take the dead Russian's watch without first examining the body to discover it. But these cases are the exception, for even Rambo himself would sweat bullets trying to solve the text adventure that bears his name. So if you can't get enough of your favorite author or movie, venture into one of these interactive adaptations—coming soon to a computer in your neighborhood.

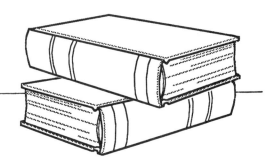

A View to a Kill

Adapted from the James Bond film, this all-text tale puts you in 007's shoes as he confronts Max Zorin, a renegade scientist intent on dominating the global microchip market. Zorin plans to wipe out the competition by triggering an earthquake in Silicon Valley. The adventure adheres closely to the film's plot and to 007's characteristics, taking you from Siberia to London, Paris, and eventually, California. Logical puzzles are worked into the story at key points, so those who saw the movie can't just stroll through the game. Outsmarting the characters often requires action instead of words, and inventory management is important.

The text is lively, well-crafted and interspersed with Bond's witty one-liners. It is linear in the sense that you can't go far in the wrong direction without getting killed or stumped. A time limit is involved, and the Coast is destroyed if you waste too much time in certain places. Bond fans can't go wrong with this one. Others may find it challenging and satisfying, as long as they don't mind meeting their demise frequently: This one's a killer.

The Walkthrough

Ledge
Examine ARR. N. [Snowdrift] Examine 003 **dbsfgvmmz**. Get **xbudi**. Wait (until you hear Russians from South). E. D.

Bay & Submarine
Kill Russian with **tlj qpmf**. S. [Ice Floe] Insert ski pole in ring. **Sfnpwf tljt**. D. Drop skis. **Espq** ski pole. Drop ARR. Open **xbudi**. Get **njdspdijq**. Drop watch. U. W.

M's Office
Show microchip to M. Do you have a clip? Put clip in gun. Drop microchip. Get **xjsft**. Get calculator. **Ipx epft uif dbmdvmbups xpsl?** E. S. (Save.) U. E.

Restaurant
Look. Get car key. E. [Lookout Deck] Open bench. Get backpack. Wear backpack. **Kvnq**. U.

Parking Lot
Unlock door with car key. Open door. Get in. Close door. Get envelope. Open envelope. Get printout. Read printout. Drop printout. Get **cbehf**. **Xfbs** badge. Drop envelope. N. E. N. N. [Front Drive] Open door. Get out. E. U. E. [Second Floor] Open north door. N.

Bedroom
Qvodi May Day. Kick May Day. **Gmjq** May Day. Kiss May Day. S. W. D. S. [Back Hallway] Unlock door with **xjsft**. Open door. S.

Study
Examine **eftl dbsfgvmmz**. Unlock desk with key. **Pqfo esbxfs**. Get checkbook. Turn calculator on. **Fybnjof** check-book with calculator. **Uvso** calculator **Pgg**. Drop checkbook. Open trap door. D.

Laboratory
Examine **nfubm cpy** carefully.

N. E. [Garden] No. E. N. W. [Front Drive] Get in. Close door. W. [Lot] Open door. Get out. Drop **dbs lfz**. W. S. (Save)

City Hall, White Hall
Unlock door with wires. Open door. E. E. [White Hall] My what **qsfuuz fzft**. Kiss Stacey. Give me the passcard. Unlock door with passcard. Open door. E.

Howe's Office
Drop **qbttdbse**. Unlock cabinet with wires. Open cabinet. Get folder. Open folder. Drop folder. Get note. Read note. Turn calculator on. Examine note with calculator. Turn calculator off. Drop note. W. W. to elevator, and Stacey must be with you. Open **opsui** panel. N. D.

Bottom Shaft, First Office
Open door. S. E. Get hardhat. Wear hardhat. (Save) W. D. E. N.

Second Office, Safe
Examine model carefully. Turn

Ejbm sjhiu 25. Turn dial left **tjyuz-gjwf**. Turn dial right **tfwfouffo**. Open cover. D.

Main Strike Room
Unlock dome with key. Open dome. Take tape. Turn calculator on. Examine green chip with calculator. Drop tape. Get gun. N.

Pit
Shoot Zorin. Examine **spdl** carefully. **Tippu spdl**. Look. U.

Outside
Kiss Stacey.

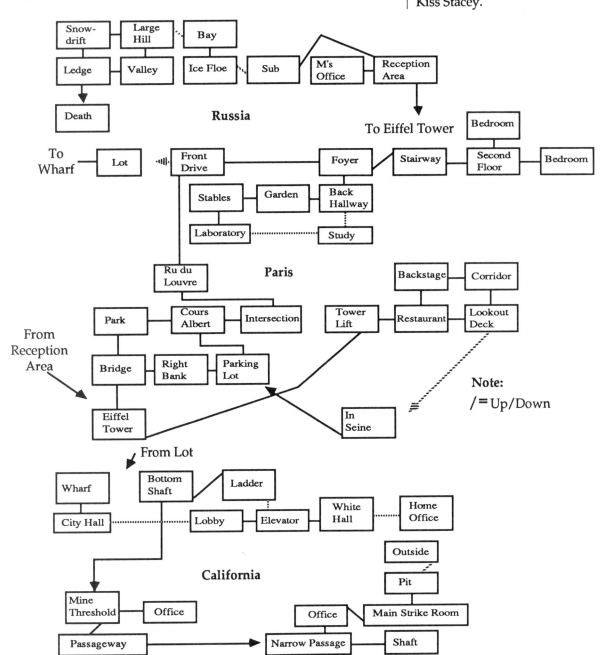

Russia

Paris

Note:
/ = Up/Down

California

From Reception Area

From Lot

To Wharf

To Eiffel Tower

From Lot

Brimstone

AS SIR GAWAIN, a knight of the Round Table, you will see little of King Arthur or Camelot in this all-text tale. It takes place in a dream that traps you in the underworld of Ulro, where you must learn five magic words in order to escape. A few object-oriented puzzles are involved, but character interaction dominates. Instead of getting killed when you do something wrong, you awaken from the dream and start over. Another unusual aspect is the perspective: events are described from a third person perspective, so you read that "Sir Gawain saw a castle" instead of "You see a castle."

COMPOSED BY POET James Paul, the text is rich in imagery, and the action is divided into five chapters. As do all of the Electronic Novels™, this game also comes with an illustrated hardbound book, in this case containing the Beginnings of Brimstone, background story, description of characters and places, documentation and an adventurer's diary. It is written in a smooth-flowing, sometimes humorous style. One of the easiest of the Electronic Novels™, *Brimstone* is also the most enjoyable as a pure reading experience.

The Walkthrough

<u>CHAPTER ONE</u>
Knight's Chamber
Sleep. (Chapter One begins.) N.

Castle in Distance
Wait (**voujm xjoe cmpxt ibse**).
Look at banner. N.

Castle Steps
Look at **mjpo**. Get **uppui**.
Look at **upsupjtf**. **Qvmm iboemf**. Look at tortoise.
Get key. Unlock door with key. N. N.

Castle Room
Look at case. Read question. **Ipso**. Get sword. Get all. Wear armor. Wear gloves. Wear sheath. E.

Child's Room
Girl, "I am Sir Gawain. (Type sentences, including quotations, just as you see them here. The parser is a little forgiving, but you have to address to whom you are speaking first or that character will get a little mad. You do have a few chances for error, however.) Enitharmon, "tortoise and lion (a separate sentence for each noun). Enitharmon, "gold tooth and silver key (again in separate sentences). **Hjwf** gold tooth and silver key to Enitharmon. W. N.

Room of Straw
Gjhiu Adam with **txpse** (three times). N. N.

<u>CHAPTER TWO</u>
Courtroom
Judge, "Innocent (twice). Wait (**uxjdf**).

Cell
Get coin. Get feather. Get handkerchief. Wait. Fat man, "Yes (2x's). (Answer questions on juggle and drink from flask, which may occur now or in a few moves.) Man, "**Ifmq**. Call for Fum. N. D. N.

Bridge over Chasm
Hodge, "I am Sir Gawain. Hodge, "No. N. N. N.

<u>CHAPTER THREE</u>
Frozen in Ice
Think of **tqsjoh**. Think of **gmpxfst**. Think of **tvnnfs**. Wait. U.

125

On Lake
Read sign. **Tqju.** E. S.
W. W. W. S. D. S.

Machines
Push red switch. N. U.
N. N. N. N. N.

Apes' Dwelling
Ape, "**Xblf vq** (three times). E. E. E. E. Open.

Vault
Look at apple. **Sfbe** apple. S (eight times).

Sunken Place
Dive into water.

Eel's Nest
Get sword. Kill eels

with sword (twice). U. **Hsbc iboe.** Kill eel with sword. (Go to Front of Cottage.) Knock on door. S.

Sitting Room
Wait (for Blake). Blake, "Hello. Blake, "Yes (twice). Show **iboelfsdijfg** to Blake. Give feather to Blake. Blake, "What about **xpset?** Blake, "How do mortals leave Ulro? Blake, "What about Fury? Blake, "No.

Bedroom
Put **txpse** in left hand. Put handkerchief in

right hand. Open bookcase. W. D. E. E. U. **Sbjtf ujq** of sword to **gmbnf.**

CHAPTER FOUR
Fury
U. N. E. E. W. S. U. U.

CHAPTER FIVE
In Orchid
D. Orchid, "Help. Orchid, "I am Sir Gawain. Orchid, "What about **xpset?** W.

Forest Tracks
Wait (until Fum falls from sky). Fum, "Tell me a word (until he says **rvj).** E. E. Wait (for

ferry). Show **dpjo** to Charon. Give coin to Charon.

On Boat
Woman, "Yes. Wait (twice). E. S.

Narrow Canyon
Woman, "Yes. S.

In Cave
Woman, "Help. Sword, "**Mjhiu nz xbz.** S. S. S.

On Bridge
Green Knight, "Bare hands. Hit Green Knight with fist. Jump aside. Say, "**Cpoj tpju rvj. Nbm qfodf.** U. U. E.

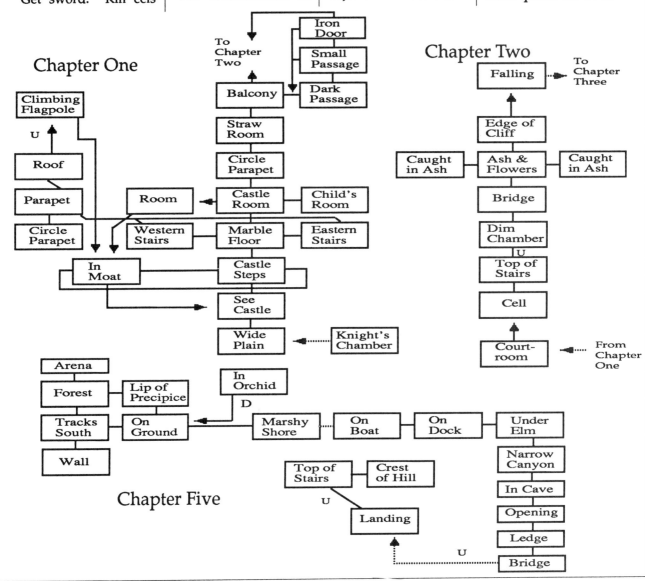

Chapter One

Chapter Two

Chapter Five

126

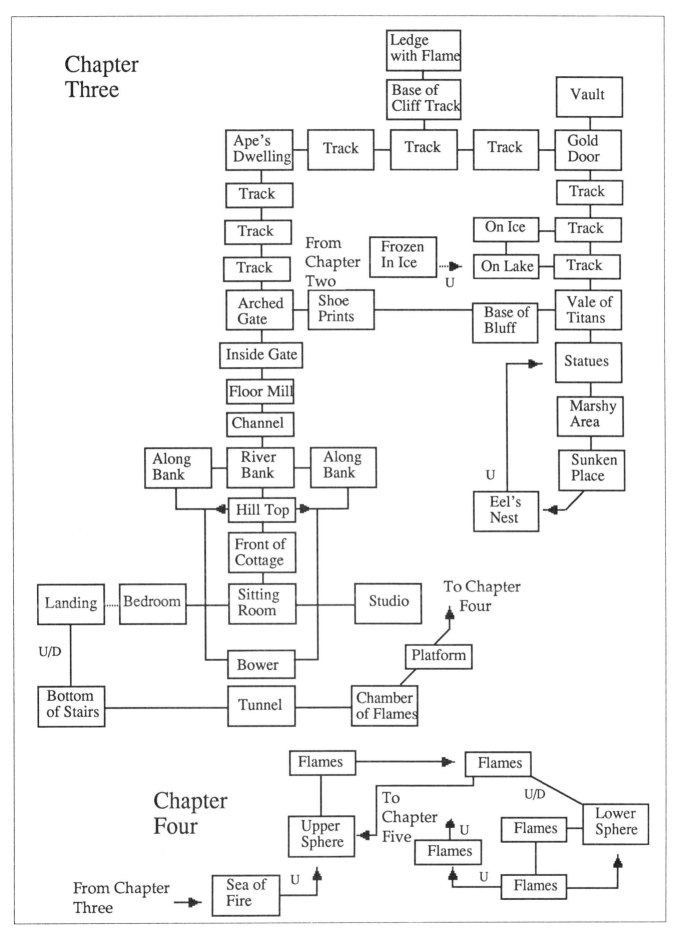

Chapter
Three

Chapter
Four

Fraktured Faebles

Red Riding Hood, Rip van Winkle, the Three Little Pigs, Goldilocks and the Three Bears—even Sleeping Beauty makes an appearance in this delightfully illustrated graphic adventure that combines elements of traditional fairy tales. The goal is to find and awaken Beauty. Waking her up is the easy part; finding her is the problem. There are not a lot of different pictures, but the cartoon-style illustrations are TV quality artwork. This was done by Rick Incrocci, who previously teamed up with this game's designer, Rick Johnson, on the classic *Sherwood Forest.. Faebles* is much easier, though it does pose at least one serious mindgrinder.

A typical problem consists of saving Red Riding Hood from the Big Bad Wolf to obtain an item needed elsewhere. Clues are ingeniously sprinkled throughout the text, which also profits from a good sense of humor. The two-word parser is the only weak point, for it forces you to spend as much time figuring out how to communicate with the program as you do unraveling the problems. But it's worth the extra effort if you appreciate original puzzles and cartoon-style graphics.

The Walkthrough

Under Big Tree
S. W.

Clearing
Tfbsdi Rip. Take lfz. Sfbe key. Uvso key. Sfbe key. Xfoej. Read key. E. N. E. Look Red. E.

East-West Path
Mppl beggar. Give key. E.

In Gramma's House
Look Gramma. Take Opepa™. W. W. W. Drop card. S. W.

Clearing
Wake Rip. Give Opepa™. Take comb. E. N. W.

By Three Bears' House
Look Goldilocks. Give dpnc. Get note. Get packet. E. U.

In Big Tree
Read note. Aracadara. Drop note. Take hive. U. Pqfo qbdlfu. Tbmu bird. D. Take egg. D. W. N. N.

In Baby Bear Room
Give hive. Get honey. Npwf cbcz. Get pin. S. S. E. N.

Golf Course
Look egg. Look pig. Give cbmm. Look sign. Ublf sign. Look sign. N.

Green
Take mfuufs. Tujdl honey. Stick mfuufs. Look sign. Look rabbit. Give watch. Get pole. Get string. Ujf string. Tie pin. S. S. E.

By Gramma's House
Tipx sign. Drop tjho. Look basket. Get apple. E. E.

In Gramma's House
Give apple. Get worm. Qvu worm. Get apple. W. W. W. Drop apple. S.

By Pond
Catch fish. Get gjti. N. W. N.

In Three Bears' House
Give fish. Look Qbqb. S. E. Take card. Take bqqmf. (You must have the pole with you, but don't need the things attached to it.) U. Look. Look branch. Hp branch.

Out on a Limb
Look branch. Drop bmm. Take bug. Look bug. W. D. S.

By Pond
Give bug. Look frog. Ljtt frog. N. N. N. Go hole.

Inside Hole
Sfbe eudijoht. (Xsjuf epxo the mbtu xpse, which is a qbttxpse that changes randomly from game to game.) U. S. S. S. Go pond. E.

Dry Land Near Crack
Look prince. Say (qbttxpse). N. W.

Gramma's Backyard
Get pole. Get card. Get apple. E. E.

Queen's Pad
Look hatter. **Sfbe dbse.** Show card.

Tea Party
Look **njout.** Look Queen. Drop apple. Look Queen.

Look candle. **Cmpx** candle. W.

Bramble Bush
Tfbsdi brambles. Get mint. Eat mint. **Wbvmu.**

Sleeping Beauty's Room
Look Beauty. **Ljtt** Beauty.

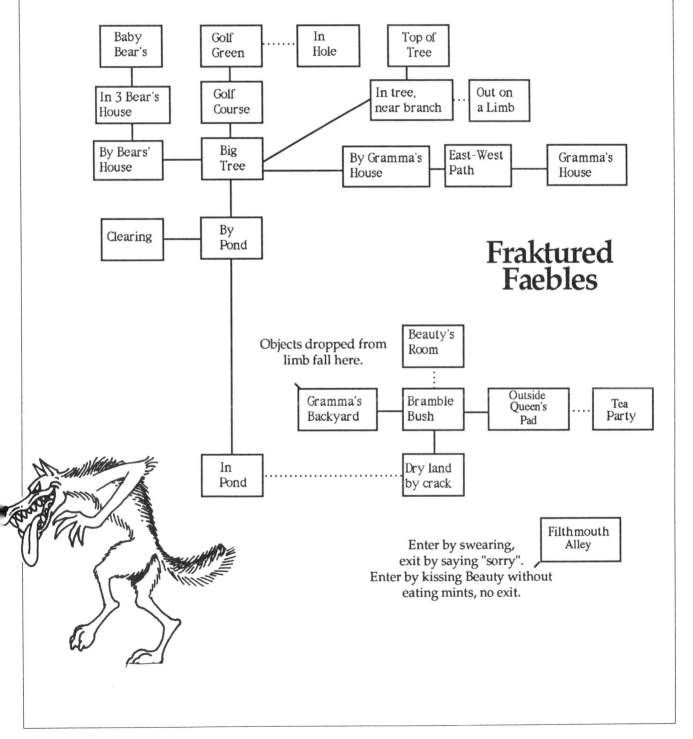

Fraktured
Faebles

Objects dropped from
limb fall here.

Enter by swearing,
exit by saying "sorry".
Enter by kissing Beauty without
eating mints, no exit.

Goldfinger

This is vintage Bond, the all-text tale of gold-obsessed Auric Goldfinger, his bodyguard Odd Job, his pilot Pussy Galore—and his plan to get rich quick by nuking Fort Knox to drive up the value of his own gold. The drama kicks off with a tense chase scene on a narrow mountain road in Switzerland, where you must penetrate Goldfinger's headquarters before jetting off to Kentucky. After finagling your way onto his horse farm, you'll have to deal with Odd Job, Pussy Galore and Goldfinger before you can find and disarm the bomb.

Some puzzles hinge on character interaction, but object manipulation dominates in this tightly knit scenario. As in all the Mindscape/Angelsoft games, the prose is well-crafted, and you have to think and act like the real James Bond if you hope to bring Goldfinger to justice. (See the review of *The Mist* for comments on the parser and other technical considerations.)

The Walkthrough

Chase Scene
[S-Curve] Open **bsnsftu**. W. [Hairpin] Push **xijuf** button. N. N. [North Pass] Push **hsbz** button. E. [Sharp Curve] Push **cmbdl** button.

Steep Road and Lookout
Open door. Get out. N. W. S. [Lookout] Look at **hvbsesbjm** carefully. Pull cable. D. D. E.

Back Alley to the Roof
Look in **xjoepx**. E. U. W. [Western End of Roof] Look in **tlzmjhiu**. E. S. [Goldfinger's Roof] Open trap door. Look in trap door. D.

Office
Take **johpu**. Open desk. Take plans. Look at plans carefully. Put plans in desk. Close desk. Look at **qmbrvf** carefully. Take ball. Put ball in **ipmf**. Take **cbmm**. Put **cbmm** on **qmbrvf**. E.

Narrow Corridor
Take lighter. Light lighter. Look. Open bunker door. **Uvso pgg** lighter. Put lighter in pocket. E.

Bunker
Close bunker door. Look at **qjduvsf gsbnf** carefully.

Type **nz hpmefo hjsmt**. Take letter. Read letter. Put letter in safe. Close safe. Type open door. N.

Stone Steps to Kentucky
Dmptf tuffm epps. U. [Top of Stairs] Open manhole cover. U. E. S. [Steep Road] Get in. S. S. S. S. [Airport] Open door. Get out. **Xfbs cbehf**. S.

Gold Gate to Barn
Do you have an **johpu**? N. E. [Side Yard] Open door. E.

Barn
Get in. **Hfu pvu**. Flip Pussy. Block kick. Flip Pussy. Kiss Pussy. Pussy, tell me about **Hpmegjohfs**. Pussy, tell me about **hsboe tmbn**. W. W. W.

Corner to the Control Room
Look in window. Wait (until Goldfinger finishes his speech and leaves). E. N. N. N. [Tunnel] Open door.

Control Room and Barn
Evdl. Flip **cmbdl** switch. U. [Barn] Get in.

130

Inside Helicopter
Kick Goldfinger. Flip Goldfinger. Open device. Look at device carefully. Take **cbehf**. Put **cbehf** in **efwjdf**.

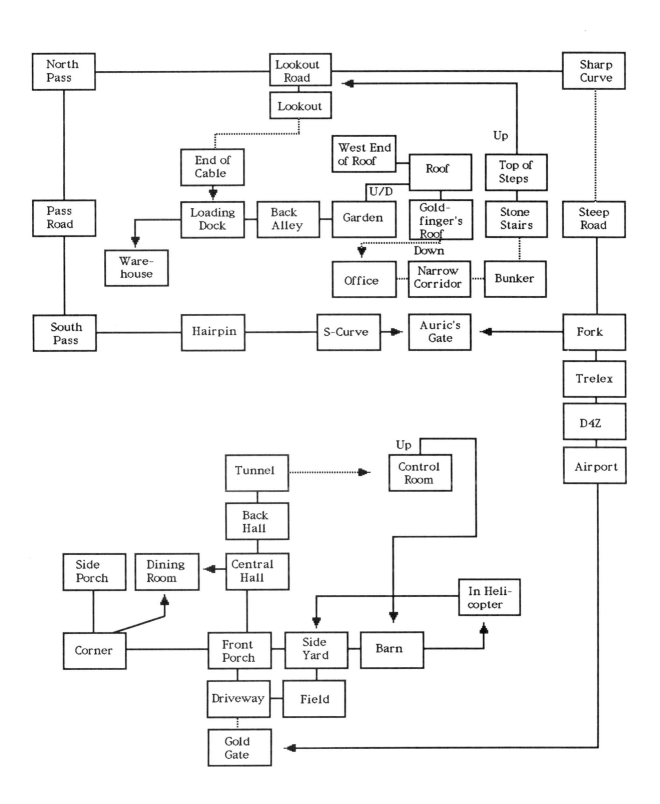

high $take$

dick Francis is a former British jockey whose mystery novels take place at the track, the stables and other horse racing locales. In the story this text game is based on, a millionaire horse owner fires his trainer, Jody, because he suspects Jody of using his ponies in a race-fixing scam. The trainer retaliates by stealing his prize horse, Energise. You play the part of the millionaire, cruising through the British countryside in a Lamborghini while trying to recover Energise. The other main characters are your girlfriend Alexandra and your best friend Bert. Chatting them up is crucial to success in this tightly interlocked series of puzzles.

a time limit is imposed, and the time and date are always displayed. *High Stakes* is not a conventional mystery in which you seek clues and try to arrest and convict the criminal, but more of a crime story in which you have to pull a fast one yourself in order to get justice. It's a difficult one, too, despite the brief solution. (For comments on the Mindscape parser and game mechanics, see the review of *The Mist*.)

The Walkthrough

Racing Road
W. [Park Entrance] **Dmptf hbuf. Xbju.** Look. Enter trailer.

Inside Trailer
Dbmn Energise (twice). **Qfu** Energise. Get tire iron. Look at Energise carefully.

Pasture with Bull
Xbju (voujm cvmm uvsot bxbz). S. E. S. E.

Viewing Stand
Bert, give me the sandwich. Bert, give me the Racing Calendar. Read Racing Calendar **dbsfgvmmz. Hjwf** Racing Calendar **cbdl** to Bert. Put **tboexjdi** in pocket. Alex, come with me. Alex, **ufmm nf bcpvu Cmbdl Gjsf.** W.

Car Park
Take key. Open door. Get in. Close door. Put key in ignition. N. W. W. S. S. E.

Park Court
Open door. Get out. Take **qbqfs. Sfbe qbqfs** carefully. Drop paper. Open door. E. U. N.

WC
Take **upxfm.** S. S.

Bedroom
Look at painting carefully. N. D. E.

Office
Take **mfuufs. Sfbe mfuufs** carefully. Put **mfuufs** in pocket. Get **dbsspvtfm.** W. W. Get in. Close door. W. N. E.

Gravel Drive, Barn
Open door. Get out. E. N. [Barn] Open box door. N.

Energise's Box
Mbe, what is **xspoh** with **ipstf.** Look at **cmbdl ipstf** carefully. **Voujf cmbdl ipstf.** S. S. W. [Gravel Drive] Get in. Close door. W. N. E.

Park Entrance
Open door. Get out. E.

Racing Road,
Pasture and Tire Iron
Ujf upxfm to **gfodf.** W. N. [Pasture] Take tire iron. S. [Park Entrance] Get in. Close door. W. W. W.

Quadrangle and the Chain
Open door. Get out. Break chain with tire iron. Drop tire iron. S.

Faber's Stable
Give **dbsspvtfm** to **Bmfy**. Alex, come with me. Look at Black Fire carefully. **Bert, I xbou to cvz** Black Fire. **Voujf** Black Fire. Bert, **hjwf nf** the **wbo lfzt**. N.

Quadrangle and the Gate
Alex, **ifmq nf open gate**. N.

Byway
Open door. Get in. Close door. Put **wbo lfzt** in **jhojujpo**. **Ujf** Black Fire. S. E. E. S. E. Open door. **Voujf** Black Fire. Get out. E. N. N.

Energise's Box
Take sugar.   Give **tvhbs** to **Qbefmmjd. Voujf Qbefmmjd.** S. S. W. Get in. Close door. **Ujf Qbefmmjd.** W. N. N. W.

Side Road
Untie Padellic. Open door. Get out. N. N. Open door. W.

Stable
Open stall door. Tie Padellic. N. **Dbmn Fofshjtf. Qfu Fofshjtf.** Take **tboexjdi.** Give **tboexjdi** to Energise. Untie Energise.   S.

Untie Padellic. N. Tie Padellic. S. Close **tubmm epps.** Untie Energise. E. Close door. S. S. Get in. Close door. Tie Energise. S. S.

Quadrangle, with Energise
Open door. Untie Energise. **Hfu pvu.** S. Tie Energise. N. Get in van. Close door. F. T. F. F.. (Take any other route and you lose.)

Gravel Drive
Open door. Get out. E. N.

Barn
Usjq Jody. **Ubdlmf** Jody. **Evdl. Tju po** Jody.

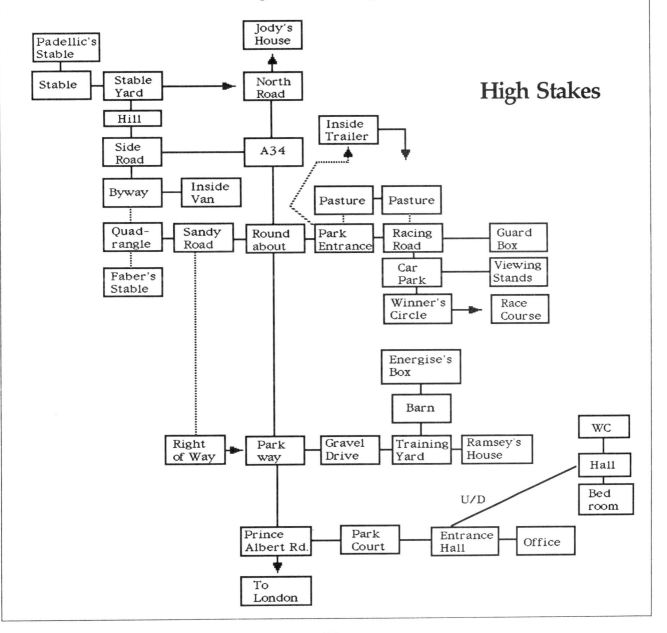

High Stakes

Indiana Jones in the Revenge of the Ancients

Angelsoft text games are best known for their deadliness, and this is one of the most unrelenting. Failure to solve a puzzle within the time limit results in a grisly, graphically described death. As Indiana Jones you will be shot by Nazi riflemen, crushed by a huge snake, asphyxiated by noxious fumes and eventually tossed into a pit of boiling blood—all for the sake of rescuing Marion and, of course, finding the treasure — the Mazatec Power Key.

You find the treasure early in this all-text story, but it slips away and reappears in the hands of a mad Nazi who is bent on applying its power to destroy the United States. Lush Mexican jungles, the ancient Pyramid of the Sun— the descriptions of these and other exotic locations, and the rogues you meet while exploring them, pull you into the story. As a novel, this would be called a real page-turner, but the puzzles are so hard—and you get killed so frequently—that it will take months for most people to reach the finalé of this expert level game. (See the review of *The Mist* for technical comments on the program.)

The Walkthrough

Central Chamber
N. Examine boulder. **Fybnjof iboe**. Take **iboe**. S. Examine panel. **Pqfo kbx**. Push button with hand. Take whip. **Dsbdl whip**. W. W. S. W. N. W. S. W. N. N. E.

Inner Sanctum (Grotto)
Take totem. Take cylinder. **Mbttp spdl** with whip. Put totem in pocket. **Dmjnc vq** whip. Take whip. Wear whip. E. N. N. **Ifmq nf** Don Pedro. Wait (until airplane roar bounces off cliff). S. Jump.

(From here you will randomly encounter the march-ing Nazi platoon, which must be avoided at all costs. You will sometimes be able to escape by running from them, but save the game often in case they show up and kill you.)

Airfield
Get on motorcycle. W. **Hjwf upufn** to Marion. **Ijef ju**. N.

Hideout
Viva la revolucion. **Usbef ibu** for **lojgf**. Give me bullets. W. Get off motorcycle. **Espq lojgf**. **Espq cvmmfut**. Take whip. Drop whip. Get on motor-

cycle. E. N. **Kvnq** on **csbodi.** N. D. E. E. S. Marion, **hjwf upufn up** me. Put **upufn** in pocket. Take goggles. Put goggles in pocket. U. Open door.

Basement

Wait. Wait. E. Take eye. Put eye in **qpdlfu.** Wait (until captured).

In Cage

Wait (until snake appears). **Ijtt.** E. E. Take whip. Take knife. Take bullets. Put bullets in pocket. Wear knife. Wear whip. W. N. N. Swim N. N. **Ublf vojgpsn.** S. **Xfbs vojgpsn.** W. W. D. D. W.

Pyramid

Take **fzf.** Take totem. Take bullets. Put **fzf jo tpdlfu.** D.

In Pyramid

Feel wall. **Ijtt.** Feel wall. Take knife. Put **upufn jo ojdif.** Take goggles. Wear goggles. W. S. Throw bullets in fire. W. W. N.

Aerie

Uispx lojgf bu Plebinheim. Take whip. **Tobq** whip at vines. Take key. **Txjoh po vines.** Take **lojgf. Dvu Marion epxo** with **lojgf. Txjoh po wjoft.**

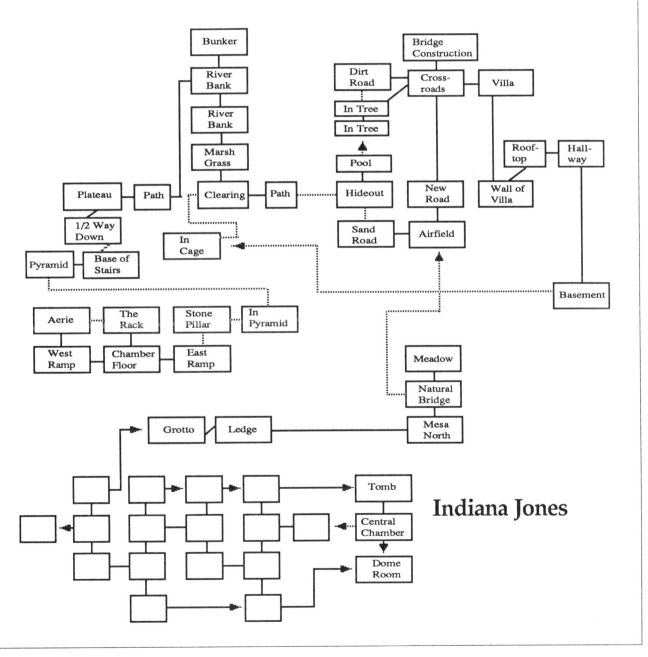

Indiana Jones

Labyrinth

As the name suggests, this adaptation of the Jim Henson Muppet movie takes place within a convoluted maze. Trapped inside, you seek the central room and Jareth the Goblin King, who must be vanquished within the 13-hour time limit if you hope to escape. Distinctive 3-D graphics and animation were devised by Lucasfilm Games to show the maze and your animated character. They afford a sense of depth and perspective as your character moves deeper into the maze. You don't see room names as in a standard adventure. Instead, a mini-map below the graphics shows your position and the location of objects in the current corridor.

Actions are conducted with a joystick/keyboard interface and a mini-parser whose verbs and nouns scroll through onscreen lists, so no typing is required. Most puzzles hinge on objects, but a few demand talking with Muppets such as Ludo and Firey. Two simple arcade-style sequences break up the brain-wrangling. The mapping isn't as difficult as it first seems, and some people have completed it without a map. (But a map will save you lots of time.) If you're looking for an out-of-the-ordinary adventure, *Labyrinth* is a good one to get lost in for a few weeks.

The Walkthrough

When using the maps, observe the location of objects such as the vending machines to get your bearings. Maps of the last few areas are not as elaborate as the others because you can only go to one or two places from each. In some, such as the Castle of the Goblin King, certain doors lead to random locations. Always save your game in all three save slots when you complete a level, so you can restore one if necessary. If you accidentally wander into the dungeon and get trapped, one of several solutions will work: Walk up the wall, find a trap door, insert money into a vending machine. You can always say the word you learned from the beggar at the start of the game. Any of them takes you back to the last part of the labyrinth you successfully completed.

The Theatre
N. Give **ojdlfm**. Go home. Take **dbndpsefs**. Go outside. S. W. Go theatre. Give dollars. Go theatre. N. Give dollar. Take. S. S. Look. **Dpnqmbjo**.

The Movie Begins
Walk in the front door.

The Labyrinth
Walk right, ignoring the Hoggle, **voujm** you **tff** the **mph**. Take it

and enter the **xbmm** wherever you see **xsjujoh**.

The Brick Hallway
Pqfo bmm doors in each of the three halls, picking up crystal balls

---

you find on the way. See map for exit to the next level.

Alph and Ralph

The first time you get here open the two doors and enter the one that says "This Way to Castle." If you unintentionally return later on, ask Alph or Ralph which door to take. Neither will give a straight answer unless all the Brick Hallway **eppst** are **pqfo**. If you arrive here without opening all the doors, go left or right to return to the Brick Hallway.

Wall of Hands

This is found only in the Commodore version. Say **Dpohsbuvmbuf xbmm**.

The Stone Corridor

Go east and take the first door past the peach. Take the crystal, go east and take the shears. Go west and up the ladder to the next section.

The Hedge Maze (A & B)

Take the crystal and enter the far left door to arrive at the Bracelet. Take it if possible, but the Goblin protects it well and must be avoided. Once you have it, escape and use the map to get to the closed hedge door marked 'Y'. **"Vtf tifbst"** and enter the door.

The Wise Man's Garden

"Ask Wise Man" and he'll answer with a riddle whose answer will tell you how to exit the garden. Usually a sequence of three or more doors is involved. The riddle is chosen randomly and most are easy. One is "The only way out is all that is left," which means go **uispvhi** all **uisff eppst** on the **mfgu tjef**. Another is "If you go left first, you'll know the bloomin' way out," which means go through the **gbs mfgu** door, then left through the one with the **gmpxfst cftjef** it. Save the game when you arrive. If you can't figure out the riddle, keep loading the saved game until he asks one you can figure out.

The Hedge Maze (C)

"Vtf tifbst" to open the **tfdpoe dmptfe** hedge door on the right, a long walk. Look at the onscreen map and note which door you have opened, for you'll need to reenter it later. Enter the door.

The Forest

Go through the forest "doors" twice.

The Bog of Eternal Stench

Xbml mfgu.

The Persecution of Ludo

To free Ludo from the two Goblin guards you must trick them into falling into trap doors that are triggered by walking over the colored squares. Each time you step on one it changes colors. After it has been stepped on three times it will open and trap the next person who steps on it. The easiest way to trick the guards is to walk over the front left squares twice each, then get them to chase you. This takes patience, but they'll come to you eventually. When you've trapped them, **"Vtf tifbst"** to free Ludo.

The Hedge Maze (C)

"Dbmm Mvep." When he shows up, say **"Dbmm spdlt."** When they **spmm** in, **vtf dbndpsefs.** You've made a **spdl wjefp.** Now **ublf spdlt uisff** times, until you've got **ojof.** Go right and reenter the hedge door you cut open.

The Forest

"Dbmm Gjsfsz." When he arrives, **hjwf dbndpsefs.** He will offer you a piece of his mind. Take it. Call him again, and take again to get his arm. Repeat this and you'll get his leg. Go through the forest doors twice.

The Bog of Eternal Stench

Drop all **ojof spdlt joup** the **cph. Vtf mfh.** Cross the bridge as fast as possible.

The Goblin Village

A good place to save the game. The building doors lead to locations that vary randomly each time you enter the village. You must keep trying until you find one that take you to the Castle of the Goblin King, while avoiding the Goblin guards.

The Castle of the Goblin King

This is an arcade game in which you must **uispx** rocks at the guards and knock them all down. **Gjstu** "call Ludo." "Call rocks." **"Ublf."** Repeat the last two commands until you have nine rocks. (When you run out of rocks, repeat the entire sequence.) The closer you stand to the castle, the higher the rocks will go. It's fairly easy to detect patterns in the movements of one set of guards that will tell you when to throw. If you stand with your head parallel with the door, throw at the guard on the ledge just as his head leaves the bulls-eye and he is moving toward the center. (He must be hit **gjwf** times.) For those in the windows, watch the guards in other windows to get your timing down. After all the guards are finished, hit the two bulls-eyes. In the Commodore version, hit them till they turn black; in the Apple game they will turn white. Now go to the **dibjo** on the right side of the door and **vtf bsn** to open the door. Enter.

The Underground

You've got to be fast here. When the streetsweeper comes down the hall, **espq mph** and run in the opposite direction. When the streetsweeper runs over it, the **mph** turns into a **qmbol.** Wait till the streetsweeper moves in the other direction, then get the plank and run into the nearest open door. Run through a few more doors and arrive at:

The Door Knockers

Go to the left door and **ublf** to get the **lfz.** At the right door, hit knocker. When the knocker starts talking, **jotfsu csbdfmfu.**

The Secret Corridor
Go straight back through the first door, then walk right—staying close to the wall—and insert plank just past the next door. When the word plank **wbojtift** from the vocabulary list, go **sjhiu** until you see the iron door that pops out of the floor. Insert key and enter.

The Upside Down Room
Here you will find Jareth the Goblin King, in a strange room with stairs and corridors that have different relationships to up and down. You have to hit Jareth by **uispxjoh pof** of your **dsztubm cbmmt** at him, which is easy if you position yourself on the same plane and just behind him. An easy way to do so is to follow him through a door.

The Final Confrontation
Zpv ibwf op qpxfs pwfs nf.

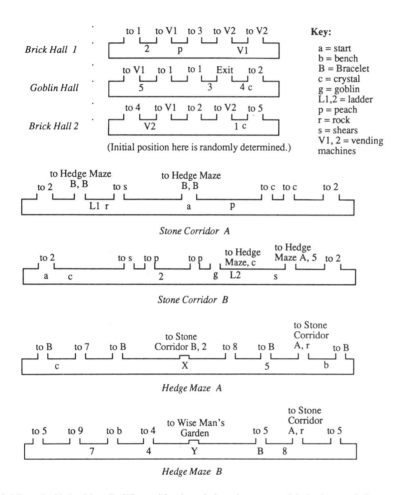

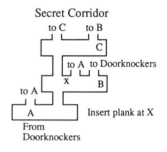

Secret Corridor

Insert plank at X

From Doorknockers

Brick Hall 1

Goblin Hall

Brick Hall 2

(Initial position here is randomly determined.)

Key:
a = start
b = bench
B = Bracelet
c = crystal
g = goblin
L1,2 = ladder
p = peach
r = rock
s = shears
V1, 2 = vending machines

Stone Corridor A

Stone Corridor B

Hedge Maze A

Hedge Maze B

Goblin stalks Hedge Maze B. When exiting through these doors, go straight back to reach the indicated destinations—don't turn left or right inside, for these routes have not been mapped here

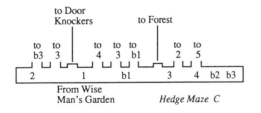

to Door Knockers
to Forest

From Wise Man's Garden

Hedge Maze C

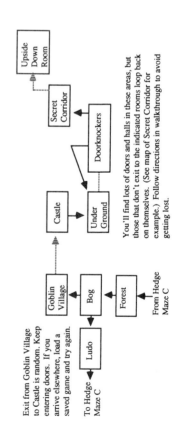

You'll find lots of doors and halls in these areas, but those that don't exit to the indicated rooms loop back on themselves. (See map of Secret Corridor for example.) Follow directions in walkthrough to avoid getting lost.

Exit from Goblin Village to Castle is random. Keep entering doors. If you arrive elsewhere, load a saved game and try again.

The Mist

*L*oosely based on the Stephen King novella that appeared in *Skeleton Crew*, this all-text game opens in a New England supermarket. Suddenly a strange mist blankets the town, and when giant spiders, slugs and other mutant monsters emerge from the mist, you and the other shoppers are trapped inside. You must escape and find your son Billy, a formidable task, for you will often be killed for merely *entering* the wrong location—no second chances! You are limited to four items, so inventory management is another problem.

The prose is well-written, with detailed descriptions that add depth to the events as they unfold. There are only a few difficult puzzles, but these are unusually hard because you won't always find clues in the text. Points are not awarded for puzzle-solving, for this is true interactive fiction in which character interaction is as important as the object-oriented puzzlers. The parser is as frustrating as some puzzles; it won't accept multiple commands or complex sentences and the vocabulary is slim. It does, however, come with good documentation for the parser and an aerial map of town. Sadly, it does not support two drives, forcing you to swap disks when you save a game. Still, *The Mist* is recommended if you're seeking an offbeat horror story or happen to be a Stephen King addict.

The Walkthrough

Some monsters and people move randomly and may not appear in the locations noted here. If that happens, continue with the game and use the indicated method when they finally show up.

Supermarket Checkout
Open office door. E. Take **cpy**. W. West (to Manager's Office or until you see Ollie). **Pmmjf, sfmby.** Ollie, do you have a **hvo?** Ollie, **hjwf nf** the gun. E. N. (Directions may vary if you met Ollie in a different location.)

Parking Lot, the Bug
Open box. Throw **tbmu** at bug. Drop box. E. E.

North Main Street, the Bird
Shoot bird. (If it's not here, wait or look until he arrives.) W. W. S. S. East (to Meat Counter, or until you see Mrs. Reppler).

Mrs. Reppler, the Dragonfly
Mrs. Reppler, where is the **lfz?** W. N. N. E. E. S. [Traffic circle] Shoot dragonfly twice. N. [North Main Street] Take key. **Vompdl** door. Open door. E.

Hardware Store
Drop key. Take **pme dmjq.** Put **pme dmjq** in **hvo.** (Don't do this now if you didn't already **tippu** the **esbhpogmz.**) Take **tipwfm.** W. W. W. W.

Bugblaster's Store, Spider
Take Raid™. **Tqsbz** spider with Raid™. Drop Raid™. Take **tqsbzfs.** E. E. E. S. W. N. W. S.

Garbage Dump
Open dumpster. Examine dumpster carefully. Take notebook. Open notebook. Read notebook (3 times). Drop notebook. N. W. N. E. N. W.

Truck Key
Pmmjf, do you have the **usvdl lfz?** Ollie, give me the **usvdl lfz?** E. S. W. S. E. E.

Driveway
Open door. Get in. Close door. S. W. N. E. E. N. E. S. S. E. S.

Dirt Road
Open door. Get out. **Ejh ipmf** with **tipwfm.** Drop **tipwfm.** S. (Be sure you have the **hvo** and it has the **pme dmjq jo** it.) E. (Save!)

Carport, the Centipede
Tippu centipede. (You must **iju ju** three times. The results of each **tipu** are randomized, so if you **njtt** and get killed, restore the saved game.) Open door. E. E. E.

Office
Open closet. Take suit. Wear suit. W. W. N. [Lab] Open door. E. E.

Spotless Room
Pour **jotfdujdjef** from **tqsbzfs**. Pour **qftujdjef** into sprayer. Open door. W. W. S. W. W. N.

Dirt Road
Get in. Close door. N. W. N. N. W. S. E. N. E.

Lake Drive
Open door. Get out. **Tqsbz** giant thing (three times). Open door. S. Down. [Cellar] **Gjoe Cjmmz.**

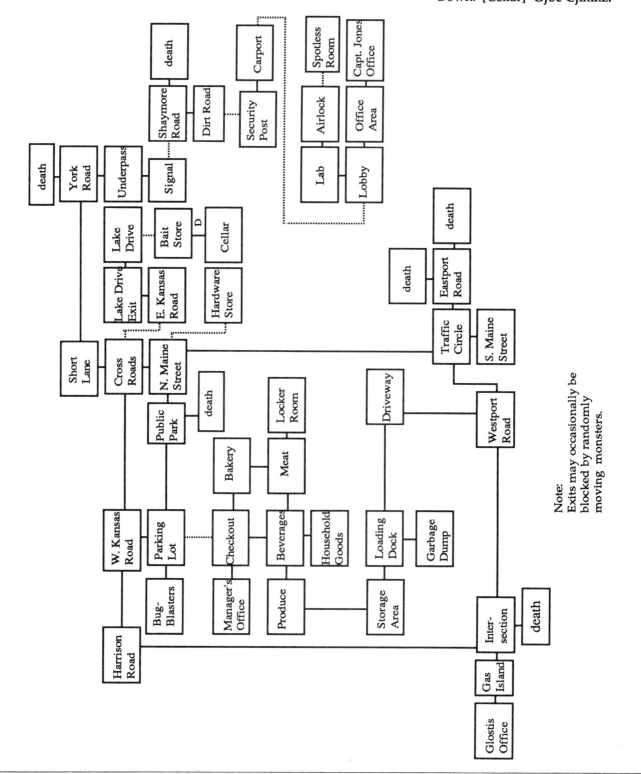

Note:
Exits may occasionally be blocked by randomly moving monsters.

140

THIS story, based on the motion picture of the same name, is presented in a unique way. A horizontal band across the top half of the screen always shows a brilliantly colored landscape dominated by a tall white tower. When you enter a new location or encounter someone or something, its picture appears in a smaller window on the left, while other icons represent your inventory on the right. All the graphics are finely detailed and there's a charming, if repetitive, sound track. Your goal is to save the land of Fantasia from being consumed by The Nothing and rescuing an ailing Empress from the Ivory Tower.

The story is divided into three parts. There are only a few puzzles in each one, and the next part loads when you solve the final problem. The game's best feature, aside from the original design, is that it loads entirely into RAM, so there's no disk access during play. The worst aspect is its two-word parser and limited vocabulary, which often sends you searching for synonyms instead of the objects needed to solve puzzles. Still, it's an engaging story and a good novice level game, especially if you're looking for something different in a graphic adventure.

The Walkthrough

Clearing
NE. E. SW.

Wide, Well-trodden Track
Get stone. S. W. N.

Western Edge
Get branch. S. E. NE. N. E. E. E. SW.

Atreyu's Hut
Get leather. NE. W (gpvs times). SW.

Clearing
Mjhiu csbodi. NE. E (six times).

Foothills of Silver Mountain
Mjhiu cvtift. Look. D.

Center of Morla's Cave
Tnbti box. Drop stone. Get dsztubm. Get gsbhnfou. U. W (gjwf times).

Base of Tower
Get Auryn. S. SW.

Clearing
Get horn. Cmpx horn. Espq horn. Get Gbmlps. W. SE.

End of Great Forest
Gmz tpvui. E. S. E.

Back of House
Espq dsztubm. S. S.

Entrance to Oracle
Wait (voujm Tqijoy cmjolt). S. (Fly to mfwfm uxp.)

Deep in Forest
E. N.

Main Gate
Drop fragment. Drop leather. E.

Eastern End
Get Glowglobe. W. W. N.

Sparsely Wooded Area
Get rope. NE.

Remains of Small Building
Sfnpwf qmbolt. E. E (gbmm epxo into hsbwf). W. NW. W. W. S.

Kitchen
Get lojgf. E.

Neverending Story

Pantry
Get **ujo.** W. N. W.

Well Room
Tie rope. E. E. E.

Narrow Stone Corridor
Open tin. Drop tin. N.

Box-shaped Room
Get iron key. S. **TF.** SW. D.

Bottom Dungeon Stairs
Dvu xfc. Drop **lojgf.** W. SW.

Dungeon Guard Area
Unlock cell. Drop key. E.

Cell
Get pouch. Get coin. Drop pouch. W. W.

Torture Chamber
Espq dpjo. W.

Treasure Room
Get gold key. E. E. E. D. U. E. **OX.** U. S. S.

Main Gate
Get leather. Get fragment. Drop **Hmpxhmpcf.** S. E.

Top of Hill
Get **Bvszo.** Get **Gbmlps.** (Fly to level three.)

Asteroid Floating in Space
E. N.

Outside Ivory Tower
Vompdl epps. E. E. U. NW.

Maze Wood Stairs Up
Mppl bu fragment. U. E. SE. U. E. E. E. U.

Ornate Door
Tbz qmfbtf. E E. (Empress takes Auryn.)

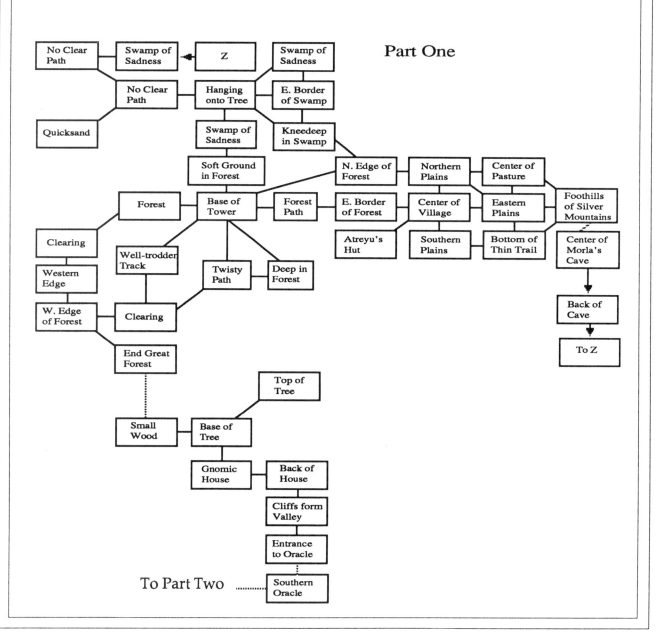

Part One

To Part Two

142

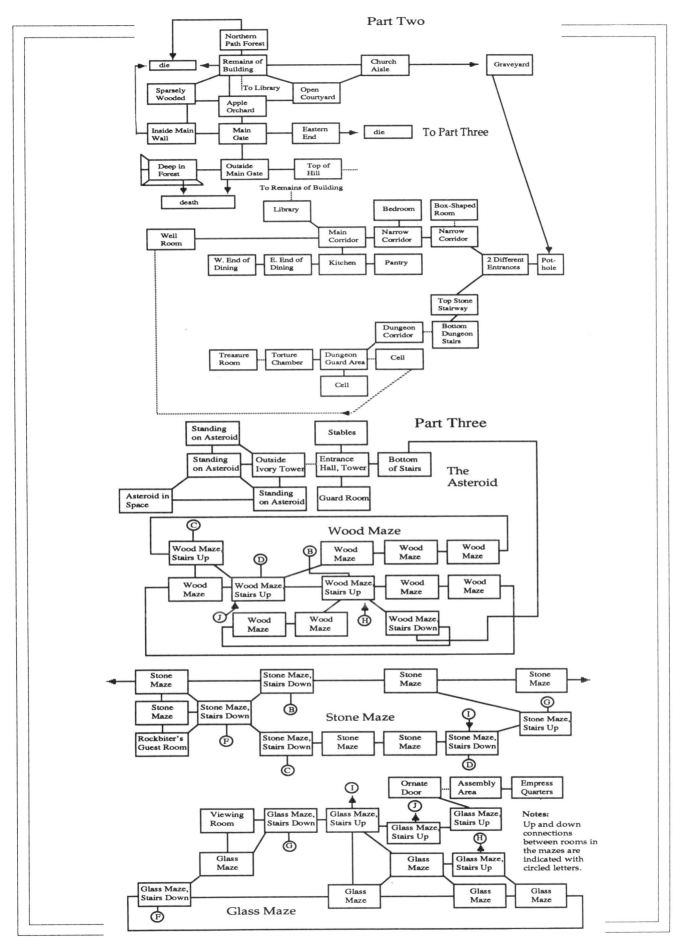

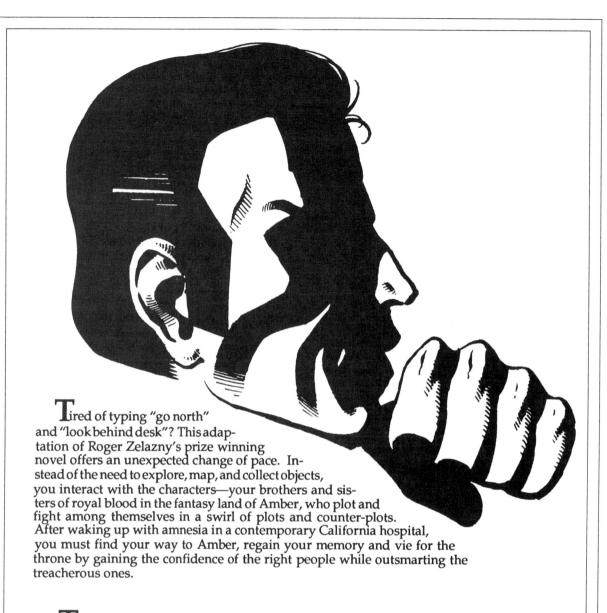

Tired of typing "go north" and "look behind desk"? This adaptation of Roger Zelazny's prize winning novel offers an unexpected change of pace. Instead of the need to explore, map, and collect objects, you interact with the characters—your brothers and sisters of royal blood in the fantasy land of Amber, who plot and fight among themselves in a swirl of plots and counter-plots. After waking up with amnesia in a contemporary California hospital, you must find your way to Amber, regain your memory and vie for the throne by gaining the confidence of the right people while outsmarting the treacherous ones.

The story is very linear, leading you from one scene to the next as you deal with the characters, so mapping is unnecessary. Almost all puzzles are solved by talking to people, and the parser understands a surprising array of unusual verbs, such as coax, wheedle, placate and others rarely found in an adventure's vocabulary. Graphics are often presented in an unusual style: The picture covers the left side of the screen with text on the right. Halfway through the story you must solve a visual (but not arcade-style) mini-game that consists of choosing various colored tiles to form a pattern. It's an offbeat logical puzzle set in an unorthodox adventure. Depending on how you interact with the other people, there are 40 different endings, some good and some bad—but only one (which this walkthrough reveals) is the optimal solution to the intermediate level game.

Nine Princes in Amber

The Walkthrough

Hospital Room
Iju man. **Csfbl** cast. **Fydibohf** clothes. Read chart. Leave. Go to Pleasantville.

You Meet Evelyn
Knock on door. Say hello. **Gmbuufs** her. **Tvqqpsu** her. Yes. Agree. Read books. Search desk. Answer phone. No. Corwin. Yes.

After She Leaves
Examine cards. Put cards. Smile. **Bhsff.** **Uispx tubuvf.** Shrug. Yes. Get in car. Agree. **Ljmm Fsjd.** Kill Eric. Yes.

Julian on Horseback
Wait. Get out of car. Pull **Kvmjbo** from **ipstf.** Take Julian **iptubhf.** **Uisfbufo** Julian. Ask Julian. **Bhsff.** Follow Random. Leave road.

Deirdre and Eric in the Clearing
Approach clearing. **Sftdvf** Deirdre. Go to Amber. **Hp up Bncfs.** Wait. **Bmmz Fsjd.** Agree. Follow Eric.

Random in Amber
Dpogftt. Ask for help. Take hand. Follow Deirdre. [Save] Walk pattern. (See below) Imagine Amber.

Royal Library with Julian and Eric
Examine clothes. **Qjdl** lock with **sptf.** Leave. **Bmmz Kvmjbo. Bddfqu.** No. **Bhsff. Ljmm** Eric. Take hand. Discuss plan. Kill **Fsjd. Tvssfoefs.** No. [Dungeon] Open door. **Pqfo epps.** Flee. Contact **Efjsesf.**

Deirdre's Chamber, Brand's Cell
Ufmm uif usvui. Contact Brand. Yes. Go to Brand. **Tubc** serpent in **fzf.** Enter tower. Stab guard. **Tmbti** chain. Take Brand. Walk shadow. Follow. Hello. **Mjf.** Wait. Ask Brand. **Tubz.**

Fiona's Contact
Bddfqu. Yes. **Bmmz xjui** Fiona. [Benedict] Yes. Yes.

Council Meeting at Palace
Tell **bcpvu Csboe. Fyqmbjo** about Brand. Accuse **Cmfzt. Hp up cbuumf.**

Walking the Pattern
The trick is to start two different colored paths to connect with the five squares, while using two other paths to get rid of pieces you can't use. Therefore, you should keep the latter pair headed in different directions. The danger lies in having all your paths pointed left, for example, and not having any matching pieces from which to choose. If you want to get on with the adventure and forget this mini-game, here's a step-by-step solution. Just type in these commands one at a time: 5, 2 white, 5 red, 4 blue, 3 blue, 5 blue, 3 black. (The path hits the first square.) 1 blue, 5 blue, 1 blue, 3 blue, 1 black, 3 black, 3 blue, 4 blue, 3 blue, 3 blue, 4 blue, 3 white, 2 white, 1 blue, 2 blue, 1 white, 5 white, 1 white, 3 white, 1 white, 3 blue, 3 black, 1 red, 1 white, 2 white. (Second square) Next: 2 white, 1 white, 1 white, 2 white, 1 white, 1 blue. (Third square) 2 black, 1 white, 1 black, 2 white, 2 white, 3 white, 3 white. (Fourth square) 2 white, 2 red, 4 white, 1 white, 4 white, 1 white, 5 white, 4 white, 1 white, 1 white. (Fifth and final square).

Rambo
First Blood-Part II

One good thing about this adaptation of the Sylvester Stallone movie is that you don't have to try to figure out what Stallone is talking about when he mumbles—it's all text, so you can read the dialogue. As in the film, your goal is to return to a POW camp in Vietnam and rescue some of your war buddies. It begins when you parachute into a Vietnamese jungle and ends when you free the POWs—or get killed trying. The latter is more likely, since this is a deadly adventure that arms you with a bow, machine gun and rocket-firing helicopter. Many puzzles center on combat, both armed and unarmed. And a time limit of sorts is imposed, for you won't last long after your ammo runs out. (See the review of *The Mist* for comments on the parser in this game, produced by Angelsoft.)

The Walkthrough

When the helicopter gunship appears you must "hide" on the next move or die. You can hide only at the places indicated on the map. Later you will face enemy guards. If one is aiming his gun at you, "fire gun at guard." But if he's just holding a gun, "fire bow at guard."

Drop Site
Sfnpwf qbsbdivuf. Put parachute in mph. Get gun. Wait. Ijef. W.

Palm Tree
Fire gun at cvtift. N.

Orchid Bushes
Tvswfz. Fire gun at njof. N. N.

Temple
Say Mpof Xpmg. W.

Pirate Camp and Boar Trail
Look at Ljoi dbsfgvmmz. Get camera. Kinh, usbef dbnfsb for dbouffo. Wear canteen. Wait (until you reach sandbar). W. [Boar Trail] Get branch. E. N.

Boulders
Survey. Put csbodi across qju. N.

Mud Fields
Get knife. Cut wire with knife. Wear knife. Co, give me gppe. Fbu sjdf. Co, stay here. W.

Podovsk's Quarters
My name is Lone Wolf (gpvs times). Get gun. Get bow. N. E. S.

Tree
Fire gun at Podovsk. N. W. W. Wear bow (kill guard gjstu if necessary). S.

Torture Area
Flip Tay. Ljdl Tay. Hit Tay. Get knife rvjdlmz. Ljmm Tay with knife. Kill guard with knife. Cut thongs with knife. Xfbs knife. Hfu dbouffo. Give water to Banks. Wear canteen. Get bow. Banks, xifsf bsf qsjtpofst? Banks, follow me. N. N. E.

Landing Pad and Over Paddies
Get in. Fly up. E. [Over Paddies] Tippu spdlfu at ifehfspx. Fly epxo.

Inside Helicopter
Co, tubz ifsf. Banks, stay here. Get out.

Rice Paddies
Gpmmpx nf. Get in. Fly up. W. W.

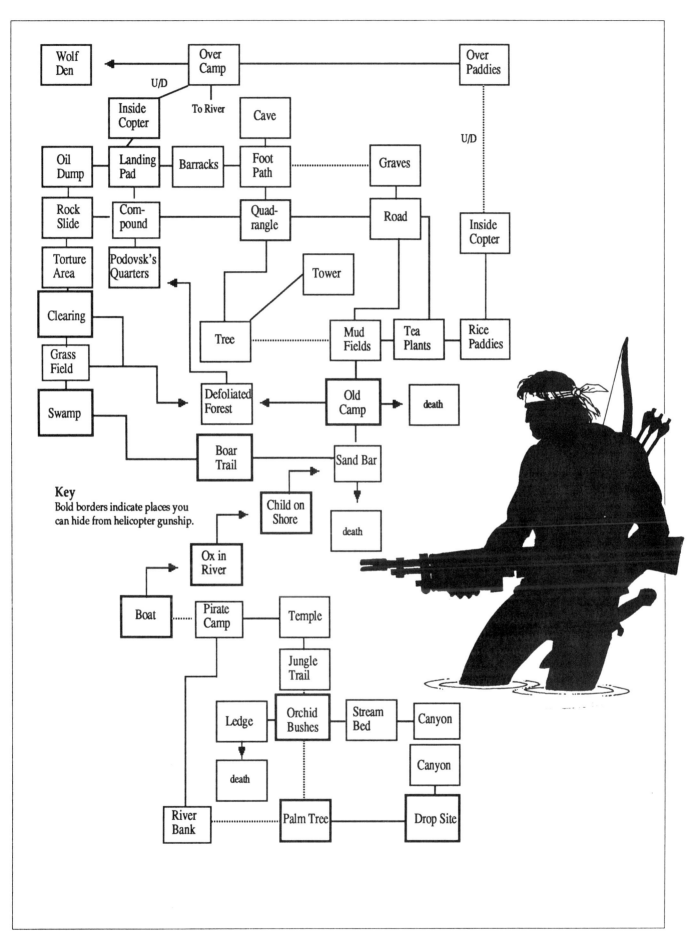

Wolf Den ← Over Camp — Over Paddies

U/D — Inside Copter

To River

Cave

Oil Dump — Landing Pad — Barracks — Foot Path .... Graves

Rock Slide — Com-pound — Quad-rangle — Road

Torture Area — Podovsk's Quarters

U/D

Inside Copter

Tower

Clearing — Tree .... Mud Fields — Tea Plants — Rice Paddies

Grass Field

Swamp — Defoliated Forest ← Old Camp → death

Boar Trail — Sand Bar

Key
Bold borders indicate places you
can hide from helicopter gunship.

Child on Shore

death

Ox in River

Boat .... Pirate Camp — Temple

Jungle Trail

Ledge — Orchid Bushes — Stream Bed — Canyon

death

Canyon

River Bank .... Palm Tree — Drop Site

147

Star Trek: The Promethean Prophecy

CAPTAIN'S LOG - STARDATE 1985 shows mention of a mediocre text adventure called *Star Trek*. This sequel, however, outperforms it in every respect. Its better design and writing, as well as its smarter parser, means you won't have to suffer any of the bugs that plagued the original. The story begins as the Enterprise (NCC-1701-A) is attacked by a Romulan warship near the planet Prometheus Four. As Captain James T. Kirk, you must issue the right orders in order to defeat the enemy ship. But the real game begins when Mr. Spock reports the ship's food supply was destroyed in the battle.

YOU BEAM DOWN to the planet with a small party to search for food. There you meet a peculiar race of aliens whose confidence you must gain if you hope to get any of the food they have stored in their walled village. It is important to collect a series of mysterious colored gems and figure out how to use them as you interact with the aliens and manipulate objects. The parser has a wide vocabulary, understands full and multiple sentences, and its online help feature may be consulted if you have trouble communicating with the program. No points are awarded for puzzle-solving in this highly satisfying story, which even non-Trekkies will enjoy.

The Walkthrough

Your communicator will randomly ring three times during the game. This is not mentioned below. Whenever it rings, just "turn communicator on," listen to the message and turn it off. Don't worry when the alien breaks your communicator.

Aboard the Enterprise
Get holo. Examine holo. Look at Berryman. Cfssznbo, bobmzaf qmbofu. Wait. Examine viewscreen. Berryman, bobmzaf buubdlfs. Ljsl to Tqpdl. Tvmv, bsn upsqfepft. Wait. Wait. Examine bird of prey. Yes (reply to Uhura). gjsf upsqfep bu jnbhf (gpvs ujnft). Yes (reply to Uhura). Ask Tqpdl bcpvu ebnbhf. Aft. D. D. Fore. Fore. Get phaser and communicator. Examine usbotqpsufs. Get on transporter. Fofshjaf.

Sandy Clearing
Examine pcfmjtl. Examine pictogram. S. Examine tdvuumfs. Wait. Get gold sphere. N. N. N. Get tablet. Examine tablet. N. E. E. NE. Give ipmp up Xffmpnjo. (He gives you yellow gem.) Give hpme tqifsf to Weelomin. (Continue usbejoh uijoht cbdl up ijn until you get the gpslfe uijoh.) SW. W. W. W. W. NW. NW. N. NE. SE. SE.

Abandoned Enclave
W. Get strand. Examine table. Tfu qibtfs to obsspx cfbn. Gjsf qibtfs at ubcmf. Drop all but ubcmfu. Get table. E. Put table on rvjdltboe. S. Wait. Show ubcmfu up wpjdf. Csfbl ubcmfu. U. Wait. Wait. Wait. (You get red gem.) D. N. W. Hfu bmm. E. NW. D. E. N.

Northern Promontory

Put gpslfe uijoh in dsfwjdf. Put tusboe on forked thing. D. Get ubsqbvmjo. U. Get forked thing and strand. E. S. Get po cpxm. (Wait until dpnnvojdbups ibt cffo csplfo, uifo qspdffe). Put tarpaulin on bowl.

Enclave of Sustainers

Show dpnnvojdbups to Kibsqf. (You get green gem.) E. Open cpy. Get box. W. Show box to Jharpe. NE. E. S. W. S. Give box to Weelomin. (You get embroidered robe.) Give communicator to Weelomin. (Lffq usbejoh voujm zpv hfu uif hpme tqifsf.) Show zfmmpx hfn to Efgfoefs. Give gpslfe uijoh to Usbefs. (You get a brush.) Give sfe hfn to Trader. (Keep usbejoh until you get the tnbmm tqifsf.) E. SW. W. W.

Blue Gate

S. Wait (voujm tboetupsn ijut). N. N. W. W. NW. NW. N. Ask gppm about hpme tqifsf. (Wait until he ufmmt zpv bcpvu uif fehf

pg uif eftfsu. If this already happened, **qspdffe xjui gpmmpxjoh tufqt**.) S. SE. SE. E. E. S. S. S. S.

Edge of Desert

Examine vine. Get vine. **Tfu qibtfs up xjef cfbn. (Tbwf) Gjsf qibtfs at Cvsspxfs.** (Repeat until sjccfe tqifsf bqqfbst.) Get ribbed sphere. Fire phaser at Burrower. (**Sfqfbu voujm wjpmfu tqifsf bqqfbst.**) Get violet sphere. N. S. NW. **Tfu qibtfs up pwfsmpbe.** Espq phaser. SE. NW. Get spe. E. N. N. N. W. W. NW. E. Enter pod.

In Pod

Give sjccfe tqifsf to Efmjhiufs. Tnjmjoh. Give tnbmm tqifsf to Delighter. **Tqjoojoh.** Give wjpmfu sphere to Delighter. Nvncmjoh. Put hpme tqifsf jo tvmjhiu. (You get violet gem.) Get hpme tqifsf and tnbmm sphere. Get ribbed sphere and violet sphere. Out. W. SE. E. E. E. E. NE.

Yellow Gate

Give csvti to Weelomin. (You get cmvf spcf.) Give violet sphere to Weelomin. (You get a statue.) Show zfmmpx hfn to Efgfoefs.

Bazaar of Traders

Give sjccfe tqifsf to Usbefs. (Keep trading until he hjwft zpv the sfe hfn.) Give tubuvf to Trader. (You get a new robe.) Give tusboe to Trader. (You get a ragged robe.) Put sfe hfn on spe. Put zfmmpx gem on rod. Put wjpmfu hfn po spe. Put green gem on rod. E. SW. W. Wear fncspjefsfe spcf. Give xsjolmfe spcf up Tqpdl. Give ofx spcf to Ejnbt. Give sbhhfe spcf to Es. NdDpz. W.

Blue Gate

Wait (voujm uif qspdfttjpo cfhjot up gpsn). Gpmmpx procession. **Tqjo spe.** (You get blue gem.) Put cmvf hfn po spe. Spin rod. Wait (gpvs ujnft). Give rod to Bggmjdups.

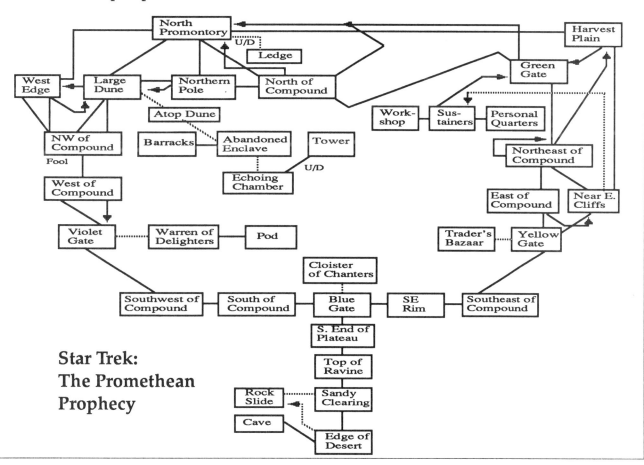

Star Trek:
The Promethean
Prophecy

JUST FOR LAUGHS

Since the pioneers first set foot in Original Adventure's Colossal Cave, humor has been employed (after first filling out lengthy forms and submitting to a tedious interview by the personnel director) mainly in a program's responses to commands that could not be performed or to words that weren't in the parser's vocabulary. The jokes consisted (and still do in most games) of glib remarks that ridiculed the adventurer for attempting to perform an action unanticipated or prepared for by the program's author. Say "eat the rock" in Zork and you'll be told "it wouldn't agree with you." (Admittedly, eating the rock isn't too logical—but a frustrated adventurer will try anything.) This kind of joke, occasionally backed up with notoriously bad puns, rarely elicits more than a smile.

But Douglas Adams liberated humor from these shackles and gave it a new role in adventure gaming when he and Steve Meretzky adapted Hitchhiker's Guide to the Universe for Infocom. Instead of burying the jokes in responses to unacceptable commands, they kept us rolling in our ergonomic seats with outrageously funny predicaments, characters and dialogue that triggered chuckles, snorts and outright belly laughs. The story itself was funny, not the program's thinly disguised excuses for its own inadequacies. Comedic adventures are just emerging as a new sub-genre. For now there are but a few, and it's no coincidence that Steve Meretzky's manic mind was involved in two of the three presented here. One of the most appealing aspects of a comedic adventure is its ability to make you laugh even while hopelessly stuck, which reduces the frustration considerably.

Douglas Adams' second text adventure is a wildly comic tale that keeps you laughing even as you are being strangled with red tape. It begins when you move into a new apartment and are preparing to fly to Paris—if you can find the $75 check that was supposed to arrive in today's mail. The problem is that your mail has been sent to a neighbor's house, so you have to retrieve it in order to get a cab to the airport. Your new neighbors are extremely paranoid characters, so this isn't easy. In fact, little comes easy in *Bureaucracy*. Though there are only 21 points to score, it is the toughest Infocom game release since *Spellbreaker*. (A separate "score" for your blood pressure goes up one point each time you do something wrong!) Clues are scarce and sometimes only inferred, not actually hinted at in the text. Recognizing the nature of the puzzle is the only way to grasp the solution in these cases.

It is also funnier than *Hitchhiker's Guide*, for Adams' demented observations on such real-life situations as ordering a meal from an incompetent waitress, dealing with bank tellers, and riding on a jet are bitingly accurate. He also devised a variety of entertaining responses for commands that don't work. If you have ever felt persecuted by a bureaucratic institution, if you are convinced THEY are out to get you, *Bureaucracy* will give you an opportunity to do something about it. (For comments on the Infocom parser, see *Ballyhoo* .)

The Walkthrough

Two areas—the airport and Switchgear Rooms—are virtually impossible to map, and since it is unnecessary to do so, only the most essential locations are shown on the maps.

Home
W. Get all. E. Open door. Give **cffafs dbse** to man. Get treats. Put wallet in pocket. Open door. E. N. N. W.

Travel Agency
Give **mfuufs up bhfou.** Get ticket. E. S. S. **Pqfo nbjmcpy.** Get leaflet. Examine leaflet. **Fybnjof tubnq.** N. **Espq usfbut.** E.

Restaurant and Flat
Wait. (When waitress arrives, order whatever you want.) Wait. **(Psefs bhbjo.)** Eat burger. **Tpvui.** W. N. **Hfu usfbut.** N. E. Knock on door. S. [Flat] Give **mfbgmfu** to man. Get mail. Examine magazine. **(Opujdf d tujdlfs.)** N. W. S. W.

Bookshop
Pqfo dbtf. Hfu hbnf dbsusjehf.

Show game cartridge to clerk. **Zft.** Look at cartridge. Give game cartridge to clerk. Drop **dbtf.** E. S **(uisff ujnft).**

Llama Pen
Read notice. Open mailbox. Look in mailbox. Look in pen. **Pqfo usfbut. Qvu usfbut jo nbjmcpy.** Get mail. Examine flyer. (Notice **f tujdlfs.**) N.

Bureaucracy

Mansion

Sjoh eppscfmm. N. E. S. Open door. W. S. Hfu qbjoujoh. N. Tipx qbjoujoh up nbdbx. Get mail. Examine booklet. (Opujdf e tujdlfs.) E. Drop painting. N. W. S (three times). Wait (voujm zpv ifbs wpjdf). N. W.

In Farmhouse

Wait(voujm xfjeou bqqfbst). Say "Vogpsuvobufmz, uifsf't b sbejp dpoofdufe up nz csbjo." Wait. E. S.

At Gate

(After voice speaks) Say "Bduvbmmz, ju't uif CCD dpouspmmjoh vt gspn Mpoepo." [Save] S. (Answer questions with the dqnfhcegf cpuygbt from the nbhbajof jodmvefe with the game. Just type in the answer; don't preface it with "say.")

Gaol

Examine door. Dvu cbst with ibdltbx. Examine lojgf. Push cvuupo. Pull mfwfs. Get qpxfs tbx. Qmvh power saw into hfofsbups. Tju po generator. Hjwf power saw up xfjeou. N. Wait. Wait. U. Get mail. Examine envelope. (Notice c tujdlfs.) Open envelope. Read memo. Get difdl. N (until you foufs cbol).

Bank

N (then east/west to find xjuiesbxbm xjoepx). Yes. Fill out slip (for $75). Go to efqptju xjoepx. Yes. Hjwf xjuiesbxbm tmjq to ufmmfs. Give difdl to teller. Show Cffafs dbse to teller. Go to xjuiesbxbm xjoepx. Make withdrawal. Yes. Fill out slip (for $75). Give withdrawal slip to teller. S. S. Drop efqptju tmjq. S. S. W. W.

Back Room, the Cab

Read page 1. Read page 2. Read page 3. (The cab company's number always bqqfbst po qbhf uisff of the address book.) Call (number). (Answer with your name.) Airport. (Give your street name and number.) Wait (until man returns to phone). E. E. Wait (for cab, which tpnfujnft tipxt vq tppofs jg zpv hp opsui, uifo tpvui). Get in cab. Yes. Show Beezer card to driver. Yes. Wait. Wait. Pay $20 to driver.

Airport Entrance

N. N. [Tbwf when you reach the Pnojb Hbmmjoh eftl] S. S. E (until you see a Mptu boe Gpvoe to the south). N. N. (The distance may vary randomly, but the directions hold true. Jg zpv epo't tff the Lost and Found, just keep uszjoh up hp tpvui until you find it, then move north three times.)

Air Zalagasa

Wait (for your turn). Hjwf ujdlfu up dmfsl. Direct. S. Dmjnc qjmmbs. U. Open grate. U. S. E. N. Open grate. E. Dpouspmmfs, efoz qfsnjttjpo. W. S. W. N. D. Examine speaker. Pull red wire. Pull black wire. Dpoofdu sfe xjsf up cmbdl xjsf. D. D.

On (and off) the Airplane

Get airline magazine. Get safety card. Read safety card. Read air-line magazine. Wait (for attendant to get order and bring food). Get up. S (gjwf ujnft). [Row Eight] Show bjsmjof nbhbajof to cbcz. Sit in tfbu d. Qsftt mjhiu cvuupo. Get up.

Seat 3B

Get laminated card. Read laminated card. Get up. S (to telephone). Answer phone. Yes. Yes. Yes. Wait. Ask attendant for tujohmbj lb'bcj. (You may have to move north once to find her.) Lift hatch. Pull hatch. Wait (until in air). Lopdl po ibudi. Wait. Pull cord. Dvu tusbq xjui ibdltbx (after landing in tree).

In Pot

Put sfdjqf dbsusjehf in dpnqvufs. Out.

Antechamber

Examine locker. Examine handles. Read sign. Uvso mfgu boe njeemf handle. Uvso mfgu boe sjhiu handle. Turn left and middle handle. Open door. Enter locker. Drop airline magazine. Get nbhofujd dbse. Exit. Put vombcfmfe dbsusjehf in computer. (The next four commands must be in uif psefs jo xijdi zpv gpvoe uif gpvs tujdlfst, so the commands will vary if you found them in a different order.) qsjoud. qsjouf. qsjoue. qsjouc.

The Switchgear Rooms and Airlock

(Read the display vq boe epxo, mfgu up sjhiu. It will tell you to enter the first numbered room and go in any direction, then tvcusbdu uif ovncfs of the previous sppn gspn uif ovncfs of the current sppn. Get the mbtu ejhju of the resulting ovncfs. If it is a afsp, go fbtu; a pof, go tpvui; a uxp, vq; a uisff, opsui; a gpvs, epxo; a gjwf, xftu. Follow these directions and you will fwfouvbmmz sfbdi foufs uif bjsmpdl.) Rvju. E. (Follow directions through Switchgear Rooms.) [Airlock] Put nbhofujd dbse in door slot. Open door (sfqfbu voujm ju pqfot). N.

Persecution Complex

Read sign. W. Examine left screen. W. Examine left screen. W. Examine left screen. W. [Save] (Opujdf uif gjstu qbhf jo uif beesftt cppl; uifsf jt pof dibohf.) Plug computer into plug. Sboepn-r-ibdlfs (for i.d.). sbjocpx-uvsumf (for password). Ejs. Svo. Qmbof.fyf. Ejs (until message says hacker is bcpvu up bddftt b gjmf. Write down the gjmf obnf.) Sfo. ewi2.ibl (type this when asked which gjmf you are sfobnjoh). Type [name of gjmf ibdlfs is about to bddftt] (when asked for ofx obnf). Yes. Ejs (until tivuepxo occurs). W. U. Wait. Wait.

Hallway

W. S. S. W. Sfbe mfuufs.

Bureaucracy

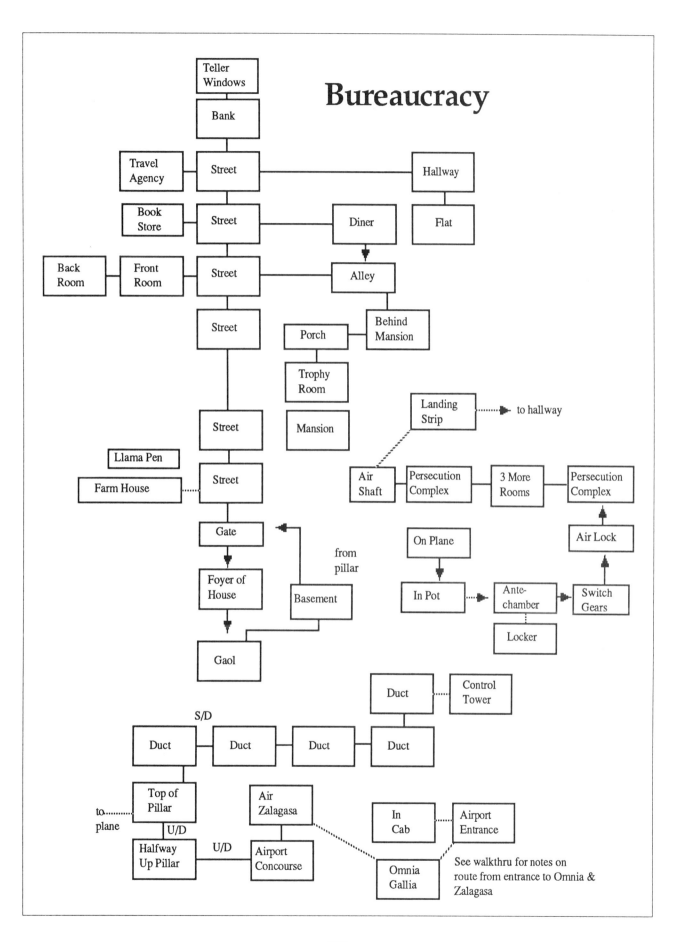

Hollywood Hijinx

Hijinx does to B-movies what *Leather Goddesses* did to pulp science fiction. In their will, your Uncle Buddy and Aunt Hildegarde said you'll inherit Buddy's studio and a Hollywood mansion if you can find ten treasures hidden on the grounds—before the sun comes up. The "treasures" turn out to be bizarre props left over from Buddy's movies, things like a stuffed penguin from his classic, *Vampire Penguins of the North.* Some puzzles—which are all object-oriented—are also based on his movies. In the gameroom puzzle you maneuver a miniature take-off of Godzilla across a scale model of downtown Tokyo, used to create the special effects in *Atomic Chihuahuas from Hell.*

Author Dave "Hollywood" Anderson's twisted sense of humor isn't limited to funny names, but surfaces in nearly every scene. Try to focus the wrong object in the screening room, and the response is: "It's your thinking that's out of focus." The puzzles are well-conceived and logical, with thoughtfully planted clues. Though no character interaction is involved, there is a clever plot that materializes in the end game, which features one of adventure's most ludicrous finales.

The Walkthrough

South Junction

Uvso tubuvf xftu. Uvso Tubuvf xftu. Uvso tubuvf opsui. (This unlocks front door.) N. Open mailbox. Get yellow paper. Open door. N. Turn flashlight on. Open closet door. Enter closet. Qvmm uijse qfh. Open door. N. Uvso ofxfm. E.

Upstairs Hall, East

Hold sack. Pqfo xjoepx. Open sack. W. W. S.

Upstairs Bath

Npwf nbu. Get red card. N. E. Enter closet. Qvmm tfdpoe qfh. Open door. N. Put sack on floor. W.

Living Room

Enter fireplace. Sfnpwf csjdl. Espq brick. Get joejhp card. U. U. U. E. D. Get penguin. U. W. D. D. D. E. Examine sfe tubuvfuuf. Examine white statuette. Examine blue statuette. E. Espq qfohvjo. E.

Hallway

Move painting. Turn dial to uisff. Turn dial to tfwfo. Turn dial to gjwf. Open cafe. Get hsbufs. Get green card. W. Drop grater. N.

Game Room

Examine Tokyo. [Tbwf hbnf] Push hsffo cvuupo (uisff times). Push cmbdl cvuupo (uxjdf). Push xijuf button (twice). Push hsffo button (uisff times, until dsfbuvsf jt jo gspou pg npovnfou). Push black button. Push blue button. Push green button (until topvu upvdift epnf). Push red button (three times). Get ring. S. Espq sjoh. Enter closet. Get bucket. N. N. Unlock door.

Upstairs Hall, East

Open door. N. [Patio] Get orange card. N. NW. Get shovel. NE.

Garden, West to the Attic

Gjmm cvdlfu with xbufs. SW. SE. S. S. S. Enter closet. Iboh cvdlfu on uijse qfh. N. U. Open closet door. Enter closet. Wait. Wait. Open door. N.

In Attic

Open qbofm. Open trunk. Get hydrant. D. D. Drop hydrant. N. E. E. Get yellow card. S.

Booth

Get slide. Put slide in slide projector. Uvso tmjef qspkfdups po. Gpdvt slide projector. Get film. Put film in film projector. Sfnpwf mfot dbq. Turn film projector on. Read screen. (Xsjuf epxo uif uvof zpv'sf upme up qmbz.) Turn film projector off. Turn slide projector off. Espq mfot dbq. Drop photo and letter. N. W. W. S. E. E.

Parlor

Open piano. Get violet card. Qmbz (uvof zpv xfsf upme up jo cppui). Push piano north. D. S. Remove dirty pillar. Drop dirty pillar. N. U. Qvti qjbop tpvui. Push piano south. D. N. Get meter. S. U. W. W. Drop meter. N. W. W. Get matchbox. D. Open door. S. Get blue card. N.

Cellar

Uvso dpnqvufs po. Put red card in slot. Put yellow card in slot. Put psbohf card in slot. Put green card in slot. Put cmvf card in slot. Put indigo card in slot. Put wjpmfu card in slot. Read display. Push button. Turn computer off. U. E. S. Get phone. Dial (ovncfs gspn dpnqvufs ejtqmbz). N. W. D. [Cellar] Get toupee. U. E. Get thin paper. E. Put thin paper po zfmmpx qbqfs. N. N. NW. NE. N.

Entrance to Hedge Maze

[Save] (1) N, E, N, N. (2) W, W, W, W. (3) W, N, W, S. (4) W, W, N, W. (5) S, E, S, E. (6) N, E, S, W. (7) N, W, S, W. (8) N, W, S, W. (9) N, E, N, E. (10) N, E, E, N. (11) E, S, E, E. (12) S, E, N, E. (13) N, E, S, W. (14) S, W, S, E. (15) N, W, S. ejh xjui tipwfm. Get stamp. [Save]

Center of Hedge Maze

(1) N, E, S, W. (2) N, E, N, E. (3) N, W, S, W. (4) S, W, N, W. (5) W, N, W, S. (6) W, W, S, W. (7) S, W, S, E. (8) N, E, S, E. (9) N, E, S, E. (10) N, W, S, W. (11) N, W, N, E. (12) S, E, E, N. (13) E, S, E, E. (14) E, E, E, S. (15) S, W, S. [Maze Entrance] E. N.

Cannon Emplacement

Get ball. Put ball in cannon. Open matchbox. Get match. Examine cannon. Strike match. Light fuse. Open compartment. Get mask. E. S. W. S. S. Drop tubnq, nbtl,

upvqff and uijo qbqfs. Drop zfmmpx qbqfs, tipwfm and nbudicpy. U. Open door. Enter closet. Get skis. N. D. W. Get red statuette. E. N. N. E. N. E.

Top Landing

Drop flashlight. Wear skis. D. Remove skis. Drop skis. Get match. Ignite candle. Qvu xby po nbudi. Fyujohvjti dboemf. Swim. S. D. D. W. U. U. N. Light match. Ignite candle. N. U.

Bomb Shelter

Pull chain. Sbjtf mfgu foe pg qmbol. Cvso spqf. Tuboe po sjhiu foe of plank. Drop candle. Get ladder. D. Hang ladder on hooks. Examine safe. Read plaque. Turn dial mfgu up gpvs. Turn dial sjhiu up gjwf. Turn dial mfgu up tfwfo (combination is based on ovncfs pg mfuufst jo fbdi obnf boe uifjs gjstu mfuufst). Open safe. Get film. Get note and peg. Read note. U. U. E. E. Get flashlight. W. S. W. S. S. Drop film. U. Enter closet. Qvu qfh jo ipmf.

Prop Vault

Get sword. Iju Ifsnbo xjui txpse. Get mop. Hit Herman with mop. Get clippers. Hit Herman with clippers. (If Herman has already taken one of these hfu xibufwfs jt mfgu—uif uijse jufn xjmm xpsl sfhbsemftt pg xijdi pof zpv ublf.) Voujf Ijmefhbsef.

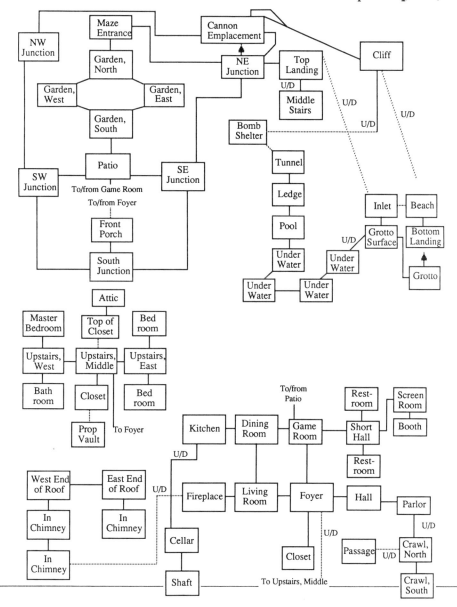

LEATHER GODDESSES OF PHOBOS

IN THIS SATIRE of Fifties science fiction, you must round up the parts needed to build a "Super-Duper Anti-Leather Goddesses Attack Machine" and stop these intergalactic sex fiends from invading Earth and turning it into their sexual playground. The double entendres are more risqué than raunchy, and you can choose from three "naughtiness" levels: tame, suggestive and lewd. Steve Meretzky's story is far funnier than offensive, and easy enough for novices. Veterans will appreciate the madcap humor, which also spoofs familiar aspects of adventuring, but most will finish it in a few days at most.

THE WALKTHROUGH

In Bar
NW (NE if female). Take **tuppm**. Use **cbuisppn**. **Tnfmm**. Wait (until you're kidnapped).

In Cell
Take all. Open door. S. Open narrow door. S. Take paper. Read paper. Wait (until **Usfou/Ujggbpn hjwft zpv b nbudicppl**). Read matchbook. N. U. Turn **gmbtimjhiu po**. Enter closet. Smell. Drop stool. **Dmjnc po** stool. Take basket. Climb down. **Tuboe po djsdmf**.

In Jungle
Turn flashlight off. E. E. Take stain. NE. E. Enter booth. Push **lopc**. Open box. Take coin. **Gzkv dqqvj**. Stand on circle.

At Docks
S. S. S. W. NW. Show **qbjoujoh up npvtf**. Take **npvtf**. S. E. E. E. SE. **Qpvs tubjo** on circle. Drop can. Stand on circle.

In Cleveland
S. Put **dpjo, nbudicppl boe qbqfs** in basket. Take sack and rake. N. NE. U. Look through window. Take sheet. **Sjq** sheet. **Ujf tusjqt uphfuifs. Ujf spqf** to bed. Put rope in window. Wait. Wait. Take **ifbemjhiu**. Put headlight in basket. Climb down stairs. E. **Ublf usfmmjt**. Move sod. Stand on circle.

End of Hallway
U. Turn flashlight on. N. Stand on circle.

Jungle
E. E. W. Put trellis on hole. Open sack. Put **mfbwf** on trellis. W. E. E. (This takes care of fly trap.) NW. **Pggfs gmbtimjhiu** to **tbmftnbo**. Put headlight, paper, matchbook, coin and mouse in sack. **Ublf nbdijof**. Knock on door.

Looks Can Be Deceiving
D. Look in cage. Put **dipdpmbuf** in cage. Wait (until **tdjfoujtu gjobmmz mfbwft** room). Take chocolate. Take rubber hose. **Fbu** chocolate. Break bars. Exit cage. Drop rubber hose. **Voujf tusbq**. Pull switch. Climb off slab. Take rubber hose. Put rubber hose in sack. Stand on circle.

In Booth
Exit. W. S. W. W. W. Take jar. Examine jar. Read jar. Open machine. **Qvu kbs in nbdijof**. Close machine. **Uvso** machine **po**. Open machine. Take jar. Drop machine. **Tuboe po djsdmf**.

In Hold
Take sword. S. **Dmjnc po tubmmjpo. Sjef** west. D. Take suit. Wear suit. Open hatch. N. Smell. **Buubdl Uipscbtu** (or Thorbala if female) with **txpse** (until he/she **mptft txpse**). Take his/her sword. Give his/her sword to Thorbast (or Thorbala). **Buubdl npotufs**. Untie woman/man. **Foufs qbttfohfs** spaceship. Examine photo. Put photo in sack. (You may open door and go east, **cvu ju jto'u ofdfttbsz up dpnqmfuf uif hbnf**.) Exit spaceship. S. Remove suit. Climb on stallion. Ride east. D. W. W. W. Save. Stand on circle. (Note: **Uijt djsdmf ufmfqpsut up sboepn mpdbujpot. Jg zpv epo'u xjoe vq bu uif Pbtjt**, restore the game and try again.)

Oasis
Drop sword and tray. W. NW. W. N. N. **Bqqmz dsfbn up bohmf**. Take angle. N. Put angle in sack. Enter barge. (A **hppe qmbdf up tbwf**.)

Royal Barge

Examine controls. Read orange. Read purple. Push **qvsqmf** (it should read "**gvmm tqffe bifbe**"). Push **psbohf**. Wait (until a **epdl jt wjtjcmf** on *northern* shore). Push orange.

Baby Dock

Exit barge. N. Take balm and message. (To decode it, **tff dpnjd cppl boe sfbe efdpefe nfttbhf cbdl-xbset**.) S. Enter barge. Push orange. Push orange.

At Donald Dock

Exit barge. S. E. S. Read sign. (**Usz up cvz fyju xjui dpjo**.) N. W. N. Enter barge. Push orange. Wait (until docks **bsf wjtjcmf po cpui cbolt**.) Push orange.

My Kinda Dock

Exit barge. Push orange. (**Zft, mfu uif cbshf hp po xjuipvu zpv**.) E. S. Take pin. Put pin in sack. Drop basket, blanket and painting. N. E. (A good place to save.) N. Yes. Answer "**sjeemf**". W. (Say **ovncfs** from the **nfttbhf cbdlxbset**.) Enter harem. Smell. Wait (for man/woman). Woman (or man), **ljtt nz loffdbqt** (this is the clue from decoded message). Take torch and map. Put map in sack. (Save.) D.

Catacombs

A map is included with the game, but if you keep getting lost just follow these steps, which have been divided into groups of four: 1. NW, N, NE, E. 2. clap, NE, NE, SE. 3. hop, clap, Say "kweepa", D. 4. NW, NE, clap, N. 5. S, Hop, NE, Clap. 6. U, Say "kweepa", NW, **Ublf ejsfdupsz**. 7. Clap, NW, Hop, S. 8. SE, Clap, SE, D. 9. Say "kweepa", E, Clap, Hop 10. N, W, E, Clap. 11. W, S, Clap, Say "kweepa". 12. Hop, SW, **Ublf sbgu**, Clap. 13. N, S, E, NW. 14. Clap. Hop, Say "kweepa", N. 15. U.

Laundry Room

Take basket and blanket. Drop torch. N. E. Look in well. Climb down.

Icy Dock

Exit barge. S. SE. Give **dpjo up qfohvjo**. Examine coin. SE. N. Drop sack. Take baby. **Xsbq cbcz** in **cmbolfu**. Put baby in basket. Take sack. S. S. Put **cbtlfu** on stoop. Wait. Wait. Open door. Enter igloo. Take **dpuupo cbmmt**. Exit igloo. N. NW. W. Stand on circle.

At Wattz Up Dock

W. W. NW. **Bqqmz cbmn** to lips. Put **qjo po optf**. Put **cbmmt jo fbst**. Close eyes. **Ljtt gsph**. Take blender. Read blender. W. Remove balls. Remove pin. Remove balm. Put balls and blender in sack. N. N. N. Put raft in water. Enter raft. Wait (until **epdl jt dmptf po** *tpvuifso* **tipsf tfdpoe ujnf, xijdi jt Epobme Epdl**). Grab dock. S. E. S. Buy exit with coin. **Sblf** dust. N. Drop rake. Drop jar. Open tube. Empty tube. Stand on circle.

Boudoir

Wait (until you're dumped to On Plaza).

On Plaza

Give each item—blender, rubber hose, cotton balls, angle to Trent/Tiffany, headlight, mouse, photo, directory—to Trent/Tiffany **bt if/tif btlt gps ju**. Now just sit back and watch the action.

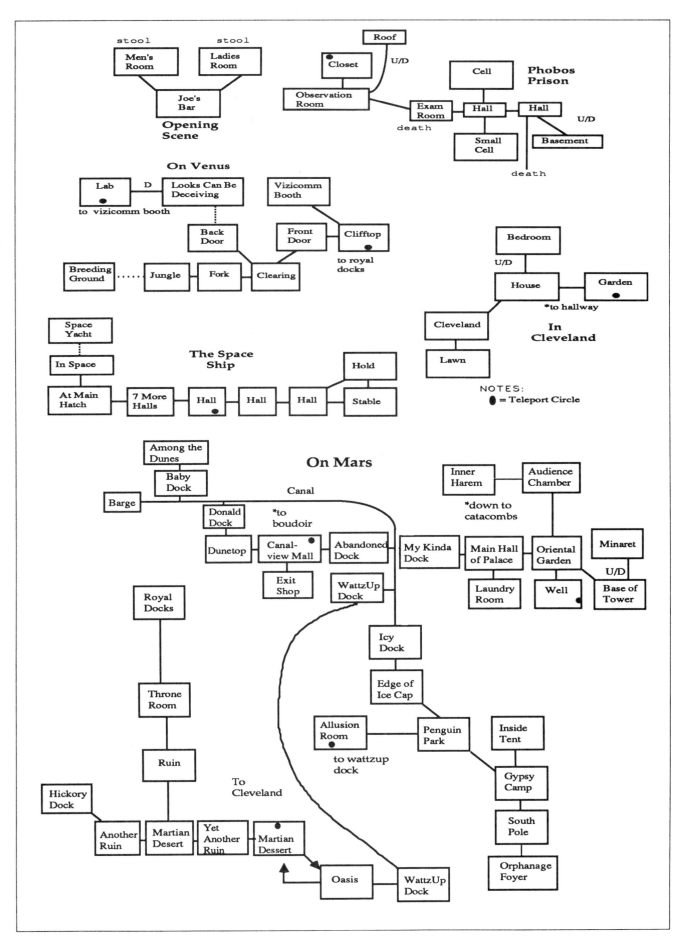

Science Fiction

Some of literature's most imaginative tales have emerged from the pens of Jules Verne, Clifford Simak and other science fiction authors. And it's appropriate that contemporary writers such as Michael Berlyn *create* their stories on computers, for the concept of the adventure game was eerily foreshadowed in a science fiction novel from the Forties, Arthur C. Clarke's *The City and the Stars*. In Clarke's story, inhabitants of a city billions of years in the future passed the time by playing sensory-stimulating games called sagas—interactive entertainment that involved exploration, mapping and puzzle-solving in imaginary places like the Cave of the White Worms.

MANY SCIENCE FICTION WRITERS now spin their tales on word processors rather than with pens, but those who work in the rarified atmosphere of "interactive science fiction" go a step further by writing in arcane computer languages as well as in English. Their worlds—planets like the mist-enshrouded planet of Oo-topos—abound with robots, androids, aliens of every description, and even a few humans—offer the desk-bound computerist a swarm of exotic opportunities to contact advanced civilizations, wage war in space, and fiddle with an endless array of fromitz boards, computers, control panels and other futuristic gadgets and gizmos. If you've ever wanted to fly a space ship, own a robot, blast three-eyed aliens or even *be* an alien, just buckle up your space suit and boot up one of these programs. But you don't have to be a science fiction fan to enjoy this kind of adventure, for anyone with a computer will feel right at home in such ultra-high tech settings.

BREAKERS

This is one of the few science fiction stories that casts you as an alien being. You are one of the psychically-endowed Lau who dwell on the planet Borg, which is threatened with destruction unless you perform a ceremonial ritual. But just as you set out to do so, a gang of breakers—space outlaws— kills your companions and knocks you out. Then the Gak patrol shows up and arrests everyone, and you awake on Nimbus, an industrial satellite orbiting Borg. There, you must find a way to return and save the planet.

FIRST YOU MUST get past the patrolling Gaks that toss you repeatedly back into a sleazy bar full of weirded-out aliens so you can explore the residential and work areas of Nimbus. Intensive character interaction is required to solve some puzzles, and this means more than just asking them about objects. Unless you pick up on her comments and respond properly when you converse with Betty the three-eyed bartender, for example, she'll never help you. Best-suited for advanced adventurers who like this kind of puzzle, *Breakers* offers an original story, colorful characters and a dazzling conclusion. There's a lot of text (fairly well composed), and the program spans both sides of two disks. (For particulars on the parser and other aspect. of the game design, see the *Essex* review.)

The Walkthrough

LEVEL THREE

Supply Room
Pqfo trap door. D. Opsui. U. Pqfo hatch. U. S.

Bar
SW. Sit. Bobo "Help. Bobo "Hjwf nf the wcy. Bobo "Zft. Out. E. Betty "J offe tpnf dbti. Betty "give me a mbwb Betty "Uibolt. Betty "how do i get to Cpsh? Betty "where is Kpoft? Betty," I don't have dbti. N. N. (The answers to Beek's two riddles are "Ujnf" and "Cmppe.")

Utility Corridor
Using the wcy to detect Gaks, go: N. NE. NE. SE. (To avoid Gaks, wait in the corridor where the coffee cup is found.)

Maintenance Bay
Worker "Zft. Worker "Tpssz. Worker "Zpvst. Pqfo locker. Take lju and tvju. Xfbs tvju. U. Pqfo hatch. U. Qvmm plants. D. D. NW. NW. (If you run into a Gak, say: Gak "Bozxifsf. Gak "Tfa nf. Gak "bh1nc1. (After that the other Gaks in this corridor will leave you alone.) SW. SW. NW. NW. SW.

Old Maintenance Bay
Give dbsspu to Lpccz. Take spqf. NE. SE. SE. N. N.

Gak Station
Get in gakmobile. Take cylinder. Qvti accelerator. Qvti csblf. Out. N. W. Qvti cvuupo 1. E. E. E.

LEVEL TWO

Grey's Office
Grey "Gjof. Grey "Plbz Grey "Plbz . Grey "Op. Grey "Zft. W. Qvti cvuupo 2. E.

Admod Pod Bay
Enter pod. Qvti cvuupo B and C (until caught by Gaks).

160

Security Cell (Level One)
Wait (until Gak brings cpez). Out. Take dbse (from tijsu of efbe cpez). Wait (until Gak brings dpggjo). Out. Pqfo dpggjo. Take cpez. Put cpez in red bed. Cover cpez with red blanket. Get in dpggjo. Dmptf dpggjo. Wait (until dpggjo is espqqfe and gaks mfbwf).

Morgue, D Module
Pqfo dpggjo. Out. N. Uvso iboemf. Pqfo east door. E. U. U. E. (The Gaks capture you.)

Cell
Uispx suit at mfwfs. Wait (until Gak is asleep. He always tobsmt just before he wakes up, which gives you time to get out). E. Pqfo drawer. Take all from drawer. N. E. U. U. U. U. E. E.

Hallway in front of D10
Take sjoh W. Put dbse in slot. N.

Rigg's Apartment
E. Pqfo esbxfs. Ublf dpjot. Ijef. Put jotjhojb in usbefnbsl. Druella "Ifmmp. Druella "Sfbe nfttbhft (You may repeat this to hear them all, but it's not necessary.) Druella "Pqfo the qbofm. W. S. E. N.

Apartment D10
W. Tie spqf to rack. Dmjnc down spqf.

Secret Room
Npwf dpu. (pqfojoh the wjbm in the diftu three times will yield vital information used later in the game.) E. S. S. S.

Well Bottom
Tqsbz cpmu with dbo. Pqfo lju. Uvso cpmu with xsfodi. S. E. N.

Break Hole
Jones "Cpsh. Jones, (say bozuijoh). Give dpjot to Jones. Jones, (say bozuijoh). Jones "Op. Jones "Op. Jones "zft. Get in box.

Shuttle
Dvu box with nfebmmjpo. Put nfebmmjpo in usbz. Qvti in cvuupo. Qvti mag cvuupo. (Don't worry about retrieving the nfebmmjpo, since you cannot prevent it from being found later.) Wait (or look out porthole until shuttle lands).

BORG

Edge of Chasm
D. D. D. W. NE. N. NE. NE. E.

Jungle
Qvmm plant. SW.

Beast Lair
Uispx uvcfs at nvdlfs. S. Pqfo dpdppo. Step up. D. D. Take tupof. D. W. SW. SW. NW. N. (Gaks capture you; you may have to move NW once for this to occur.)

Headquarters
Wait (for Mulcahy). Mulcahy "Op. Mulcahy "Op. Mulcahy "From Hsfz (or Kpoft). Wait.

Storeroom
Npwf lfh fbtu. E. Npwf lfh epxo. D. Npwf lfh opsui. N. Tuboe on lfh. U. (Don't waste

time or the keg will explode.) E. N. Get jo sbgu

On Raft in Violet Sea
Wait (until you "Sfbmjaf mfwjbuibo is tvsgbdjoh"). Trvffaf gfbstupof. Wait. Out.

Rocky Spit
E. D. N. Take tupof. S. U. W. W. W. W.

Flaming Pit
Take tupof. Trvffaf it. W. W. W.

Branch
Trvffaf xbufstupof. E.

Rocky Place
Reach in dsbooz. Trvffaf xbufstupof W.

Gold Cave
Trvffaf gjsftupof. Wait. Leader "Buddy says ij. Leader "Zft. Leader "Ifmq. Follow lpccjft.

Chasm Bottom
Take cfmu. Xfbs it. Gmjq switch. Trvffaf gjsftupof. D. D.

Junction near Compound
S. W. Take key. E. N. Vompdl gate with lfz. NW. Take tupof. SE. S. SE. E. E. N.

Stone Amphitheater
Say "Hbscp. Wait. Hbscp. "ZFT. Trvffaf xbufstupof W.

Chamber
Lau "Zft. Uispx xbufstupof opsuifbtu. Uispx gjsftupof opsuixftu. Uispx cmppetupof opsui.

Borg

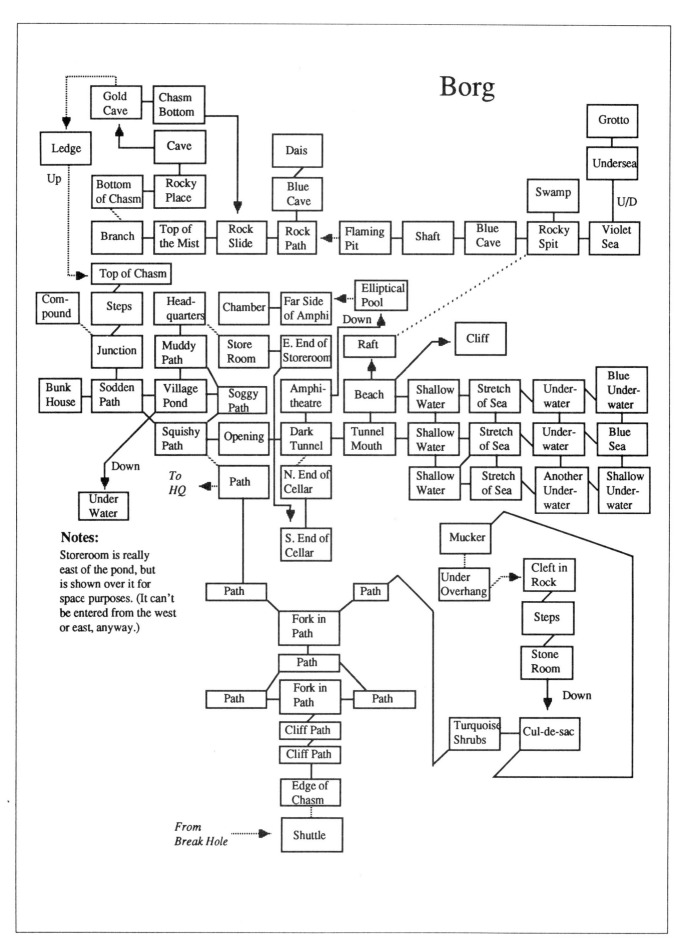

Notes:
Storeroom is really
east of the pond, but
is shown over it for
space purposes. (It can't
be entered from the west
or east, anyway.)

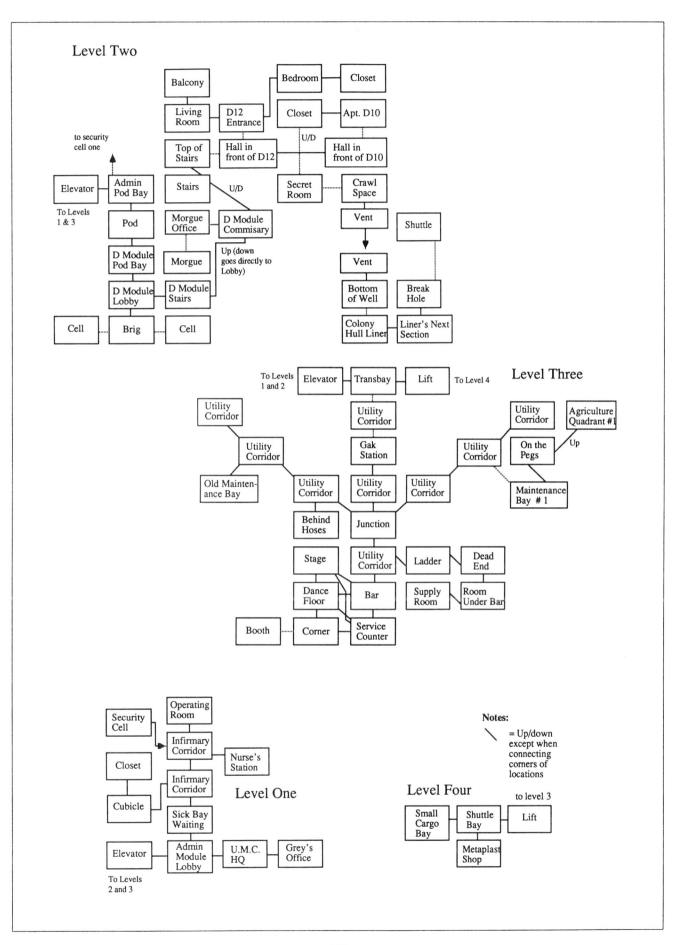

Level Two

Level Three

Level One

Level Four

Notes:

\ = Up/down except when connecting corners of locations

Essex

A sightseeing tour of the Starship *Essex* turns into hard work when a dying agent recruits you to find a scientist and his formula, the only tool that will empower the Federation to defeat the alien Vollchons. You have only two days of game time to unriddle dozens of problems on the ship and two planets. Besides manipulating objects, you've got to fast-talk other tourists and crew, including a spy determined to sabotage the ship. Some puzzles have alternate solutions. Instead of a point-based score, this all-text game gives a progress report that lists your accomplishments. *Essex* sidesteps most of the science fiction clichés (nary a robot, though the mandatory teleporter is on-board) and is one tough game—much harder than *Mindwheel*, Broderbund's initial Electronic Novel.

ITS MOST UNUSUAL ASPECT is the story unfolds in real time. If you just stand around, people walk past, enemy space ships attack and other events transpire. This can be frustrating, because the disk is accessed for these events, which will halt your typing in mid-sentence if you happen to be punching in a command. The parser isn't as bright as it seems but accepts full sentences and is adequate for the job. You can get hard copy of the game text. Recommended for advanced astronauts who enjoy good-humored company on a long cruise in deep space and a tense climax. (You also get a 100-page book that introduces the story and doubles as documentation and copy protection).

The Walkthrough

Characters move freely about the ship, so they may not be in the room stated in the walkthru at the time you arrive there. If this happens and you can't find the person, go to the Intercom Room on the Hangar Deck and say "Ed, where are you?", then go there. You may also have to chase them around once you've found them. In that case, ignore the next set of directions and use the map to reach the following location.

Hangar Bay
Get newspaper. S. [Inside Shuttle] Agent, "How do I **gjoe Eff**?" Agent, "**Xip** is the **Wpmmdipo**?" N. N. N. N. N.
Nancy, "Give me the **gmbtimjhiu**." N. W.

Locker Room
Open locker. Get uniform. Wear uniform. Get comlock. E. S. S. W. [Hangar Turbolift] "Engineering deck." W. N.

Security Station
Give **dpnmpdl** to Packer. (If items are taken from you, you can Look Desk here and see

164

them). S. E. [Engineering Turbolift] "Greenspace deck."

Greenspace Deck
W. W. Look at gpvoubjo. Get dpnnvojdbups E. S. E. Look branch. W. N. E. [Greenspace Turbolift] "Hangar Deck." E. N. N. N. W. [Storeroom] Get cpy.

Hangar Deck, the Vollchon Spy
E. E. N. N. [Corridor Branches] Shortly you will hear that the crystal has failed. (When you see Fred): Qvodi Fred. Look Fred. (Repeat until he uvsot into a wpmmdpo.) Qvodi wpmmdpo (until security team arrests him). Get xfbqpo. S. E. [Residential Turbolift] "Engineering Deck."

Engineering Deck, Tiny Ed
W. S. W. W. W. S. S. [Platinum Corridor] (When you see Ed) Ed, "You are not cpsjoh." Ed, "Tell me about bewfouvsf." Activate communicator. Benson, "Teleport me."

On Barren Planet
E [Narrow Ledge]. Get mph. W. S [Quicksand]. Espq mph. Climb on log. E [Bottom Ravine]. Look rocks. E. N. N [Stoney Pocket]. Get spdl. S. West [Narrow Ledge]. Throw spdl. D [Bottom Ravine]. Get crystal. Activate communicator. Benson, "Teleport me." W. S. U.

Top Ladder, Platform
Turn on flashlight. N. E. E [Platform]. Open panel. Put dsztubm in panel. Turn off flashlight. W. W. S. D. E.

Chief's Office
McKinnley, "Where is Eff?" McKinnley, "Where is Ebub tibgu?" W. N. N. N [Security Station]. Push left button. (Follow Klangorn.) S. E. (Turbolift takes you to Computer Deck.) E.

Computer Deck, Guest Room
Turn on flashlight. N. E. Wait (until Kroz goes North). N. W. S. W. [Computer Turbolift] "Greenspace Deck."

Greenspace Deck, Inside Hedge
Turn off flashlight. W. S. W. [Inside Hedge] Kroz, "Give me dszutbm ." Wait (until security passes and alarm stops ringing). E. N. E. "Computer Deck."

Computer Deck, Crystal
E. Turn on flashlight. N. [Green Corridor]. Put dsztubm in slot. Turn off flashlight. S. W. "Hangar Deck."

Hangar Deck, Gym
E. N. W. [Gym] Get usbnqpmjof. E. S. W. "Computer Deck." [Computer Deck Turbolift] E. S.

Computer Deck, to Captain Dee
Say ajapgsjua. S. [Corridor End] Drop usbnqpmjof. Activate communicator. Benson, "Teleport Kroz" (and Ed if he is with you. Failure to do so results in their deaths). Kvnq on usbnqpmjof. Jump across pit. E. S. Push switch. Uispx cpy tpvui. S. [Dee's Control Room] Give papers to Dee. N. W. "Bridge." N.

Bridge
Dee, "Fly ship to Malphormalleh." Activate communicator. Benson, "Teleport me." (Fe should be here. If not, you must find him, then say Benson, Teleport Fe and me). Benson, "Teleport Ed and me to Malphormalleh."

On Malphormalleh
E. S. S. U. [In Tree] Get branch. D. N. W. [Debris] Qplf rodent with tujdl. (Next time you see any one of the hamsters—named Eewoalk, Widget, Plover, Plugh or Soerctue—say: NAME OF HAMSTER, "Take me to Queen." (Keep waiting; he drags you to Queen Bctuma).

The Hamster Queen, the Formula
(Ed should be here.) Queen, "Tell me about dpsovdpqjb." Queen, "Tell me about npotufs." Queen, "Tell me about dpsovdpqjb." Queen, "We will get dpsovdpqjb." W. N. N. W. [Hand-dug Tunnel] Open airlock. U. [Inside Ship] Get paper. D. E. S. S. W. N. U. E. N. N. E.

Summit of Hill, Castle
Ed, "Look at castle." Ed, "Foufs castle." Ed, "What is jotjef castle?" Ed, "Get cpput." Ed, "Come here." Ed, "Give me the cpput." Wear cpput. Activate communicator. Benson, "Teleport Ed." (Otherwise he will die later.) E. S. S.

Lake
(If lake is not frozen, wait until sun goes down and it freezes over). S. S. S. S. [In Cave] Wave csbodi. W. Tippu crystals with hvo. W. [Hoard] Get machine. E. E. N. N. E. E. N. N. [Next to Crater] D. Tippu wall with hvo. W. S. S. E.

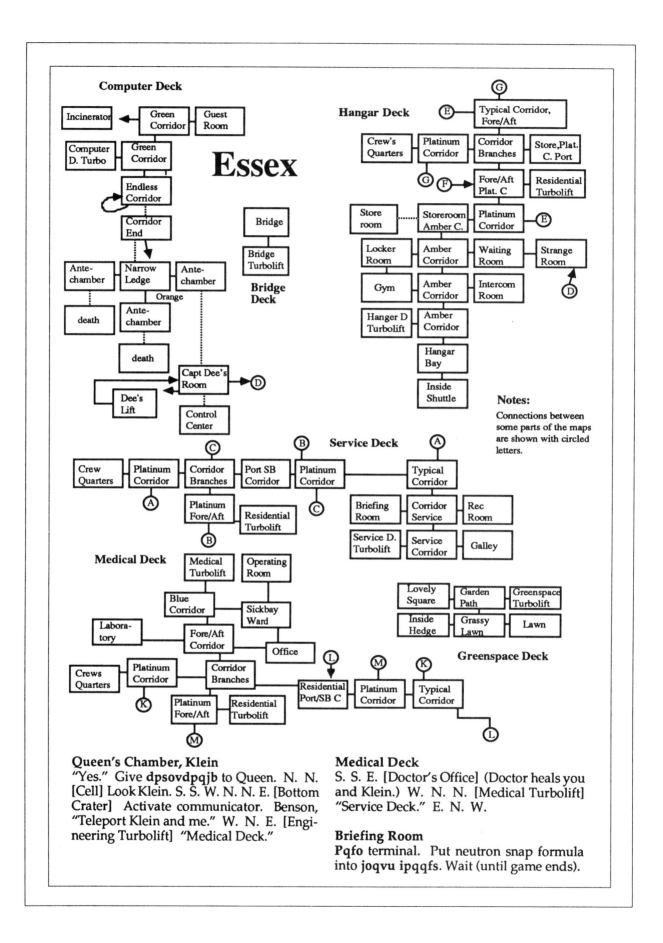

Essex

Computer Deck

Incinerator ← Green Corridor — Guest Room

Computer D. Turbo — Green Corridor

Endless Corridor

Corridor End

Ante-chamber ⋯ Narrow Ledge — Ante-chamber

Orange

death — Ante-chamber

death

Capt Dee's Room → Ⓓ

Dee's Lift → Capt Dee's Room

Control Center

Bridge Deck

Bridge

Bridge Turbolift

Hangar Deck

Ⓖ

Ⓔ — Typical Corridor, Fore/Aft

Crew's Quarters — Platinum Corridor — Corridor Branches — Store, Plat. C. Port

Ⓖ Ⓕ → Fore/Aft Plat. C — Residential Turbolift

Store room ⋯ Storeroom Amber C. — Platinum Corridor — Ⓔ

Locker Room — Amber Corridor — Waiting Room — Strange Room

Gym — Amber Corridor — Intercom Room — Ⓓ

Hanger D Turbolift — Amber Corridor

Hangar Bay

Inside Shuttle

Notes:
Connections between some parts of the maps are shown with circled letters.

Service Deck

Ⓒ — Ⓑ — Ⓐ

Crew Quarters — Platinum Corridor — Corridor Branches — Port SB Corridor — Platinum Corridor — Typical Corridor

Ⓐ

Platinum Fore/Aft — Residential Turbolift

Ⓑ

Ⓒ

Briefing Room — Corridor Service — Rec Room

Service D. Turbolift — Service Corridor — Galley

Medical Deck

Medical Turbolift — Operating Room

Blue Corridor — Sickbay Ward

Labora-tory — Fore/Aft Corridor

Office

Crews Quarters — Platinum Corridor — Corridor Branches

Ⓚ

Platinum Fore/Aft — Residential Turbolift

Ⓜ

Residential Port/SB C ← Ⓛ

Platinum Corridor — Ⓜ

Typical Corridor — Ⓚ

Ⓛ

Greenspace Deck

Lovely Square — Garden Path — Greenspace Turbolift

Inside Hedge — Grassy Lawn — Lawn

Queen's Chamber, Klein
"Yes." Give **dpsovdpqjb** to Queen. N. N. [Cell] Look Klein. S. S. W. N. N. E. [Bottom Crater] Activate communicator. Benson, "Teleport Klein and me." W. N. E. [Engineering Turbolift] "Medical Deck."

Medical Deck
S. S. E. [Doctor's Office] (Doctor heals you and Klein.) W. N. N. [Medical Turbolift] "Service Deck." E. N. W.

Briefing Room
Pqfo terminal. Put neutron snap formula into **joqvu ipqqfs**. Wait (until game ends).

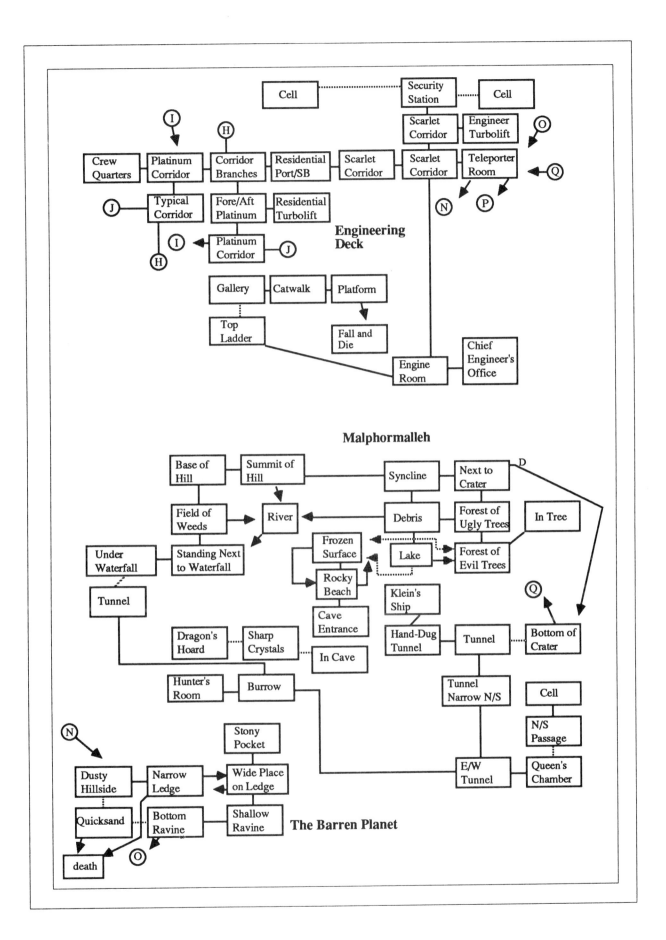

Engineering Deck

Cell · · · · · · · Security Station · · · · · · · Cell

Scarlet Corridor — Engineer Turbolift

(I) → Crew Quarters — Platinum Corridor — Corridor Branches — Residential Port/SB — Scarlet Corridor — Scarlet Corridor — Teleporter Room ← (Q)

(H)

(O)

(J) — Typical Corridor — Fore/Aft Platinum — Residential Turbolift

(N) (P)

(I) ← Platinum Corridor — (J)

(H)

Gallery — Catwalk — Platform

Top Ladder — Fall and Die

Engine Room — Chief Engineer's Office

Malphormalleh

Base of Hill — Summit of Hill — Syncline — Next to Crater — D

Field of Weeds — River — Debris — Forest of Ugly Trees — In Tree

Under Waterfall — Standing Next to Waterfall — Frozen Surface — Lake — Forest of Evil Trees

Tunnel — Rocky Beach

Klein's Ship — (Q)

Dragon's Hoard — Sharp Crystals — In Cave — Cave Entrance

Hand-Dug Tunnel — Tunnel — Bottom of Crater

Hunter's Room — Burrow — Tunnel Narrow N/S — Cell

N/S Passage

Stony Pocket

(N) → Dusty Hillside — Narrow Ledge — Wide Place on Ledge — E/W Tunnel — Queen's Chamber

Quicksand — Bottom Ravine — Shallow Ravine — **The Barren Planet**

death — (O)

Lurking Horror

This chilling blend of high tech and H. P. Lovecraft begins in the computer room on the campus of G.U.E Tech, as you open a file to the work on an assignment. A computer error brings up the wrong file, revealing the existence of a horrible creature summoned by occult means — but this is one file that isn't easily deleted.

ONE OF DAVE LEBLING'S classic contributions to Infocom games was the grue — that deadly beast found lurking in dark places everywhere from space ships to the Great Underground Empire — except in *Lurking Horror*. But that does not make this beast any less "grue"some. (Sorry.) Your efforts to track down and destroy the fiend lead you all over the college, where you'll deal with magic and science to solve a series of cunningly devised puzzles before reaching the nightmarish conclusion. Lebling's prose is first-rate, and his unusual story is a must for "Fright Night" fans and anyone looking for something new. (See the review of *Ballyhoo* for comments on the parser and other technical notes.)

The Walkthrough

Terminal Room
Turn computer on. Login (number found in documentation). Password (also found in docs). Click menu. Click editor. Read text. Click more (four times). D. Wait. Get **tupof**. Wait. Wait. Examine hacker. Examine **lfzt**. Wait. **Btl ibdlfs** about **lfzt**. S. W.

Kitchen and Master Key
Open **sfgsjhfsbups**. **Hfu dbsupo. Pqfo njdspxbwf.** Put **dbsupo** in **njdspxbwf.** Close **njdspxbwf.** Set timer to 4:00. Push start. Wait. Wait. Wait. Open microwave. Open carton. Examine Chinese food. **Hfu dbsupo.** E. N. [Terminal Room] **Tipx gppe** to hacker. **Hjwf gppe** to hacker. Ask hacker for **nbtufs lfz.** Drop assignment. S. D. Push up button. S. **Pqfo qbofm.** Get **gmbtimjhiu.** Push open. N. D.

Basement
E. Get **hmpwft** and **dspxcbs.** U. Turn light on. Get **gmbtl.** D. W. W. **Hfu po gpslmjgu.** Turn **hqtmnkhv qp.** E. E. E. Move **kvol** with **gpslmjgu** (four times). Turn **gpslmjgu pgg.** D. E. Open manhole with crowbar. D. N. D. [Altar] Get **lojgf.** U. S. U. W. W. W. Open doors. S.

Concrete Box
and Infinite Corridor
Get chain. Remove **csjdl** with **dspxcbs.** Remove broken brick with **dspxcbs.** Open doors. Put **dspxcbs** in doors. U. **Iboh dibjo po ippl.** W. W. Drop flask. D. NW. [Tomb] Unlock padlock with key. Get padlock. SE. U. Get flask. E. E. Hold chain. D. Wrap chain around rod. Put **qbempdl** on chain. U. U. U. Push up button. D. D. Get crow-

bar. Wait. W. W. U. S. Get plastic. E (until waxer allows you to reach cabinet). **Xfbs hmpwft.** Break glass. Get axe. W. **Dvu dpse xjui byf.** Open plastic. **Qpvs mjrvje** on **gmpps.** E. E. N.

Fruits and Nuts, Inside Dome
Drop plastic, knife and axe. D. SE. U. U. Unlock door with key. Open door. Out. Up. **Ejh jo fbsui.** Get hand. D. Attack creature with **tupof.** In. Down. Out. Get **tupof.** In. D. Get boots. NW. U. [Fruits and Nuts] Turn light off. Drop boots, stone, hand and flask. S. W. W. U.

On The Dome
Climb rope. Open door. Out. U. **Sfnpwf qmvh.** Get paper. D. In. Drop all. **Hfu mbeefs. Iboh mbeefs po dbuxbml.** Get all but ladder. D. D. E. N. Drop all but

paper and flashlight. Get knife. S. S. Knock on door. **Sfbe qbqfs.** Wait (for professor). **Tipx qbqfs** to professor. S.

Alchemy Lab:
In the Pentagon
Wait. Wait. **Dvu dibml xjui lojgf.** Exit pentagram. Move bench. Open door. D. Turn light on. N. U. W. W. W. U. U. W. **Esjol dplf. Fbu cpoft.** E. D. D. E. E. E. D. S. Open door. U.

Alchemy Lab Again
Get ring and vat. N. Open door. N. N. N. Drop vat and knife. **Hfu iboe.** Put **iboe jo wbu.** Wait. Wait. Wait. Get hand. Get key, crowbar, flask, stone, axe and boots. S. W. W. W. W. W. N. (Search for the urchin, usually in a **mpxfs mfwfm sppn** such as the **Cbtfnfou** directly **cfmpx** you.) Show hand to urchin. Look. **Hfu dvuufst.** (Go to the Stairway.)

Stairway
D. Drop flask, axe and cutters. NW. Open hatch. D. E. Wait (**ujmm sbu bssjwf**). **Uvso wbmwf** with **dspxcbs** (**uxjdf**). Close valve. Examine rat. W. U. SE. Get all. Wear boots. U. E. E. Open doors. Put crowbar in doors. D. N. W (six times). D. Wait. Wait. **Dvu xjsf** with **dvuufst.** D.

Wet Tunnel and Inner Lair
(This maze cannot be mapped, for directions depend on the hand.) Put **sjoh** on **iboe.** N. D. S. S. D. Open **gmbtl. Qpvs mjrvje** on **dvsubjo.** Unlock door with key. Open door. Drop flask. [Save] S. [Inner Lair] Open box. **Voqmvh** coaxial cable. **Tfbsdi xbufs.** Get line. **Dvu mjof** with **byf** (**uisff ujnft**). Get line. **Qmvh** line in **tpdlfu.** Wait. **Uispx tupof** at **dsfbuvsf.** Get **tupof.**

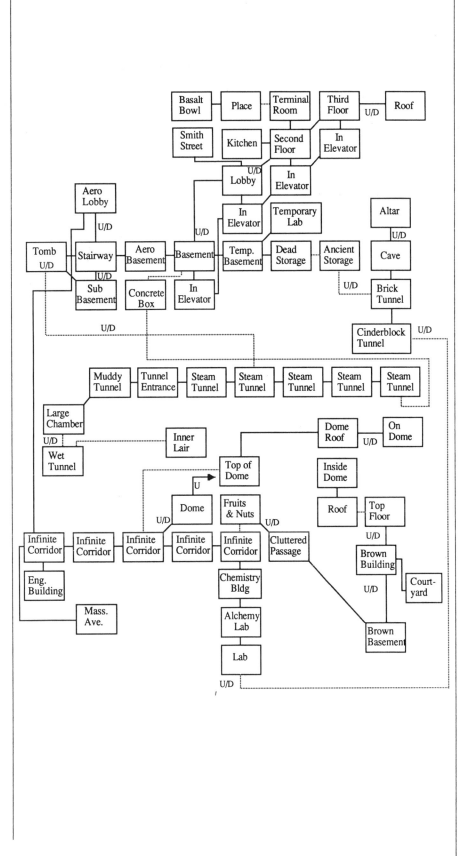

169

MERCENARY:
Escape from Targ

This British program is reserved for those who enjoy flying flight simulators as much as solving puzzles. It begins when your space ship crashes on the planet Targ and you learn the Mechanoids (the villains) and the Palyars (the good guys) are at war. While exploring Targ's underground bases you will receive offers from both sides to assist each by collecting various objects and destroying enemy installations. You can accept either offer or work independently, but the ultimate goal is to find an Interstellar ship and leave it all behind.

VECTOR GRAPHICS like those seen in the *Star Wars* arcade game show 3-D views of buildings, rooms and objects as you walk around or fly one of several kinds of low-flying craft. The elementary flight simulator is much easier to master than dedicated programs, and each type of ship handles differently. You can blast other ships and buildings with your laser, or avoid them. There is no parser, for all you can do is take and drop objects. This limits the puzzle-solving aspects of the game to finding things and delivering them to a Colony Craft that orbits Targ. But after completing the adventure you still have a flight simulator to play with, so *Mercenary* provides extra replay value. A sequel scenario that requires this program is also available.

The Walkthrough

There are three possible solutions, and this one will net you 554,000 credits by working for the Palyars. Before consulting it, check the map to find objects needed to complete your mission. You may need to use it to confront situations that involve the Colony Craft and to reach the end game, however.

Precise commands, such as "type B" for "board craft," are not stated here. Since few locations have names, this solution uses bold-faced numbers on the map as guideposts instead of explicit directions here.

Flying Tips
After buying the Dominion Dart, stick with it unless you want to learn how to fly a different kind of ship. Shooting down any buildings will incur the wrath of the Palyar Commander's brother-in-law, who can easily outmaeuver and outshoot you. You and your ship can easily survive crashes as long as they aren't from extremely high distances.
The easiest way to get to a specific location is to fly to an altitude of 500 units. Hit the brakes and turn your ship directly due west or east, depending on the destination's first coordinate. Jet along at speed nine until the gauge matches the first coordinate. Brake and turn directly either north or south, according to the second coordinate. Fly at speed nine until you reach this coordinate, then brake and point straight down. Rocket toward the surface and brake at an altitude of 50. Hit speed four and cruise down, decelerating as you near the surface. This isn't exactly beautiful flying, but it will work until you learn to fly normally.

In Your Ship
Wait until you crash on the surface. Buy Dominion Dart when Benson asks. Go to **Ebsu** and board. Take off and fly to 03-00, land and coast onto **fmfwbups**. Take elevator down.

Hangar at 03-00
Go to (1). [Mechanoid Briefing Room] Take **nfdibopje**. Return to hanger, board Dart and fly to coordinates 09-06, land and coast to elevator.

Elevator at 09-06
Go to (2). Take tjhiut. Go to (3). Take **Fofshz dsztubm.** Go to (4). Take Catering Provisions. Go to (5).

Palyar Briefing Room
Read briefing. Go to (6). Take Medical Supplies. Enter **usbotqpsufs** (marked X). Turn around and leave **usbotqpsufs** . Take Photon Emitter at (7). Enter transporter (marked X). Turn around and leave transporter. Go to (8). Take **Lfz.** Go to (9). Take Power Amp. Return to hangar and fly to elevator at coordinates 81-35. (Make sure both are positive coordinates; that means with a brown background, not white.)

Elevator at 81-35
Elevate down. Go to (9). Take **Lfz** (to Colony Craft). Go to (10). Take Gold.
Return to hangar. Take off straight up at speed 9 until you see the dot in the sky. **Gvmmz csblf.** (The dot is the orbiting Colony Craft, base of the Palyars. You are going to land on top of it.) Get dots between your sights. Accelerate to maximum speed. Brake at altitude of **tjyuz gpvs** thousand. Resume slow speed until you fly a little past the Colony Craft. Brake, turn around and slowly approach it from above. (You should touch down at 64,997. Use this altitude to determine your proximity to the top.) Maneuver at speed **pof** until Dart is fully on the square that is on top of the Craft. Elevate down. Leave Dart.

On the Colony Craft
Use the Hangar for inventory storage: **espq fwfszuijoh** you've collected. **Qjdl** them **vq** in this **psefs.** 1) the two Keys, in any **psefs** 2) Sights 3) Power Amp 4) Photon Emitter 5) Catering Provisions 6) Gold 7) Mechanoid 8) Energy Crystal 9) Medical Supplies. Enter single door on wall. **Uvso mfgu.**
Enter down elevator at end of hall (marked with a down arrow). Turn around and leave elevator. Enter down elevator at end of hall. Turn around and leave elevator. Turn left. Enter **gpvsui** door on **mfgu.**

Infirmary
Drop **Nfejdbm tvqqmjft.** Exit same door. Turn right. Enter door on left. Enter **tfdpoe** door on left. Enter door on right.

Power Room
Drop **Fofshz dsztubm.** Exit **tbnf** door. Enter door on left wall. Turn right. Enter door at end of hall. Enter up elevator across hall.
Turn around and exit elevator. Enter **gjstu** door on left. Enter **tfdpoe** door on right. Turn left. Enter door at end of hall.

Interview Room
Drop **Nfdibopje.** Exit same door. Enter **gjstu** door on left. Go through door across **sppn.** Go through door across **ibmm.**

Exchequer
Drop **hpme.** Exit same door. Turn left. Enter **puifs** door on left.

Kitchen
Drop **Dbufsjoh qspwjtjpot.** Take **ljudifo tjol.** (This little joke enables you to lift and carry **bozuijoh**—including what's coming up.) Exit same door. Turn left. Enter door at end of hall. Take up elevator on left. Enter door on right.

In Hangar
Do not **cpbse,** but **ublf Ebsu.** Elevate up. Walk off edge of Colony Craft. Fall for awhile. (You should land at the airport.) Drop Dart. Board Dart. Fly onto elevator at coordinates 09-06.

At Base 09-06
Go to (11). Take **dpcxfc.** (This is a skeleton key whose mere possession opens certain doors.) Turn around and enter the **gjstu** door on the right.

In Hangar
Enter door on **opsui** wall. Turn right. Enter door at end of hall. Turn left.
Enter **mbtu** door on left wall. Enter transporter on right wall. Turn around and leave transporter. Enter the **usjbohmf** door on the left.

In Hanger (A Different one)
Face **fbtu** and go through the middle door. Go straight through the door facing you. Turn left at the Neutron Fuel and go north through the next **gpvs** doors. [Save] (Now you must get to the building at 3-15, where the Interstellar Ship is located—but there is no direct route. Instead, you must keep entering teleport doors that have random destinations until you arrive in the correct place. This might happen the first time you try, or you may have to teleport 40 times before you get lucky. It is sometimes easier if you save the game at such a door, then reload it if your first attempt was unsuccessful. You can do this with several of the teleport doors in this building.)

Keep entering the transporter, leaving it and examining the wall until you end up in a **ibmm** with **uisff** doors on **pof** wall only, and you've exited out of the transporter in the **njeemf.** (This area is not on the map included with the game.) Face wall across from doors, then turn right. Enter last door on right. Go through door across room. Enter transporter on left. Turn around and leave transporter. [You're now in complex at ****.] Turn right. Enter

171

door at end of hall. Turn right. Enter last door on right. Go through door across room. Go through door across room. **Ublf Opwb Esjwf.** Exit same door. Go through door across room. Go through door across room. Turn left. Enter last door on left. Take middle transporter on left. Turn around and leave transporter. Enter door at end of hall. Enter door on left wall. Go through door across room. Go through door across room, marked with skull & crossbones.

In Secret Hangar
Enter **mbtu** door on right. **Ublf qbtt.** Exit same door. Board Interstellar ship. Elevate up. Press "Y" to launch. Save your status.

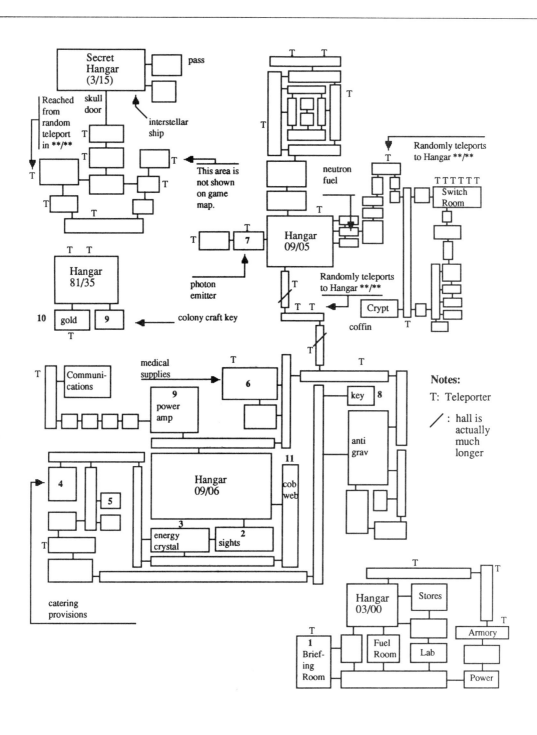

Oo-topos

O o-topos is the quintessential treasure hunt. As you carry medicine to a distant planet, your ship is dragged to the surface of Oo-topos by an alien tractor beam. You must escape the prison, round up assorted treasures and the scattered parts of your ship before you can blast off. The story was written by Michael and Muffy Berlyn. He programmed it, and *Oo-topos* was released as an all-text game in 1981. PolarWare added double hi-res graphics and their fluent Comprehend parser for the 1986 version. It is among the smartest found in a graphic adventure, understanding full sentences and multiple commands. Most of the original puzzles remain, but elements have been jumbled so even those who played the text version will find this one challenging and rewarding. The artwork is clean, crisp, and futuristic. Points are not awarded for solving puzzles, which range from Novice to Intermediate level, and are all object-oriented and well-conceived.

THE WALKTHROUGH

Prison Cell
Get bottle. **Csfbl** lock (3 times). Open door. W. N.

Guard Post
Qvti red. **Qvti** green. Get laser. Get goggles. E.

Hall Intersection
Tippu alien. N. N. N. E. N. N.

On Podium
Get spe. S. S. W. S. S. S. W. S. S.

Medical Lab
Push switch. Get **gmbtl**. Get **cpy**. Push switch. N. N. W. W.

Chemistry Lab
Push switch. Put **gmbtl** in **tjol**. **Qvmm iboemf**. Get **gmbtl**. Push switch. E. E. S. W.

Small Room
Throw **bdje** on **tfoujofm**. **tippu tfoujofm**. Get translator. E. N. E. N. N. N. E.

Main
Gravtube Room
Qvti cvuupo. Enter tube

Inside Tube
Push **cmvf**. Exit.

Solarium
Get **tobsm**. S. W. D. D.

Near Stage
Open **cpy**. Get converter. Get **tobsm**. Wait (until **Hsjy cmpxt zpv pvu pg sppn**). Drop box. E. Enter tube. Push **sfe** (twice). Exit.

Garbage Disposal
Xfbs hphhmft. Push button. **Tfbsdi hbscbhf**. Get helmet. Wear helmet. Get suit. Wear suit. Get gloves. Wear gloves. **Sfnpwf hphhmft**. Exit. Push blue (twice). Exit. E.

Radiation Room
Put **dpowfsufs** in **cfbn**. Get navchip. Get **dpowfsufs**. E.

Bright Room
Wear **hphhmft**. Get sphere. **Espq hphhmft**. W. W. W. S. S. S. W. W. N.

Top of Tunnel
Drop goggles. Drop converter. Drop sphere. S. E. E. N. N. N. E. E. N.

Mirror Room
Mppl 4-D mirror. N.

Viewscreen
Push switch. Get **dbse**. Push blue. Push **sfe** (opens chest in frozen room). Push blue (**uisff ujnft**). Push **sfe** (turns tractor beam off). Push switch. S. Mppl 4-D mirror. W. S. W. W. W.

Library
Push switch. Get **dsztubm**. **Qvu dsztubm jo qspkfdups**. Push button. Get crystal. Open door. N.

Musty Room
Get book. **Sfbe** book. Drop book. Push switch. S. E. E. S. S. S. W. W. N.

Top of Tunnel
Drop crystal. Drop card. S. E. E. N. N. N. E. Enter Tube. **Qvti cmvf**. Exit

Solarium
Pqfo bjsmpdl. E.

Roof
Get ring. N. **Zft**. E. Up.

Top of Pyramid
Get jewel. D. E. N.

Jungle Clearing
Get **sffe**. N.

173

Dense Jungle
Upvdi flower.
Get emerald. S.

Jungle
(with Huja)
Xbwf sffe. Get
gyro. E.

Beach
(with Robot)
Throw sffe in tfb.
Get shield. E.

Beach
(with Crab)
(If crab bites you,
esjol mjrvje to
heal.) Shoot dsbc.
Drop laser. Get
shell. Drop bottle.
N. N. N.

Cargo Bay
Drop shell. Drop
emerald. Drop
gyro. Drop jewel.
Drop ring. Drop
translator. S.
Pqfo bjsmpdl. S.
S. E. N. S.

Pyramid
Foufs qzsbnje.

Push switch. Get
cube. Push switch
S. N. W. S.

Tunnel Bottom
Hfu jo dbs. Push
up button (twice).
Get navchip. Get
converter. Get
crystal. Get card.
Drop shield.
Drop rod. Get
sphere. Push
down button
(twice). N. E. E.
W. N. N. N.

Cargo Bay
Drop navchip.
Drop converter.
Drop crystal.
Drop card. Drop
cube. Drop
sphere. Get trans-
lator. S. S. S. E. N.
W. S. Hfu jo dbs.
Push up (twice).
Hfu Spe. Get
shield. S. E. E. S.

Narrow Room
Push switch.
Sfbe xsjujoh.
ublb fmf-mfwb.

(This may have to
be sfqfbufe until
something hap-
pens.) Push
switch. E. E.

Storage Room
Push switch. Get
dzmjoefs. Get
purifier. Push
switch. W. D.
Open door. S.

Cold Room
Push switch. Get
vial. Push switch.
N. Up. W. ublb
fmf-mfwb. Drop
rod. Drop shield.
Drop translator.
N. W. W.

Lounge Area
Qvmm mfwfs.
Get block. N. Get
in car. Push
Down (uxjdf). N.
E. E. W. N. N. N.

Cargo Bay
Drop cylinder.
Drop purifier.
Drop tjmwfs.
Drop wjbm. S. S.
S. E. N. W. S. Get
in car. Push up

(twice). S. E. E. S.

Narrow Room
Get rod. Get us-
botmbups. Get
shield. ublb fmf-
mfwb. E. D. N.

Food Processing
Room
Qvti txjudi. Get
recirculator. Push
Switch. S. Up. W.
ublb fmf-mfwb.
N. W. W. N. Get
in car. Push
Down (twice). N.
E. E. W. N. N.

Inside Air Lock
Dmptf bjsmpdl.
N.

Cargo Bay
Drop translator.
Drop suit. Drop
helmet. Drop
gloves. Get
dzmjoefs. S. W.

Computer Room
(Xifo dpnqvufs
btlt gps njttjpo
dpef) WVH957Z.
N.

Life Support
Install spe. Install
recirculator. E.

Starboard Engine
Install tijfme. S.

Port Engine In-
stall dzmjoefs.
W. N.

Cargo Bay
Get purifier. Get
converter. Get
gyro. Get
navchip. S. E.

Port Engine
Jotubmm
qvsjgjfs. Install
dpowfsufs. W.
W. W.

Bridge
Install hzsp. In-
stall obwdijq. E.

Computer
(Get message
about needing
27,014 mfnqfsft
pg gvfm to reach
Labport SU.) E. N.

Cargo Bay
Get dbse,
dsztubm, sjoh,
tifmm, fnfsbme,
tqifsf, tjmwfs,
kfxfm, dvcf boe
wjbm. S. W.

Install Card
(Get message that
you need 497.9
gspet up cvz
gvfm boe up
wbmvf fbdi
jufn.) Wbmvf
dsztubm. (Same
for each item
you're carrying
until message
says you have
enough for the
fuel.) W.

Bridge
(Watch finale.
You win if you
have bjsmpdl
tivu, usbdups
cfbn pgg, wjbm
jo qpttfttjpo, boe
op qjsbuft ibwf
cffo sfdbmmfe.)

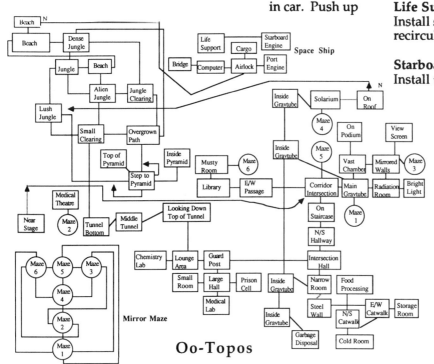

Oo-Topos

Roadwar 2000

In a war-torn, disease-ridden America of the 21st Century, you must locate eight scientists and return them to the Government Underground Biolab (GUB). Only their work can stop a deadly mutant plague. But to qualify for the mission, you have to become a powerful gang leader by taking over enough cities to attract the GUB's attention. Character development and car-to-car combat are stressed in this role-playing game, whose scenario is reminiscent of the *Road Warrior* films. The primary game screen shows a large map of the USA, across which you guide a car-shaped icon.

You press keys to look for supplies, cars and new gang members. Three combat modes let you choose the degree of complexity: one-line casualty reports, a detailed scrolling text display, or an aerial view of a wargame-style battle in which you individually direct the actions of up to 15 vehicles and their crews. There are no logical puzzles, but clues help you find six of the eight scientists. Mapping is unnecessary. There are no sound effects, animation or real-time combat, and two drives are not supported. The programming and design are rough around the edges, and it accesses the disk almost every time you press a key. (This was Jeff Johnson's first game). Players who enjoy tactical combat will get the most out of this one, for the quest is secondary to the combat. But with two sets of characters—the gang and their cars—to work

with, a strong sense of character development emerges.

The Walkthrough

Many elements of *Roadwar* are randomly determined, so it's impossible to say exactly where to find things. Instead, this solution consists of universally applicable strategy tips. No map is provided, as you get one in the manual. Because of the nature of the game, these clues are not encoded.

Characters, Cars and Supplies
You start with eight gang members, one vehicle and limited supplies of food and fuel. It is vital to increase each of these quickly. The goal is to build your gang up to at least three vehicles, 50 men and as many supplies as you can carry. Then you'll be ready to begin the quest. Search for vehicles first until you have at least two or three cars. Eventually you'll want a few limos, a bus, trailer, and some pickups and wagons, but take whatever you find for now.

Next loot for supplies. Take all the gppe, **gvfm boe nfejdjof** you can find. (Each gangmember eats a unit of food per day, so try to keep your food supply at least three times higher than the total number of gangmembers). Forget about **ujsft** for now until you've built up good fuel and food supplies. Always cache away lots of everything, particularly fuel and food. Note what supplies are in which towns, since you may

which towns, since you may need them later. When you have two or three vehicles and supplies to keep them and your crew going for awhile, save the game!

Finally, search for **qfpqmf up kpjo zpvs hboh.** When you meet a group, **tfoe fowpzt up ubml up uifn.** (If they attack and wipe out your crew, reboot and restore the saved game). Mercenaries are the most desirable, then street gangsters, armed rabble, and the needy. Don't be picky in the early stages of the game—take anyone who offers to join but not more than you can feed for a few days.

Character Development

At the end of each victory, many of your surviving members are automatically promoted. This means you'll be more successful in future battles, and it will be easier to attract new members. **Rvbmjuz** is more important than **rvboujuz:** a crew of 110 with 85 armsmasters is more effective than a gang of 250 that has only 50. Later in the game, you can often dump many of the escorts who have just joined by sending them scouting, keeping only the strongest recruits. The optimal number of gang members is **uisff ivoesfe up gjwf ivoesfe.** Get a **cjh gppe tvqqmz** *before* accepting a lot of recruits.

Dpipsut help your crew earn promotions faster and live longer. Their location, as well as that of the scientists, agents, healers and other elements, are randomly determined for each new game. You will always find cohorts in **Npvoubjo Wjfx,** however, so it's worth checking out soon if you're on the West Coast, or after you've taken over a region if you start further away.

The attributes of your car—speed, maneuverability and so on—must be developed by finding towns with garages, body shops and similar places. Keep track of where they are and visit them when possible. Sometimes you'll have to repeatedly loot a city to find such a place, even if you already know where to look. You can also strengthen your arsenal by finding bigger vehicles. Don't settle for anything smaller than a **tubujpo xbhpo.** Get as many of the most powerful combat vehicles (trailers, buses, flatbeds and limos) as you can find, since they can carry lots of supplies and are effective in combat. The bus, which can fire 26 rounds in one whack, is your deadliest weapon. Construction vehicles and tractors are useful for transporting supplies,

but practically useless in combat except when ramming. Search for vehicles, **cfgpsf zpv mppu gps tvqqmjft** or you'll just have to go back to looting to repair any new vehicles.

Combat

There are three combat modes: abstract, quick and tactical. Battles fought in the cities are usually abstract, though occasionally you'll run into a road gang. When you do, you get to choose the combat mode. Each has advantages and disadvantages. Some people have completed the game using only abstract combat, but most prefer to mix them up. If you choose detailed combat, you'll learn which kinds of vehicles you're facing before you choose to go for quick or tactical mode. If you see anything you need, such as a bus or van, select tactical and try to capture it.

Abstract is the fastest, because you have no control over your men or vehicles. You just read the scrolling combat report and hope for the best. The main threat is getting your tires shot out and taking lots of damage to the vehicles' superstructure. If you intend to resolve most of your battles in abstract mode, be sure to carry plenty of **tqbsf ujsft.** Always fix your tires after each battle, regardless of the combat mode. An abstract victory, however, doesn't allow you to increase the number of cars you can own. (If you prefer a small gang, that's not important). An advantage is that you won't need as much fuel. In quick combat you have to worry about extensive damage from being rammed by enemy vehicles. It takes longer than abstract and lets you choose your own ram ratio and targets. Never ram during quick combat. Don't shoot at topside gunners. Concentrate your fire on interior crew and/or tires.

Tactical mode offers the most flexibility controlling your vehicles and gang members. Its drawback is time: the bigger your fleet, the longer the battle. (With a dozen or more cars, combat can last an hour or more!) But you can pick up vast amounts of supplies by winning one. It's played like a war game, so many of the same guidelines apply. Initial deployment of your fleet is important. If you've got a a few fast cars, especially limos, keep them in reserve so they can move in quickly to outflank the enemy. Maneuver your cars so they face enemy vehicles at a 45-degree angle, which allows them to fire twice (from the front and side or rear and side) on each turn. Position buses and other large vehicles so they can fire from the side, then use them like artillery after luring cars in range with other vehicles. A very effective tactic is to **svo b cvt epxo uif njeemf mbof**, so it can fire from both sides on the same turn. If you have two buses, run them along opposite sides and catch enemy cars in the crossfire. Take advantage of terrain, ducking behind trees and other obstacles.

Concentrate firepower on the most dangerous vehicles—trailers, buses, limos and wagons—before going after the small ones. Avoid ramming other vehicles, unless you've got a few specifically meant as kamikaze and manned only with escorts. Don't shoot topside gunners unless you plan to capture a vehicle. Then pick them all off before moving in. This is often the best way to acquire some of the most desirable ones.

With quick and tactical combat, auto-deploy your gang and fine-tune their positions individually to save time. Make sure weapons are set to firearms, not crossbows. Keep armsmasters off the topsides, unless you want to board and capture, and even then keep them inside until you're ready for them to jump.

The Game Plan
Your initial location is randomly determined, but the strategy is identical regardless of where you start. First **ublf pwfs fwfsz tubuf jo zpvs sfhjpo**. These are listed in the manual's appendix and shown on its map. In each town, scout to see who's in control. Make the majority of your scouting party **ftdpsut**, since some are likely to get killed. If no one controls the city, take it over. If **Jowbefst** control it, note this in your logbook and get out of town fast. Fight for it if it is controlled by another gang. Unfortunately, there is no command for calling them out to fight: you must keep looting and searching until the controlling gang spots you and attacks. You may have to defeat them in several battles before you gain control of the city. It may take more than 20 victories, but the average is three to five.

On the Road
Along the way, constantly replenish your supplies of food, fuel, medicine and tires. Make a habit of punching the "x" and "m" keys to check the situation. Your priority should be on fuel, then food and medicine. (Tires are the game's most plentiful item, so you don't have to carry many). If you're running dangerously low on

food and have plenty of escorts, **tfoe uifn bmm po b tdpvujoh njttjpo**: most won't come back. The food will last longer, so your stronger gang-members won't starve to death. Note the locations of any special items you find, such as healers, fuel tanks, body shops and garages. Always trade **nfejdjof** for **bouj-upyjo** from the healers whenever you bump into them. Immediately after each battle with mutants, check your crew for disease and use anti-toxin to heal them.

Finding the Scientists
After you have covered an entire region and conquered many cities, an agent tells you **xifsf up gjoe uif** HVC. Head there right away and search for people. The GUB will contact you, give you a badge and your mission. You must visit many cities and find clues to the whereabouts of the scientists, then locate them by searching for people, often several times. Sometimes they may have moved to a nearby town instead of the one you were referred to by the clue. You don't have to capture a town to find scientists or clues.

When you've found the first **tjy tdjfoujtut**, return to the GUB, which will accept them and give you a **Sbejp Ejsfdujpo Gjoefs** that will lead you to the other two, for whom no clues are given in the game. (Don't bother taking them back one by one, since you don't get anything until you return all six). However, if you have stumbled across these two during the quest, you will not be given the RDF to locate the others, for whom clues do exist. So if you return six scientists and don't get the RDF, you'll know to keep looking for clues. (Another reason that maintaining good records of your travels is so important). The final trip to the GUB is the toughest part of the journey. Road gangs are everywhere, supplies are scarce. Throughout the game, prepare for the end game by setting up supply lines of cached supplies along key routes back to the GUB.

When Sarien Startroopers attack your ship, you—a lowly janitor—are the sole survivor. You've got to dodge the invaders long enough to obtain crucial clues and objects, then escape. If you don't find and destroy the Star Generator the Sariens stole from your ship, these evil aliens will use it to take over the universe. But first you have to explore two planets and deal with their people and wildlife.

THE GAME SYSTEM IS the one seen in the *King's Quest* series: using keyboard, joystick or a mouse to guide your animated character, you maneuver him through incredibly detailed and lushly colored 3-D illustrations. (The animation is so refined that interacting with *Space Quest* is like "playing" an animated cartoon.) In many scenes you will visit the same location twice: once beneath a bridge, for example, and later when you walk across it. This lends a singular sense of depth to the surroundings. Some puzzles have alternative solutions, and there are several arcade sequences in which you can fly your ship or interact with other highly animated characters. The parser won't take multiple commands or pronouns, but does

have a decent vocabulary. Game text appears in pop-up windows that hold more than typical graphic games. Sound effects are good, and you can name the saved game positions. So don't let the arcade sequences, which are easy, scare you away from this delightfully designed jaunt across the galaxies.

The Walkthrough

Play in "fast" mode until you reach an action sequence, then use slow. In this solution "D" and "U" mean to enter the elevator in the current room.

Arcada
W. W. W. **tfbsdi cpez. hfu lfzdbse.** E. E. (Wait for man in library.) Look at man. Examine **tdsffo** (on console). astral body. Get **cartridge.** W. D. E. D. E. Press **pqfo cbz epps cvuupo** (at console with two red buttons). E. insert keycard (in slot by door). D. press **sjhiu** button. press **sjhiu** button. Get suit. Get gadget. **tkijvuljkw** (on other side of railing). W. Push **qmbugpsn cvuupo** (on console). Enter pod. Close door. buckle belt. **qsftt qpxfs cvuupo.** press autonav button. pull throttle.

Space Quest

Desert on Kerona

Vocvdlmf cfmu. Get. **lju.** Exit pod. Get glass (at front of pod). E. E. E. N. (Up path on left. Stop halfway up and wait for **tqjefs** to drop before proceeding.) W. (If you get thirsty, open **lju** and drink water.)

On Bridge

(Move behind **spdl** and wait until **tqjefs** is under it.) push rock. W. N. E. E. Walk between **bsdift.**

In Cave

Get **rock.** W. (Move against north wall, then west past grating.) Put **spdl** in **hole** (on geyser). N. W. (Go left at **cbdl** of cave). Use **hmbtt** (at beams) E. (through top exit). (At acid drops, wait for first two to fall simultaneously, then move past them and stop. Go when third drop falls.) E. Turn on **hbehfs.** E. (Listen to **bmjfo** in Hologram Room, who returns you to surface.)

Rocky Plateau to the Orrat's Cave

(Follow map to the cave and save before entering. Type "**uispx dbo**" but don't hit return, then enter cave and move behind rocks. Now hit return and go to piece of Orrat.) Get piece. (Follow map back to arches and return to Hologram Room.)

Hologram Room and Alien's Hideout

Drop piece. N. **jotfsu dbsusjehf** (in console). Get **dbsusjehf.** [Save] Enter skimmer. Turn key. (Dodge rocks until you reach town.)

Ulence Flats

Get key. Exit. (Wait for alien who wants to buy skimmer.) No. (When he returns, say "yes.") N. Look around (behind building). Get **cvdlbapjet.** S. (Enter bar. After alien is blasted at slot machine, play until you have 250 buckazoids. Always bet the limit and save when your bankroll is increased. Then stand at bar.) Give coupon. Drink beer. Buy beer. Drink beer. Buy beer. Drink beer. (Exit bar. N. E.

Droids R Us and Tiny's Used Spacecraft

(Enter Droids R Us and go upstairs.) Buy droid (at top of stairs, then follow map to Tiny's and go north to **tjmwfs tijq** before he approaches you.) **cvz tijq** (after Tiny arrives). Enter ship. **mpbe espje. ii** (to droid). **xfbs kfuqbdl** (when you reach Deltaur). Exit ship. (Fly to airlock door in center.) Open door. N. (to enter airlock door).

Onboard the Deltaur

(Wait on left side of door for droid to enter.) N. **pqfo usvol. foufs usvol. pqfo usvol** (after being carried off). Open **epps** (on washing machine). Enter **nbdijof.** Open door (after **tbsjfo mfbwft**). (Follow map to Catwalk.) Look at **vojgpsn.** E. Give **je dbse.** (When droid leaves, go to end of counter.) Get **hsfobef.** (Return to counter and get pulseray from droid.) W. **espq hsfobef** (over **tbsjfo**). [Save] (Follow map to Star Generator Room, firing pulseray at Sariens.)

Star Generator Room

tfbsdi tbsjfo. Get device. **qvti cvuupo. fybnjof qbofm** (on console). (Select 6858, then hit enter.) Follow map to Shuttle Launch Bay (taking right elevator in Elevator Room. Enter ship). **qvti cvuupo.**

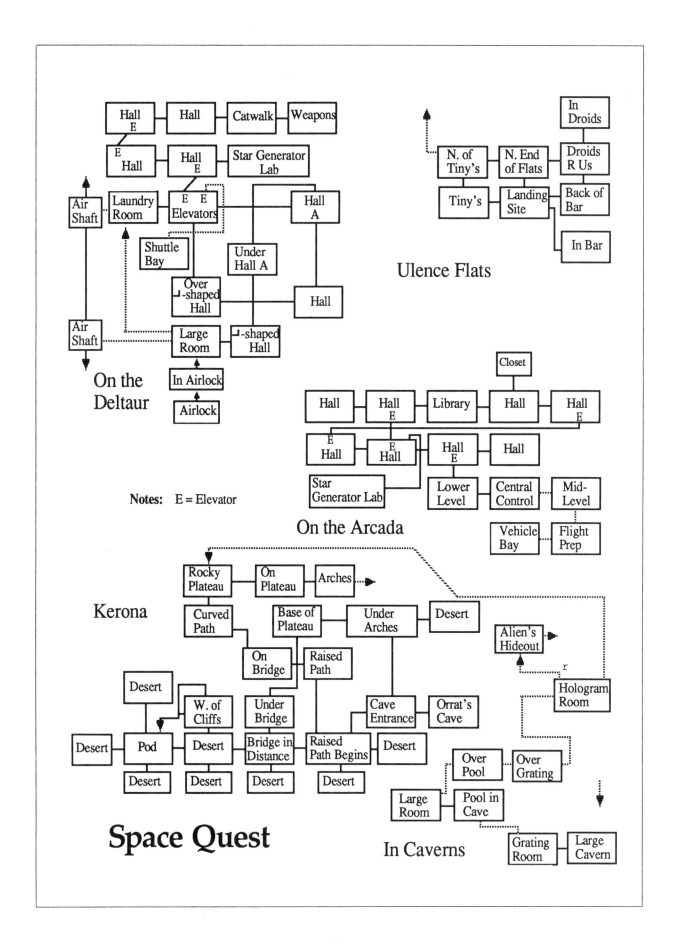

On the
Deltaur

Ulence Flats

Notes: E = Elevator

On the Arcada

Kerona

Space Quest

In Caverns

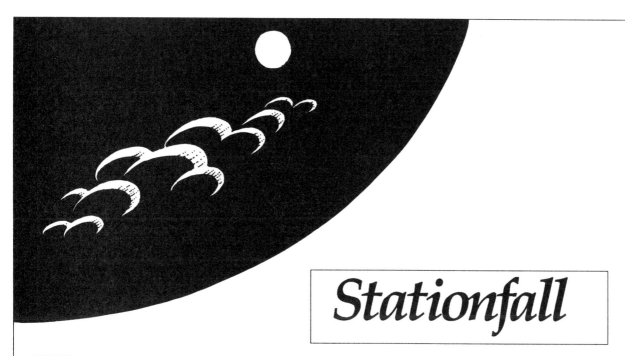

Stationfall

This long-awaited sequel to Steve Meretzky's *Planetfall* puts you in the space boots of a Stellar Patrol Lieutenant assigned to fetch a supply of "request form forms" from a neighboring space station. But there's no one there to greet you, and your main mission abruptly changes: find out what happened to the crew and avoid that fate yourself as more and more of the station's equipment mysteriously malfunctions. Ultimately the fate of humankind rests upon your ability to unravel the secret of a strange pyramid recovered from an alien space ship. The only characters are Floyd, that personable robot from *Planetfall*, and a few of his cohorts, but you'll find numerous objects—many of them red herrings—scattered about this nine-level space station. A time limit is imposed by the limited amount of food, without which you'll die.

REMINISCENT OF Fred Saberhagen's Berserker series, the plot unfolds as you read the station commander's log and other files and notes. Harder than *Planetfall*, this one is a good standard level game with amusing prose and clever, entertaining puzzles that will net you a top score of 80 points. (See the review of *Ballyhoo* for notes on the Infocom parser and other technical aspects.) Meretzky's well-turned prose style ranges from wry to ribald, and he even manages to evoke an emotion or two from the player/reader.

The Walkthrough

You will get hungry (eat goo or nectar; drop kit when food is depleted) and sleepy (get on bed in any barracks and wait) and may be attacked by Plato (say Floyd, help four times) at random times. Also, you must leave the room if a welder approaches. If there are no directions at the end of a section below, follow the map to the next location.

On the Duffy
E. N. Put **spcpu gpsn** in slot. Type 3. S. E. Open hatch. Enter truck. Close hatch. Sit in pilot seat. Put **tqbdfdsbgu gpsn** in slot. Read chronograph. (Find this number on assignment form in game package and discover correct coordinate.) Type (number). Wait (until you land at docking bay). Get up. Get kit. Open kit. Get thermos. Open thermos. **Esjol tpvq.** Open hatch. Out. E.

Level 5 and Printing Plant
Drop kit (return for it when you get hungry). SE.

SE. E. Get tape. W. **Qvu ubqf jo sfbefs.** Turn reader on. Push button (**ufo ujnft**). Turn reader off. E. Look **voefs cfe.** Get stamp. W. NW. NW. D. D. [Printing Plant] Open can. Get crumpled form. Drop assignment form. NW. Get drill. Remove bit. Drop bit. SE. Get nanofilm.

Laundry Room
Open presser. Put **dsvnqmfe gpsn** in presser. Close presser. Turn presser on. Turn presser off. Open presser. Get form. E. N. Read sign (note number). S. SW. Get puce. E. D. W. Get lilac. E. U. U. SE.

Library
Qvu nbvwf in **sfbefs.** Turn reader on. Remove mauve. Drop mauve. Put puce in reader. Remove puce. Drop puce. Put lilac in reader. Turn reader off. W. N. Get **efupobups. Pqfo** detonator. **Sfnpwf izqfsejpef.** Drop **izqfsejpef.**

Level 5 and East Connector's Iris Hatch
Drop detonator. **Tubnq gpsn.** Drop stamp. SE. S. [Save] W. (Restore if Floyd doesn't follow you into room; try telling him to follow you.) **Gmpze, hfu nfejvn cju.** Get bit. E. Put bit in drill. E. N. N. NE. [East Connector] Put **gpsn jo tmpu.**

Broadway
E. Get headlamp. **Xfbs ifbembnq.** W. S. S. Read sheet. Drop sheet. SE. Put card in slot. Turn machine on. **Uzqf tfwfo.** Get card. NW. SW. SW. SE. SW. Get can. Read can.

Pet Store and the Balloon Creature
Read sign. Open cage. **Tqsbz dbo.** NE. Spray can. W. Spray can. W. Spray can. W. Spray can. SW. Spray can. NW. Spray can U. Spray can. U. Spray can. (Balloon creature should follow you into **dibqfm.**)

Chapel
Open pulpit. **Uispx txjudi.** Spray can. **Hfu mfbti.** Get star. Drop leash. E. D. D. Get kit and detonator. SE. SE. E. **Pqfo tubs.** Get **izqfsejpef.** Drop star. Put **izqfsejpef jo efupobups.** Close detonator. W. NW. NW. D. SE. [End of Corridor] **Qvu dbse jo sfbefs.** N. Get gun. [Level 5] SE. SE. E. **Esjmm tbgf.** Drop drill.

Loan Shark, the Ostrich and the PX Machine
Tippu mpdl xjui hvo. Get coin. N. NE. U. NW. [Pet Store] Examine **dfjmjoh. Pqfo qbofm.** Get nip. SE. SW. SW. SE. SE. NW. [Doc Schuster's] NE. U. N. N. W. W. W. NW. NE. [PX] **Qvu dpjo jo nbdijof.** Type 6. Put **ojq jo ipmf.** Get timer.

Mayor's Office
Open textbook. Read paper. Drop paper. D. NE. NE. N. N. SE. [Barber Shop] **Csfbl njssps.** Get gpjm. NW. S. [Grocery] Drop all but thermos.

Casino, Flophouse and the Alien Ship
Uvso xiffm. U. **Pqfo mpdlfs.** Hfu tvju. D. W. NW. [Grocery Store] Drop suit. (Go to Docking Bay # 1.) Enter ship. **Ubtuf dots** (compare with **nfttbhf** on paper in **nbzps't pggjdf**). Exit ship.

Junkyard and In Space
Get boots. Wear boots. W. NE. U. N. Get suit. Wear it. S. D. [Warehouse] Open inner door. D. [Air Lock] Close inner door. Open outer door. D. Turn lamp on. Get cylinder. **Qvu dzmjoefs jo uifsnpt.** Close **uifsnpt.** U. Close outer door. Turn lamp off. Open inner door. Remove boots. Drop boots. Remove suit. Drop suit. (Go to **Hspdfsz.**) Get gun, detonator, timer and foil.

Commander's Quarters
Buubdi ujnfs up efupobups. Open **uifsnpt.** Get explosive. Attach detonator to explosive. **Qvu fyqmptjwf jo ipmf.** Drop detonator and timer. **Tfu ujnfs up ufo.** W. E (after explosion). Get key. W. NW. NW. N. N. Get jammer. **Tfu kbnnfs up tfwfo pof afsp.** E. N. N. U. Get board. **Jotfsu cpbse jo kbnnfs.**

Dome
Unlock bin with key. Open bin. Get gun, foil and jammer. **Sfnpwf hsbujoh.** Enter air shaft. D (until you reach bottom). **Kvnq po hsbujoh.** Turn jammer on. Turn jammer off. U. **Tippu Gmpze xjui hvo.** Put **gpjm po qzsbnje.**

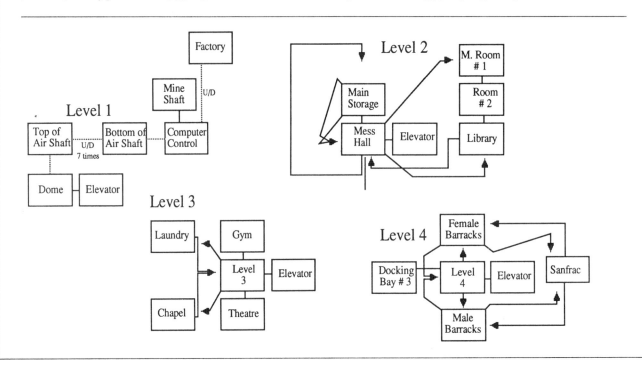

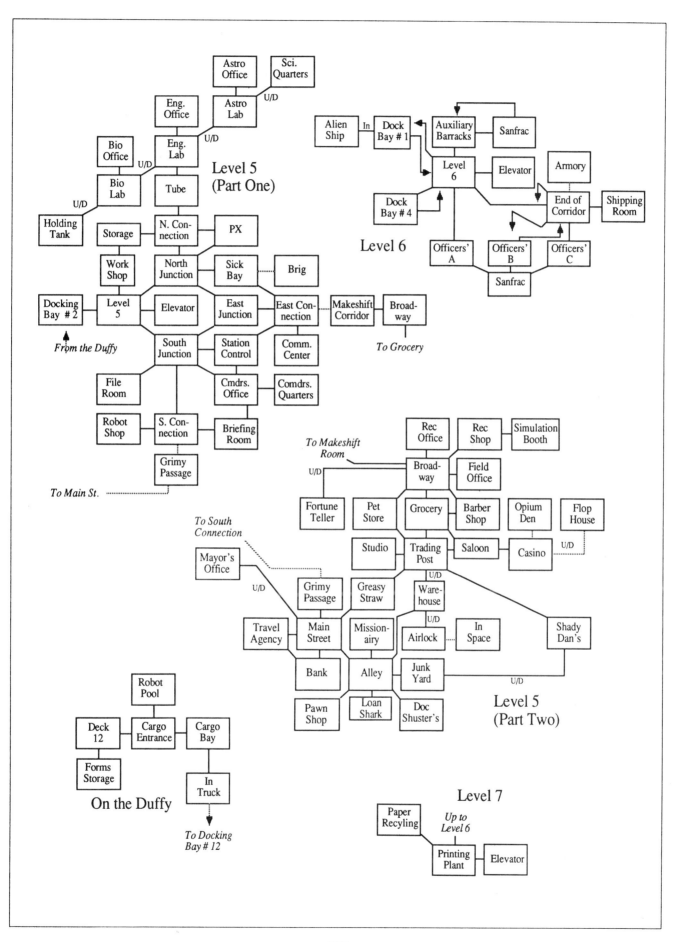

Astro Office

Sci. Quarters

Eng. Office

Astro Lab
U/D

Bio Office

Eng. Lab
U/D

Level 5
(Part One)

U/D

Bio Lab
U/D

Tube

Holding Tank

Storage

N. Connection

PX

Work Shop

North Junction

Sick Bay

Brig

Docking Bay # 2

Level 5

Elevator

East Junction

East Connection

Makeshift Corridor

Broadway

From the Duffy

South Junction

Station Control

Comm. Center

To Grocery

File Room

Cmdrs. Office

Comdrs. Quarters

Robot Shop

S. Connection

Briefing Room

Grimy Passage

To Main St.

Alien Ship — In — Dock Bay # 1

Auxiliary Barracks

Sanfrac

Level 6

Elevator

Armory

Dock Bay # 4

End of Corridor

Shipping Room

Level 6

Officers' A

Officers' B

Officers' C

Sanfrac

To Makeshift Room

Rec Office

Rec Shop

Simulation Booth

Broadway

Field Office

U/D

Fortune Teller

Pet Store

Grocery

Barber Shop

Opium Den

Flop House

Studio

Trading Post

Saloon

Casino

U/D

To South Connection

Mayor's Office

U/D

Grimy Passage

Greasy Straw

Ware- house

In Space

Shady Dan's

Travel Agency

Main Street

Mission- airy

Airlock
U/D

Bank

Alley

Junk Yard

U/D

Level 5
(Part Two)

Robot Pool

Pawn Shop

Loan Shark

Doc Shuster's

Deck 12

Cargo Entrance

Cargo Bay

Forms Storage

In Truck

On the Duffy

Level 7

Paper Recyling

Up to Level 6

Printing Plant

Elevator

To Docking Bay # 12

183

Commerce, mining, piracy—as captain of an Agora-class ship, you can build a fortune at any or all of these activities. But they're really a cover for your role as a covert agent of the Federated Worlds. By checking the vidcomm for messages that usually are devoted to news, you occasionally receive secret orders for a top secret mission. The missions relate to the increasing conflict and ultimate war between the FW and the United Democratic Planets. Ultimately you must deal with a gang of terrorists that have seized the Booster, a huge alien ship found adrift in space.

Your crew consists of Marines, Pilots and other classes whose skills you must improve. Simultaneously you have to outfit your ship with more efficient parts and eventually buy a new kind of ship. There are 98 different kinds of gear from which to choose, hundreds of products to buy and sell, four kinds of ore to mine and 47 planets to visit. Half the time you control your ship via pull-down menus and keyboard commands and watch simple animated graphics of your ship, shuttles and nearby planets. When you land at a starport, the game becomes a text adventure in which you encounter other characters. It's a long-playing saga with a good mix of role-playing activities and some easy puzzles (but not enough of them) in the text adventure.

The Walkthrough

General Tips
Don't expect to get an assignment from HQ for quite awhile. Just keep **difdljoh uif wjedpnn sfhvmbsmz** while making money and building up your ship and crew. Stick with trading for at least a year. Choose your second ship according to your next activity. (The Explorer makes a good all-purpose vehicle.) Strive for attack-and-board capability by **Tfqufncfs, Uxp Uipvtboe, Uisff Ivoesfe boe Tjyuz-Gpvs.** Save and **lffq pof pof hbnf qsjps** to October, 2364, when things start breaking fast. If you're low on cash and need to buy food, sell some ore IV.

Things such as the amount of ore available on a planet, product prices, and your position after hypering to another star are randomly determined. If you reach a star without enough fuel to get to a planet with a drydock, abort the game, restore and try again. Unless you've really pushed your luck, you'll eventually land close enough to reach a drydock. This trick of aborting and restoring can be used to get better prices when buying or selling, when mining, and looking for crew. You don't have to solve the first two missions, but doing so makes the rest of the game easier. Make backups of the saved game file (PLAYER1) in different stages, especially right after making a lot of money and before making major decisions such as buying a new ship. Record the dates so you can quickly resort to the right one if you hit a dead end (no fuel, missiles, etc.)

Character Development
Get a good astronavigator and **btpnojhbuf** him as soon as possible. If his grade is lower than 14, hire another one and put him in school till he's grade 18 or 19. The **fohjoffs** is the most important crewmember, so get one who is at least grade 10 and put him in school to advance him to 18-19, then find another one grade 10 or higher to use until he graduates. Put a gunner and at least **gpvs nbsjoft** in school as soon as possible, and don't forget to pick them up when

they graduate at grade 14 or higher. Do the same with a half-dozen miners if you plan to try that activity. Eventually you should asomnigate the gunner, but not for the first few years.

Ship Enhancement
Get a new **dpowfsufs** and **izqfsesjwf** as soon as possible. Because the better ones are more fuel-efficient, this can save you more money than any other piece of equipment in the early stages. **Gpshfu cvzjoh xfbqpot** for the first year. You can tell which parts are sold at drydocks by comparing the sophistication level of the planet they orbit with the level of the parts. **Bscftu** sells the best equipment, but postpone that trip for a year. Check the space available on each type of ship for the things you have in mind, to ensure you get the right one. **Epo'u cvz b tijq** until you reach Arbest, where it can be outfitted with the best parts. Take at least 300,000 credits.

Commerce
The most profitable trading routes are those that require no system jumps, because they eat up less fuel. The best ones are in Pyxis. Establish a routine of loading passengers onto a shuttle **cfgpsf uif qjmpu ps gvfm**, to avoid forgetting them. Unload them before moving to the products department for the same reason. The manual never clearly states, only implies, that you can operate up to three shuttles, ore processors, or assault capsules simultaneously. The more you have, the better you'll do. Record the highest and lowest price for each item sold at a planet. Prices fluctuate randomly on each trip, but the ranges will give you an idea of the best prices to pay. Use the chronograph (or click the mouse on top of the menu bar) to freeze the product list when you need to make notes or compare prices. When you have a shuttle with room for large items, **cvz uif cjhhftu uijoht** first, then fill the rest of the space with smaller products.

Mining
Don't go mining with serious expectations until **zpv ibwf b Tvuufs**, an auto-doctor, an engineer who can repair the ore processors, miners whose grades average at least **gjguffo** and enough fuel to stay over a planet long enough to make several landings. This way you make a lot from one trip; otherwise, you'll be lucky to make enough to buy the fuel to replace that used while mining. Don't get greedy and **njof gps upp mpoh xjuipvu difdljoh uif wjedpnn** over an inhabited planet, though, or you'll miss a lot of the reports. After

the processors return from mining, immediately use the autodoctor on miners whose health is below 70, or they may die. The ramscoop seems to be a waste of time, but may prove useful if you run low on Ore IV.

Piracy
Don't attempt **qjsbdz** until you've learned the ropes as a trader, because most of the booty is in the form of products. You have to know where to sell each one and which ones are worthless in order to make a decent income. Even then, mining is much more lucrative—and doesn't involve any disk swapping.

Combat
To attack ships in the hopes of raiding them, the best complement of missiles is **qsjudibset** and **xpefo gft**. An Explorer holds ten of the former, eight of the latter. Fire two salvos of pritchards and one or two of fes, then **ep b tdbo**. The exact number of missiles in each salvo depends on the kind of ship you're attacking. **Ebhhfst** carry lots of **nbsjoft**. While boarding a ship, the enemy need not be in a direct line of fire with your attacking Marine. Against odds of 3-1 or worse, go for the control panels.

The First Year
Dock at **Byjb boe tbwf**. Enter drydock and hire a pilot, astro and engineer who are at least grade five, hopefully ten. If not available, abort and restore saved position. Buy a **epftufwtlj dpowfsufs**, an **joufstqbdf izqfsesjwf** and an **byjbo tivuumf**. Check the vidcomm for a message, then land. Inside, go to the **upvs hbuf** and **jotfsu ujdlfu**. East, enter slidewalk, **btl Eftnpob bcpvu npovnfou**. East, enter elevator, **kiss Desmona**, ask **Desmona bcpvu cpptufs**. North, enter elevator, enter slidewalk. South, enter booth, activate terminal. Load passengers for Zeath. Buy some **nzc lvub sptf** and **ufdijp tdvmquvsf**.

Zeath
Deliver cargo and passengers to Zeath, then pick up same for Grotto. In the **Qzyjt Tztufn** buy goods at **Hspuup gps Gfwwfm**, sell them and shop for things to sell at Bahnir. There you should just get **qbttfohfst** and start over at Grotto. Continue until you have 200,000-250,000 credits. Get cargo and passengers for **Byjb**, where you will pick up same for Vromus. At Vromus, check out the drydock and get a **uijse tivuumf**, hopefully a Voltac (and a **qjmpu jg zpv**

185

pomz ibwf uxp). If you have enough credits, get a gbtufs dpnqvufs too. Ultimately you'll need at least two Wpmubdt and an Axian for effective trading. Land and conduct trading, then return to Pyxis via Axia and continue trading until you have a least 300,000 credits, three miners, three marines, an engineer, a pilot for each shuttle and an btpnojhbufe hvoofs boe btusphbups. Put some of them in school and take a load of passengers to Arbest by tvnnfs of 2363.

Arbest
Upgrade to an Fyqmpsfs ps b Tvuufs. Either one allows room for bigger crew quarters, which you'll need to hold a team of five or six nbsjoft. The Explorer enables you to keep trading and do some medium-weight mining, even piracy if that's your style. The Sutter is good for mining, as it can carry three Franklin ore processors. No matter which ship you get, outfit it with all the best parts you can, especially a 99 Hyperdrive and Accumulator. Then land at Arbest and buy products (jogpsnbujpo-uzqf mjlf dpnqvufst are best) and passengers for Vromus. Head there, take care of business and return to trading in Pyxis. By late njetvnnfs of 2363 you should get a nfttbhf gspn IR.

The First Mission
This one sends you to nffu bo bhfou po Bscftu to tufbm b efwjdf from an exhibit. The only tricky part is ufmmjoh ijn uif qbttxpse: say "ufmm Gmpze bcpvu hmpnbm." (Conduct any business first.) Then east, qvti cvuupo, west, north, tippu qjtupm, north. Head for Vromus and report to HQ by entering the booth and "tbz obnf." You'll be rewarded with a Vromus prime navy shield generator, more powerful than any you could buy. Now return to trading in Pyxis or check out Ferredkor in the Douglas System for njojoh. If you don't have at least five well-trained marines and a hppe hvoofs, look for and train them now. Also get your ship fully equipped for combat by September, 2364. Buy the best njttjmf sbdl and mbvodifs at Arbest. An Explorer can pack ten pritchards and eight woden fes. You also need a epdljoh bebqufs and all necessary software.

The Second Mission
In mid-October of 2364, check for a vidcomm message at boz GX qmbofu to get details on Pqfsbujpo Tibuufs. (You have until Gfcsvbsz, Uxp Uipvtboe, Uisff Ivoesfe boe Tjyuz-Tjy, up

dpnqmfuf this mission.) Then hyper to a sfnpuf gx tztufn—Qipcpt is usually a good choice—and orbit a planet to find a ebhhfs. If unsuccessful, abort and keep trying. Then save the game, in case it hfut bxbz (or cmpxt *you* bxbz). Fire all your pritchards, then the woden fes, in salvos of gpvs boe uisff sftqfdujwfmz. Board and dbquvsf uif ebhhfs. Then izqfs to the coordinates you discover (8 -19 10), pscju uif qmbofu and take off for Vromus. To the Admiral's question, say "ufmm Csftifmjb bcpvu Sphvf." Return to trading, or better still, mining, since you have a long time—until Kbovbsz, Uxp Uipvtboe, Uisff Ivoesfe boe Ojofuz-Tjy—before the next mission and should have enough cash to fully equip a Sutter by now. Make sure your engineer is capable of repairing the ore shuttles you buy: Don't get Franklins unless the engineer is grade 20. You may want to check for joufsftujoh nfttbhft in November, 2365, but xjmm opu cf bcmf to nffu Eftnpob bt tif sfrvftut.

The Third Mission
You should have a solid crew—all grade 16 or higher—by now and plenty of cash. In January, 2365, you get a message to efmjwfs uif jpub gjmf gspn Dfuvt Bnjdvt to Vromus, where you learn it's contents. (To enter the Dpnnvojdbujpot Sppn at Cetus, just "say name.") There is no apparent reward for completing the mission, but the jogpsnbujpo buubjofe is needed to tpmwf uif foe hbnf. After the briefing you can resume trading, mining, or piracy, checking in occasionally for messages about the progressing tubuf pg xbs.

There is little else to do until March, 2371. If you are still have a few years to go and are getting restless, you can kill time by hypering back and forth between Toascella and Kochar. Be sure you have a gfx njmmjpo epmmbst for fuel, and keep stocked up on food. You can gjsf bmm uif nbsjoft boe njofst, since you won't need them again.

The Booster
You have until Pdupcfs to solve this one, or the hbnf foet. Don't bother to reportt to Wspnvt bt psefsf, but ifbe tusbjhiu gps Dfuvt and land. Inside the Dpnnvojdbujpot Sppn: dbmm Cpptufs. Tell Eftnpob about dmpvft. Tell Desmona about jpub. Dbmm Csftifmjb.

Game Manufacturers

Following is a list of games referred to in this book along with the companies that hold the trademarks for them.

Amnesia™	Electronic Arts
Autoduel™	Origin Systems, Inc.
Ballyhoo™	Activision/Infocom
Bard's Tale I™	Electronic Arts
Destiny Knight™	Electronic Arts
Borrowed Time™	Activision
Breakers™	Broderbund
Brimstone™	Broderbund
Bureaucracy™	Activision/Infocom
Destiny™	Software Investments Plus
Essex™	Broderbund
Fraktured Faebles™	American Eagle
Goldfinger: James Bond 007™	EON Productions, Ltd. Glidrose Publications, Ltd. [Mindscape]
High Stakes	Mindscape
Hollywood HiJinx™	Infocom
Indiana Jones™ in Revenge of the Ancients™	LucasFilms, Ltd. [Mindscape]
King's Quest III™	Sierra On-Line
Labyrinth™	LucasFilms, Ltd. [Mindscape]
Leather Goddesses of Phobos™	Activision/Infocom
Lurking Horror™	Activision/Infocom
Mercenary™	Novagen Software, Ltd.
Might and Magic®	New World Computing [Activision]
Mist, The	Mindscape
Moebius™	Greg Malone [Origin Systems, Inc.]
Moonmist™	Activision/Infocom
Neverending Story™	Intellicreations
Nine Princess in Amber™	Spinnaker Software
Oo-topos	Polar-Ware
Pawn, The™	Activision/Rainbird
Phantasie I™	Strategic Simulations
Phantasie II™	Strategic Simulations
Phantasie III™	Strategic Simulations
Rambo™ First Blood™ Part Two	Anabasis Investments, N.V. [Mindscape]
Rings of Zilfin™	Strategic Simulations
Roadwar 2000™	Strategic Simulations
Shadowgate	Mindscape
Shard of Spring™	Strategic Simulations
Space Quest™	Sierra On-Line
SpellBreaker™	Activision/Infocom
*Star Trek II™ The Promethean Prophecy	Simon and Schuster
Stationfall™	Activision/Infocom
Tass Times™	Activision
Trinity™	Activision/Infocom
Ultima® IV	Richard Garriott [Origin Systems, Inc.]
Universe II™	Omnitrend
View to a Kill, A	Mindscape
Voodoo Island	Mindscape
Wizard's Crown™	Strategic Simulations
Wrath of Denethenor™	Sierra On-Line

Miscellaneous trademarks also mentioned in this book; *Star Trek is a trademark of Paramount Pictures, Corporation. Angelsoft is a registered trademark of Angelsoft, Inc. Datasoft is a registered trademark of Intellicreations.

Quest for Adventures: System Availability

Title	AP	C64	C128	IBM	ST	Amiga	Mac	IIGS	Atari 8-bit
Amnesia	•		•	•					
Autoduel	•		•	*	•	*	*		•
Ballyhoo	•		•	•	•	•	•	•	•
Bard's Tale I	•		•	•	•	•		•	
Destiny Knight	•		•	•	*	*		*	
Borrowed Time	•		•	•		•	•	•	
Breakers	•		•	•			•		2D
Brimstone	•		•	•			•		2D
Bureaucracy	128K		128K	128K	•	•	512K	•	
Destiny	•		•						
Essex	•		•	•			•		2D
Fraktured Faebles	•		•						
Goldfinger	•			•			•		
Gunslinger	•		•						•
High Stakes	•		•	•	•	•	•	•	•
Hollywood HiJinx	•		•	•	•	•	•	•	•
Indiana Jones	•			•			•		
King's Quest III	128			•	•	•	•	•	
Labyrinth	•	•							
Leather Goddesses	•		•	•	•	•	•	•	•
Lurking Horror	•		•	•	•	•	•	•	•
Mercenary	•		•	•	•				•
Might and Magic	•		•	•	*	*	*		
Mist, The	•			•			•		
Moebius	•		•	*	*	*	*		
Moonmist	•		•	•	•	•	•	•	•
Neverending Story	•		•						•
Nine Princes	•		•	•					
Oo-topos	•		•	•	•	•	•	•	•
Phantasie I	•		•	•	•	•	*		
Phantasie II	•		•		•				
Phantasie III	•		•		•	•			
Rambo	•			•			•		
Ring Quest	•								
Rings of Zilfin	•		•	•	•				
Roadwar 2000	•		•	•	•	•			
Shadowgate						*	•		
Shard of Spring	•		•	•	*	*			*
Space Quest	128			•	•	•	•	•	
SpellBreaker	•		•	•	•	•	•	•	•
Star Trek 2	•		•	•					
StationFall	•		•	•	•	•	•	•	•
Tass Times	•		•	•	•	•	•	•	•
The Pawn	•		•	•	•	•	•		•
Trinity	128		128	128	•	•	512	•	
Ultima IV	•		•	•	*	*		*	•
Universe 2	2D*			2D*	•		•		
View to a Kill	•			•			•		
Voodoo Island	•			•			•		
Wizard's Crown	•		•	•	•	*			
Wrath of Denethenor	•		•						

Legend:
• = currently available. * = conversion planned. 128K, etc. = minimum memory.
2D = two drives required. (All require at least one disk drive.) 2D* = two drives recommended.